Empowering
Electric and Gas Utilities
with GIS

Bill Meehan

ESRI PRESS
REDLANDS, CALIFORNIA

ESRI Press, 380 New York Street, Redlands, California 92373-8100

Library of Congress Cataloging-in-Publication Data
Meehan, Bill, 1949–
    Empowering electric and gas utilities with GIS / Bill Meehan.—1st ed.
      p. cm.
    ISBN 978-1-58948-025-4 (pbk. : alk. paper)
    1. Electric utilities—Technological innovations—Economic aspects—United States. 2. Gas industry—
    Technological innovations—Economic aspects—United States. 3. Electric power plant equipment industry—
    United States. 4. Geographic information systems. I. Title.
    HD9685.U52M44 2007
    333.793'20285—dc22
    2007025563

Ask for ESRI Press titles at your local bookstore or order by calling 1-800-447-9778. You can also shop online at www.esri.com/esripress. Outside the United States, contact your local ESRI distributor.

ESRI Press titles are distributed to the trade by the following:

In North America, South America, Asia, and Australia:
Ingram Publisher Services
Toll-free telephone: (800) 648-3104
Toll-free fax: (800) 838-1149
E-mail: customerservice@ingrampublisherservices.com

In the United Kingdom, Europe, and the Middle East:
Transatlantic Publishers Group Ltd.
Telephone: 44 20 7373 2515
Fax: 44 20 7244 1018
E-mail: richard@tpgltd.co.uk

Cover design by Savitri Brant
Interior design by Jennifer Jennings

Cover photos by (clockwise) Comstock Images—Industrial Strength/Jupiterimages, Comstock Images—Power and Energy/Jupiterimages, Photolink/PhotoDisc/Getty Images, and Russell Illig/PhotoDisc/Getty Images.

Contents

Foreword

"Energy is a critical component in sustaining Utah's vibrant economic growth and preserving our unparalleled quality of life. With just the right blend of ambition, brain power, and diverse natural resources, Utah stands ready to lead the charge in energy efficiency, renewable and alternative energy development, and new and innovative technologies."

The above quote is on our state's energy home page and it is more than mere words. Meeting our growing energy needs is a daunting challenge in today's complex world where there are many competing demands on our resources and a broad spectrum of additional cross-cutting issues to address. In Utah, we have established a comprehensive energy policy that puts into action the important combination of initiative and resources as expressed on our Web site.

Fundamental to Utah's energy policy is a comprehensive plan for energy efficiency and conservation. The Western Governors' Association has set a goal to increase energy efficiency 20 percent by 2020. Our state will work to meet this goal five years sooner, thereby saving energy and money for Utah's citizens and businesses.

Accomplishing this goal along with our other energy priorities will be challenging. Dramatic improvements in efficiency, advanced energy technologies, and enhanced alternative energy development cannot simply be realized by working harder. We need to be open to new thinking and innovative methods of resource allocation, and we must desire to see things from different perspectives. Sometimes looking back at some old sciences, like geography, can help us gain new insights.

That venerable science of geography has taken on a new twist. Geographic information system (GIS) technology has transformed the way we view maps, spatial relationships, and location. GIS gives policy makers, private industry, and utilities advanced decision making, communication, and collaboration tools to use in ways we had never dreamt of when we were studying geography in high school. Breakthrough technologies like GIS are critical to help us deal with the many challenges we face when assessing how best to meet our energy needs.

GIS reveals trends. It shows us patterns, like our energy use or our ability to capture energy in creative and efficient ways. GIS helps us to formulate answers to tough questions, like where to site a wind farm or sequester emissions.

GIS can also help us accomplish key components of our energy plan, including our efforts to work with utilities to improve efficiency in power generation, transmission, and distribution. It can assist our assessment of cost-effective methods to reduce energy losses in production and distribution. As we look to work with our utilities to continually enhance service while maintaining the highest levels of safety and reliability, we believe that the geospatial technical evaluations provided by GIS can help identify the most effective alternatives for resource placement and development.

Bill Meehan's book *Empowering Electric and Gas Utilities with GIS* illustrates how this wonderful, emerging technology based on the ancient science of geography can transform the way utilities do business. It outlines how utilities can become more efficient in the large ways, like deciding where to build a new power plant, to more operational ways, like optimizing the travel paths for their line trucks. Bill's use of the hypothetical utility, AnyTown Energy, helps us understand how a typical utility operates without integrated use of GIS technology. Then the book shows us the dramatic improvements utilities gain when they embrace GIS. While *Empowering Electric and Gas Utilities with GIS* is certainly about energy efficiency, it is also about helping the utility be as responsive as possible to customers and to the communities they serve.

I urge all those interested in innovation to carefully examine this fascinating picture of how the old science of geography packaged in new and exciting ways can bring significant improvement to one of our nation's most critical industries, electric and gas utilities.

—Governor Jon M. Huntsman, Jr.
State of Utah

Preface

Today, most utilities recognize the strategic value of good data. It's hard to imagine operating a complex infrastructure without an up-to-the-minute understanding of its condition and configuration. Yet, many utilities don't have an enterprise view of their distributed assets that a geographic information system (GIS) would provide. Some see GIS strictly as a fast way of making maps. They may be making incremental improvements in the operations but are missing greater opportunities.

Do any of the following situations sound familiar?

1. Utility A decides to interface its newly converted distribution mapping system with a brand new commercially available outage management system. The distribution maps look fine but no one built relationships between the conductors, the poles, the transformers, the streets, or the customers. Can anyone fix the digital mapping system? Sure, with a ton of money. So, Utility A decides to maintain the operating network separately in the outage management system. Opportunity missed.

2. Utility B spent millions on an automated mapping/facility management (AM/FM) system in the mid-1990s. It converted old operating drawings to beautiful, crisp, clear computer-generated plots. A distribution operating manager wants Utility B's new Global Positioning System (GPS) tracking to interface with the AM/FM system. The AM/FM manager sheepishly confesses that the old maps were converted "as is" based on the old mapping standards. For the AM/FM system to conform to the new GPS standard, the utility would have to reconstruct the locations of all the facilities to a new consistent land base. The operating manager opts for an independent vehicle tracking system not linked to the AM/FM system. Opportunity missed.

3. Utility C, a major gas company, closes a deal on a new enterprise resource planning (ERP) system. The chief financial officer (CFO) wants the ERP's plant accounting module integrated with the distribution mapping system. Unfortunately, the mapping system is a file-based computer-aided design (CAD) system and Utility C never mapped its service pipes. The files don't coordinate with the accounting system. It would take a major overhaul to link to the ERP so the CFO abandons the idea. Opportunity missed.

Progress is about gradually improving on past accomplishments. Breakthroughs are leaps forward to uncharted territory. Progress makes the process work better using tried and true methods. Breakthroughs require new ways of thinking to transform the business.

When a utility executive asks: "Show me all the places in my infrastructure where a single event could take the system down," that is an invitation for a breakthrough, and GIS is the vehicle.

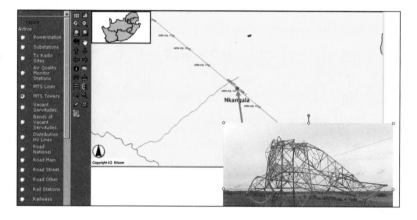

Figure A Employees of Eskom, the Republic of South Africa's government utility, use GIS tools to view extensive transmission line data on an intranet site.

Courtesy of Eskom

GIS is about discovery. It's about visualizing trends for better decision making. It's about finding weaknesses in your infrastructure before disaster hits. GIS is most powerful when utilities integrate it into the information technology infrastructure. This allows utilities to visualize the data through intelligent maps in their multiple systems: customer service, supervisory control and data acquisition (SCADA), work management, financial, and human resources. They can capture spatial information on rainfall, wetland areas, and sacred burial grounds from outside sources and consolidate it for new decision-making tools. GIS can dramatically change the way utilities view their customers, shareholders, employees, and the communities they serve.

Empowering Electric and Gas Utilities with GIS is not about making maps with a GIS. Instead, it's about how GIS can transform the utility business in big and small ways. Enterprise GIS transforms businesses by lowering costs and hassles, greatly improving

Figure B Electric distribution systems can be complicated, such as this maze of wires and connections.

Photo by Lindsay Herdstrom, ESRI

decision making, and communicating to utility executives in ways they may never have experienced before. Nearly every aspect of the electric and gas utility business involves location. So, GIS is a means to capitalize on the value that location brings to utility processes.

Much of what I present in this book is based on my first-hand experience as an engineering and utility operations manager and executive. At Massachusetts' largest investor-owned electric and gas utility, I was involved in all aspects of transmission, substation and distribution engineering, supply chain, and operations. I was the champion, visionary, and manager in charge of the comprehensive GIS. I've faced many implementation challenges but I've seen how GIS can empower electric and gas utilities in many routine and dramatic ways.

This book is for utility managers and executives. It informs electric and gas line operational managers about GIS. Line managers can apply the insights to their own business problems.

This book is also for GIS professionals who are seeking opportunities in the gas and electric business. It introduces them, in a nontechnical way, to the pressures and challenges utilities confront. GIS professionals include vendors, conversion contractors, consultants, and programmers. This book presents a detailed business case for enterprise GIS and provides a template for those already working with GIS who want to expand its use throughout their company.

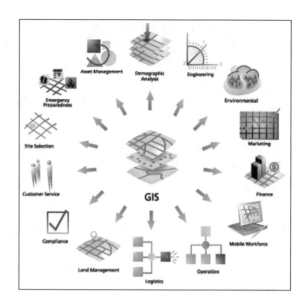

Figure C   Most of a utility's processes require spatial information.

Source: ESRI

Empowering Electric and Gas Utilities with GIS is also for chief information officers, chief technology officers, and information technology managers. It gives them insight into some of the real-world problems facing utility operations people and demonstrates how geospatial technology can improve operations.

As the title of this book suggests, GIS is a powerful technology that goes far beyond mere mapmaking. An enterprise approach to GIS encompasses a broad spectrum of data analysis to help utilities maximize efficiency, reduce risk, and serve the public.

—Bill Meehan
   Redlands, California

Acknowledgments

This book would not be possible without the hard work of the electric and gas user community. Members of that community have fully embraced GIS, advocated broad use of GIS in their companies, and made remarkable progress. This book could not have been completed without their leadership and vision. Dozens of their successes are contained in this book, but there are hundreds more throughout the community. What is impressive is the willingness of these visionaries to share their stories. They have made a significant difference in the performance of their companies. Utilities run smoother, save money, and better serve their customers and communities because of their work.

At ESRI, Laurence Litrico, our electric and gas industry coordinator, and Christine Truett, our administrative assistant, have been instrumental in helping me wade through the maze of logistics to get this work completed on schedule. A special thanks to Lew Nelson for providing the resources and support I needed to go on when frustration began to take its toll.

Thanks to the staff at ESRI Press. Mike Kataoka, my editor, provided the right blend of professional editing and moral support for the project. He supplied steady guidance and counsel. Kathleen Morgan provided much needed support in the permissions process. Jennifer Jennings and Savitri Brant contributed a brilliant design for my work and our user community's graphics. Thanks also to Jay Loteria for terrific artistry and Colleen Langley for precision copyediting. Heartfelt thanks go to Judy Hawkins who, from the very first time I approached her about this project, inspired me to complete it.

Thanks to Governor Jon Huntsman, Jr. of Utah for crafting the foreword.

The ESRI staff—Jeff Rashid and the electric and gas sales team; Tim Rankin, Pat Dolan, Lindsay Hernstrom, and the technical marketing team; Don Carson, Maroun Mounzer, and the professional services team—provided numerous stories, strategies, and ideas that are incorporated into the book. Roxanne Cox-Drake inspired this book by her work on the ESRI newsletter Energy Currents, along with the brilliant editing, writing, and compilation work of Barbara Shields. Carl Sylvester and Jim Geringer deserve a special mention for reviewing the manuscript. Of course, without the spectacular GIS software by ESRI, none of this would even be possible. Thanks to Clint Brown, Scott Morehouse, David Maguire, and their teams.

I thank all those customers, distributors, and business partners who have agreed to include their work in this book: Klaus Gerlick, Informi; Jens Henrik Sorensen, Aalborg Utility Department; Alex Hollis and Tom Coolidge, Advantica; AED-Sicad; Mike Williams, American Electric Power; Randy Patterson, Energen (Alagasco); Ted Wadzinski, Alliant Energy; Curt Kirkeby, Avista; Don Smith, Chelan Public Utility District; Lynne McNulty, Basin Electric; Ken Hilfiker, Chugach Electric; Larry Wilke, City of Burbank; Larry Callis, Kevin Brown and Darris Friend, Gainesville Regional Utilities, John Meier, City of Leesburg; Brad Benson and Bobby Curry, City of Lexington; Gary Bailey, City of Medicine Hat; Doug Elliot and Rita McMahon, City of Painseville; Pat Hohl, City of Riverside; Imagem; Marjorie Xavier, Companhia Paranaense de Energia, Brazil; Denzil McGill, Coserv; Bilal A. Hassan and Khatib & Alami, Electricite Du Liban; Enspiria; Liza van der Merwe, Eskom; Saed Abu-Helwa, GISTEC and the UAE Federal Electric and Water Authority; Terry Allen and Brad Schaaf, GeoFields; Jesse Glasgow, PhotoScience and Georgia Transmission; Jeff Grussing, Great River Energy; Rajesh Mathur, ESRI India and Gujarat Gas; Nargis Ladha, Hydro One; Baron Buckingham and Frank Mynar, Idaho Power; Ken Beville, Kissimmee Utility Authority; Keith Brooks, Kootenai Electric; Landworks; Michael Dannemiller, Lower Colorado River Authority; Mike Buri, Nashville Electric Service; Jenny Overhue, Nebraska Public Power District; North Delta Electricity Distribution Company; Northeastern Rural EMC; Ron Brush and Rob McElroy, New Century Software; John Wingfield, the New York Power Authority; Eric Kobosh, Opvantek; Greg Fox and Jana Laflair, Origin GeoSystems; Bob Harmon, Orlando Utilities Commission; George Suzuki, ESRI Japan and Osaka Gas; Patterson & Dewers; Power Engineers; Gathen Garcia and Ted Kircher, Public Service Company of New Mexico; Kevin Ruggiero, PPL; Mark Warner, Questar; RouteSmart; Bob Bernard, Saint John Energy; Myron Doherty, ESRI Canada and Salmon Arm Forest District; ESRI China and Shanghai Municipal Electric Power Company; Timothy Miller, Shenandoah Gas; David Breland, Southern Company; ESRI Sweden and Svenska Kraftnät; Tadpole Technology; Erika Murphy, Telvent Miner & Miner; Northeastern Rural Electric Corporation; Steve Murphy and Ian Fitzgerald, Truckee Donner Public Utility District.

I am particularly grateful to these special folks: Cindi Salas of CenterPoint Energy, whose enthusiasm for the vision of GIS continually inspires me; Linda Hecht, who got me started at ESRI; Jeff Meyers who is a model of commitment to the value of GIS in utilities; and Jack and Laura Dangermond, who make all of this possible.

A final thanks goes to my loving wife Shelly, who had to endure lonely evenings while I was in my office working on this project. Her patience, love, caring, and understanding keeps me going.

1

The utility enterprise: Getting down to business

The fire started in a manhole outside a huge power substation one hot, muggy July evening. It damaged nearly all the underground distribution cables feeding a major part of the city, affecting homes, office buildings, and several large manufacturing plants in the region. The devastation impacted thousands of people within a 20-mile radius. Police, firefighters, and utility employees worked around the clock. Emergency shelters housed displaced residents. Thousands of people went without air conditioning during the continuing record hot spell. AnyTown Energy endured negative press. Irate customers deluged the call center. It took several days and millions of dollars before AnyTown Energy repaired the cables and restored all the power.

In this hypothetical disaster involving AnyTown Energy, a fictitious utility, a coordinated geographic information system (GIS) would have enabled the company to spot problems before the fire started.

Many of the cables were running very close to their upper limit, although none at or above their rating. The engineers had performed the cable ratings analysis correctly. Electrical dispatchers were closely monitoring the situation prior to the fire. Based on good engineering and operating principles, the fire should not have started.

Further investigation revealed that a high-pressure steam line feeding a hospital laundry from a nearby power plant crossed the distribution duct bank that led from the substation into the manhole. The steam line was about six feet above and perpendicular to the duct bank. The utility built the steam line several years after it had installed the duct bank and calculated the cable ratings. The steam line raised the temperature of the distribution cables, causing them to overheat and subsequently ignite. As each circuit breaker tripped out, its cable burned and the remaining cables overloaded and burned as well.

Two issues emerged. First, the steam and distribution system data was not coordinated. The utility had no information to show that the steam line was close enough to the distribution cables to impact the thermal ratings, even though the utility owned and operated the distribution system, the power plant, and the steam system. Second, the backup cables traveled through the same manhole as the main cables. So the fire destroyed the main cable feeds and most of the backup feeds. Operating drawings showed each circuit separately on its own CAD (computer-aided design) created map. But these drawings did not show the geographic relationship of the cables to each other. There was no coordinated data or system in place that could answer the question, "Are there locations in our infrastructure where a single event, such as a fire, could cause significant risk to both primary and backup systems?" There was no system in place that could show the relationship of the utility's steam distribution system to its electrical system.

GIS and the utility industry

GIS provides more information than is visible on a static map. In the preceding scenario, the electrical dispatchers looked at all the cable maps, but couldn't find the problem. GIS helps users discover new things from spatial information that can aid in making decisions such as whether to lower the operating limits on electrical cables or where to expand a gas distribution main. GIS can answer questions like, "Are wetland areas close to major oil-filled equipment?" or "Are there gas leaks near major electrical switching equipment?" or "Where do transmission lines cross natural gas pipelines?" GIS could help users discover transmission line access paths within flood zones. It could figure out what would happen to transmission towers near the epicenter of an earthquake. GIS users can analyze the data to answer many questions and map the results.

Electric and gas utilities have many processes that relate directly to the operations of pipelines, power plants, and poles. Other processes relate to the business of running any large enterprise, such as accounting, customer service, and management. An enterprise GIS provides a platform of spatial information to serve nearly all the major elements of the electric and gas utility business, not just those pertaining to engineering or operations.

More and more companies, including utilities, are bringing an enterprise approach to their decision-support systems to broaden their view of their tactical units. The growing importance of enterprise resource planning (ERP) systems within utilities confirms this.

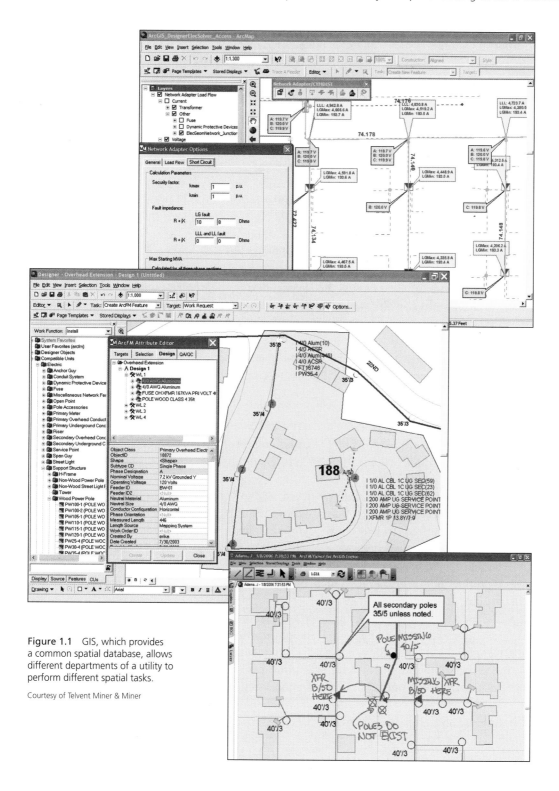

Figure 1.1 GIS, which provides a common spatial database, allows different departments of a utility to perform different spatial tasks.

Courtesy of Telvent Miner & Miner

Corporate planners designed the ERP systems to integrate the back-office systems, such as finance, payroll, human resources, customer care, and supply chain. Enterprise GIS expands the principle of integrating information as broadly as practical throughout a company, city, or even a country.

Utility companies implement enterprise GIS for two reasons. One, spatial information is important because nearly everything a utility does involves some kind of geographic location. And two, utilities see the business benefit of integrating activities. Since location is often the common denominator of tasks, enterprise GIS can reduce costs, improve decision making, build better collaboration and communication, and ultimately close the gaps in the utility's strategic performance targets. In an enterprise GIS, location data and spatial analysis for the utility assets are available to anyone in the company. Broadening the reach increases opportunities for strategic decision making.

AnyTown Energy may have avoided the cable fire if it had coordinated information on its enterprise spatial data. Likewise, utilities that can associate reliability incidents with tree trimming activities can better assess the effectiveness of their vegetation-management program. Utilities could also discover a correlation between customer attitudes and automated meter-reading applications with coordinated information. New sensor technologies imbedded in equipment, such as transformers and valves, can pinpoint a utility's assets in the field, learn their behavior in real time, and make faster decisions. For example, utilities can route crews to the precise location of a problem area, saving time and increasing customer satisfaction.

The utility GIS enterprise architecture

So what did AnyTown Energy lack? The utility had a sophisticated network of servers, routers, and PCs with a modern database management system. It had complex cable thermal simulation programs and steam network analysis programs. It had plenty of data about the electric and steam systems. Yet, information available to the utility was incomplete. The applications didn't work together. The workflows didn't connect. The steam department didn't have access to data from the electric department. What the utility lacked was an enterprise GIS architecture that aligned with the overall utility information framework.

That architecture includes these interrelated components:

- Workflow and process models identify the master processes and subprocesses that drive the business.
- Data models describe the data, structure relationships, and behaviors that are needed for the workflows in a logical and disciplined way.
- Geodatasets are the utility data itself. They include all the land, facility, and imagery data that pertains to the utility's operating area.
- Visualization and output products are tools to help make decisions, perform tasks, and communicate.
- Integration framework allows for spatially enabled corporate systems.
- Physical system includes the hardware, operating systems, processes, tools, database management system (DBMS), and networks that make the GIS function.

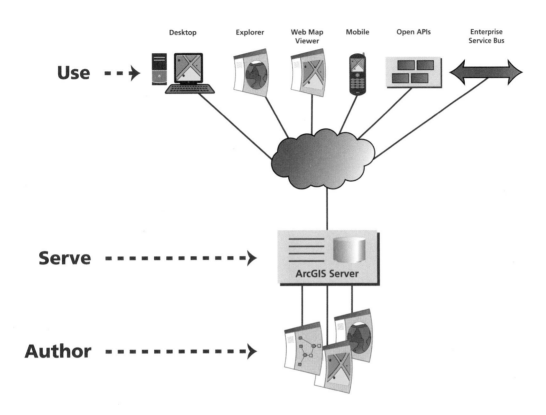

Figure 1.2   A utility can author, serve, and use asset information throughout its operation with an enterprise GIS.

Source: ESRI

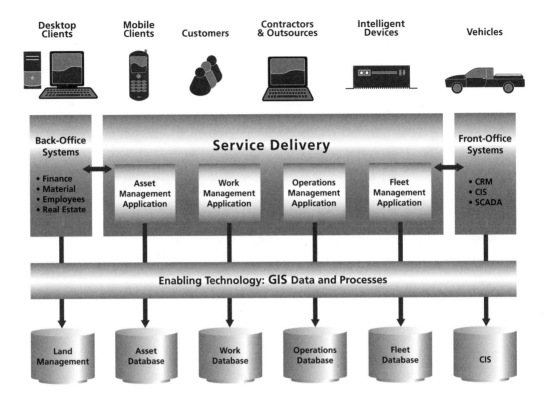

Figure 1.3   An enterprise GIS architecture aligns with the overall utility information framework.

Source: ESRI

Workflow and process models

Dozens of critical master processes exist in a utility. Examples might be restoring power after a storm, rendering an accurate bill and collecting the payment, paying property taxes, complying with a regulatory reporting requirement, hooking up a new customer, or filing an annual statement with the U.S. Securities and Exchange Commission. Every process contains a workflow. As stated earlier, most utility processes have some element of location associated with them. So nearly every workflow and process model within a utility requires something from the GIS.

Since GIS typically evolves from the mapping groups, utility workers tend to associate GIS only with utility mapping. So those responsible for the operating maps can fall into a trap. They believe that producing accurate-as-built maps is the GIS' only critical business need. Some utilities spend an enormous amount of time on the workflow of mapping, like detailing the design, annotation placement, and level of detail. This minimizes the strategic value GIS provides to the rest of the organization while elevating the importance of the map products. In the hypothetical story above, AnyTown Energy had replicated exactly the old cable distribution maps using a CAD system. It never set up a workflow to check to see if backup cables ran in the same manholes as primary cables. Further, there was no workflow that crossed from the steam department to the electric department.

GIS is more than simply producing the standard operating maps utilities have been so used to dealing with. GIS is a critical element, either directly or indirectly, in nearly every electric and gas utility workflow.

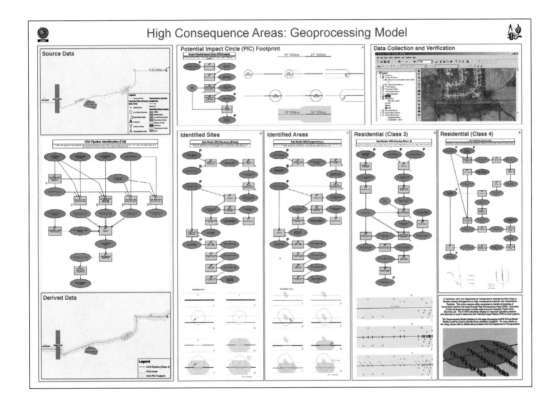

Figure 1.4   High consequence area process flow is created in the geoprocessing framework as part of a GIS.

Utility operations: United Arab Emirates

Federal Electricity and Water Authority (FEWA), United Arab Emirates (UAE), implemented an enterprise GIS for its electric and water utilities. GIS makes the utility's asset database readily available to staff members in the Ajman emirate. The GIS-enabled corporate Web site helps FEWA deliver quick and efficient maintenance and service to the company's 175,000 customers.

GIS has improved efficiency in overall operations. FEWA owns six power generation plants and provides electric, gas, and water services to northern emirates. Before GIS was implemented, data maintenance had been erratic and time-consuming. Keeping track of changes was difficult because hard-copy maps and digital CAD drawings were shared among the utility's different departments.

FEWA called on GISTEC, the ESRI software distributor in UAE, to develop a system that met the utility's needs and resolved its data management problems. GISTEC implemented enterprise GIS software that included state-of-the-art asset management solutions to improve FEWA business processes and workflows.

A central GIS was established in conjunction with supervisory control and data acquisition (SCADA) to enhance FEWA's technical maintenance and management of electric and water assets. This combination served to optimize resources of time, personnel, and support material during normal daily activities. FEWA's widespread area of operations includes remote areas in Ajman, Umm al-Quwain, Ras Al Khaimah, and Fujairah, so the challenge was to get GIS to all the company's service areas. GISTEC configured a system that met FEWA's specific business requirements and made GIS accessible to the entire utility.

GISTEC soon launched the GIS-enabled intranet site, which provided access to the company's CAD data and other databases. High-resolution QuickBird (satellite) imagery provided a backdrop of FEWA's area of operations for facility data layers. The intranet site provided an effective project communications tool among different users who were encouraged to provide input and share knowledge.

Data collection was a major part of the project because it involved extensive surveys in fifteen communities in Ajman. GISTEC, with its subcontractor MAPS geosystems, undertook the task of updating data by field collection and final data conversion. Several types of features were collected directly from the field, such as meters and substations. Specialized ground-penetrating, radar-detection techniques were used to collect consumer house-connection lines data. Data was merged with land records, photographs, and maintenance history information. Deployment processes included performing system acceptance tests, training end users, and setting up the complete system implementation in the areas of operation.

FEWA's enterprise GIS consists of one central geodatabase for storing and retrieving multiutility asset information. A set of core ESRI software products manages the database, including ArcSDE, ArcIMS, ArcGIS, and ArcPad. Other core software includes ArcFM from Telvent Miner & Miner, Oracle, and Citrix.

From *Energy Currents*, fall 2006

Figure 1.5 The Federal Electricity and Water Authority of the United Arab Emirates has a centralized GIS to view network assets.

Courtesy of Federal Electricity and Water Authority, United Arab Emirates

Data models

Once the workflows are established and process models built, the data models need to be constructed. In its simplest form, a data model is a structured way of describing the data needed in a workflow. Unified Modeling Language (UML) is the standard format for most data models. When described by UML, the data model presents the data in a structured object-oriented way. The purpose of the data model is to capture in one document three essential components of data used in the workflows and process models:

- attributes, such as the rating in kilovolt amperes [kVA], and the phase and manufacturer of a transformer
- relationship, such as the relationship of a pole to a wire or a steam line to an electrical distribution duct bank
- behavior, such as whether material type values are valid for a gas main

Some of the data needed in a workflow may come from outside the utility, such as street opening permit data, indigenous population protected areas, or zoning overlays. The complete data model includes all types of data generated internally and externally. There are data models for land information, gas and electric distribution, electric transmission, pipeline, customers, and many others, depending on the workflow and process models.

AnyTown Energy's data model would include all the attributes of the electric system and the structures that support the cables. It could include relationships to other facilities that have significant impact on the performance of the electrical cables, such as a nearby high-pressure steam line.

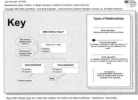

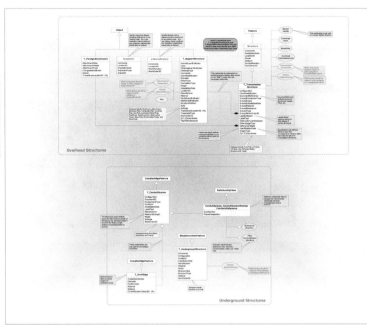

Figure 1.6 ESRI maintains an extensive collection of free, downloadable data models, including models for electric and gas distribution and transmission.

Source: ESRI

Figure 1.7 Leesburg staff members can lay data, such as network gas lines shown here, on aerial photography.

Courtesy of City of Leesburg, Florida

Facilities management: City of Leesburg

The City of Leesburg, Florida, uses GIS in many of its departments to keep costs low and service quality high. Leesburg's different municipal services were on multiple software platforms and the maps were in a variety of formats. For its new GIS, Leesburg chose the ESRI ArcGIS platform combined with Telvent Miner & Miner's ArcFM to create facilities management solutions.

It was initially thought that the city's eight-member GIS division would be the principal user. After a needs assessment, it became clear that other departments wanted to use GIS. The city decided to make GIS available to electric and gas department engineers for network design.

ESRI and Telvent Miner & Miner, an ESRI business partner that specializes in GIS implementation for utilities, developed a data model tailored to specifications of its other utilities. For example, domain changes were made to show the type of materials that workers use. Also, preferences in terminology were modified to specific department usage.

Staff designed a tracing application in-house using Telvent Miner & Miner's Designer software. The Designer product provides an integrated environment for preparing construction work sketches, workflow management, structural and network analyses, automated layouts, and job cost estimates. It provides an automated means to update the baseline corporate GIS database based on changes to the electric, gas, and water distribution facilities shown on a work sketch. This helps engineers create different versions for planning and extending lines.

The City of Leesburg contracted out the facility's inventory with Southeastern Reprographics, Inc. (SRI), which recorded facility data using GPS. This helped staff members see results right away because they could lay data over aerial photography and see how well it matched. This has been useful for making adjustments.

From GIS for Municipalities and Cooperatives

Geodatasets

The data model describes the structure of the data to be used in the enterprise GIS, while a geodataset is the data itself. Much of the data resides within the utility. However, since workers from a variety of departments (such as the electric and steam departments) captured and created the data over long periods of time, the data is often inconsistent. For example, information about a specific pole may exist in easement records, plant accounting records, operating maps, streetlight billing reports, and work-order documents. Yet the information may be all different. Obtaining or creating good data often represents the largest cost of a comprehensive enterprise GIS. Not surprisingly, the more complete, timely, and accurate the data, the more valuable a resource the data is for the utility. The data for both the electric and steam systems existed at AnyTown Energy, but it was not in a form conducive to good decision making.

Visualization and output products

With the information created through GIS, utility employees can make better decisions, communicate those decisions more clearly, and deploy resources in a more coordinated way. That means the output products need to communicate effectively. Early digital mapping systems, called automated mapping/facility management (AM/FM) systems, were devoted to the exact replication of existing hand-drawn maps. Employees were unable to see new relationships or potential dangers, such as a steam line crossing an electric duct bank. Devotion to exacting map representations inhibits new and creative ways of visualizing utility geographic data. Today, GIS users present mapping data for the specific media, whether the Internet or wireless and hand-held devices. Therefore, these maps are free from the old-fashioned mapping conventions that applied to hand-drawn maps. As utility managers continue to see the strategic value of GIS, the requirement to precisely replicate the old hand-drawn or AM/FM-based maps will fade.

If AnyTown Energy had a simple visualization of both the electric and the steam systems in one view, the dispatchers would have had a vivid warning of the disaster that was about to happen.

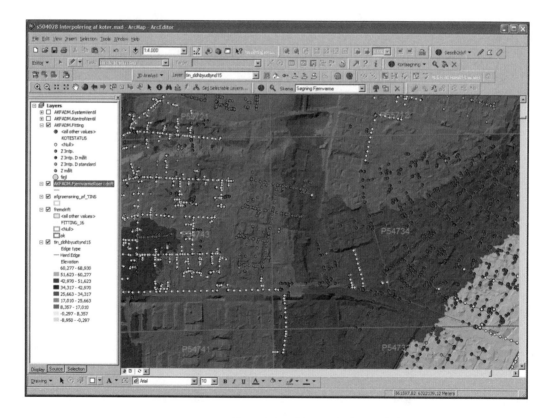

Figure 1.8   Different utility lines, including district heating, power cables, water, and gas lines, are shown on this map.

Courtesy of City of Aalborg, Denmark

An enterprise approach: Aalborg, Denmark

Aalborg, the fourth largest city in Denmark, has implemented various GIS-based civic initiatives, including the "Active Map of Aalborg" and "Digital Democracy in Rural Areas." By providing easier access to municipal information via the Internet, these mapping services keep citizens better informed and involved in the local decision-making process.

One of Aalborg's many noteworthy endeavors was the consolidation of all municipal utility companies into a single agency responsible for gas, electric, district heating, water, wastewater, and waste disposal management. A key element of the amalgamated Aalborg utility agency was the centralization of all GIS efforts. GIS data and services are provided by a single department which ensures that each utility is working from the same updated maps and data. This has further allowed the Aalborg municipality to streamline government and improve services because critical information is readily available to the various city departments.

After Aalborg developed an extensive geodatabase, the GIS department created utility-specific data models. The Aalborg geodatabase is updated daily and contains approximately 600 feature classes. Some of the feature class data comes from the integration with other systems, including supervisory control and data acquisition (SCADA), customer billing systems, network modeling systems, cadastral data, aerial photography, technical basemaps, and separate databases.

The municipality began to construct functionally integrated and coherent data models to support the development of its spatial databases. The designs needed to be dynamic and compatible with existing data. The models gave Aalborg a high degree of flexibility and more freedom to compare and analyze data.

Aalborg integrated its GIS with its financial system, which provides the city with a spatially enabled assets management tool, giving a complete overview of the municipality's assets from a geographic perspective. This includes detailing all in-ground infrastructure, such as pipelines and their age, condition, and expected life span.

The enterprise GIS has enabled Aalborg to develop a highly intelligent database along with a network surveillance system that allows supervisors to continually monitor all transactions throughout their system and perform analysis and control procedures. For example, the real-time SCADA system can determine whether a recorded leak is critical and requires immediate attention. Collected information is displayed in a logical and organized fashion in the GIS to facilitate any remedial action.

From *Energy Currents*, summer 2005

Integration framework

Enterprise GIS needs to become part of the overall utility information technology (IT) framework. Since GIS can apply to nearly all aspects of the utility, it makes sense that the spatial information be readily available to all IT systems throughout the enterprise. Today, there are many examples of utilities integrating their GIS through common integration frameworks. Utilities have the ability to publish their GIS data and other corporate data through Web services accessed by outside agencies. They can also be Web service consumers. They can use their GIS as a location-based service framework for locating employees or equipment using standard field devices. Web services can be an effective way to extend the GIS to external providers and government agencies. Utilities could subscribe to a service from an organization responsible for keeping data current and can seamlessly integrate in the utility's enterprise GIS. For example, if a transmission department needs to know the status of vegetated wetlands surrounding a proposed site for a transmission line, it could gather the information from the local government's conservation commission Web service.

If our fictitious AnyTown Energy had a common operating model or view of all its data, including historical loading, weather forecast data, as well as the geographic data, it could have created corrective actions, determined financial impacts, and developed contingency plans.

The physical system

Servers, desktop PCs, enterprise application integration (EAI) buses; and software, networks, routers, operating systems, storage devices, wireless devices, and DBMSs play an integral role in effectively deploying enterprise GIS. The physical system must be coordinated with process models and workflows. AnyTown Energy's CAD files that contained the electric cable system data were not part of an overarching IT enterprise framework.

Enterprise GIS to unify the utility

Building an enterprise GIS is about improving critical business processes that have a spatial component, which most utility processes have. Workflows and process models must be examined in the context of the core IT systems such as billing, customer service, finance, supply chain, work management, outage management, and supervisory control and data acquisition (SCADA) systems that underpin the business processes. Enterprise GIS is one of the underpinnings of the total utility IT infrastructure. GIS, viewed as a spatial information architecture, has the potential to unify the processes within a utility and enables utilities to see problems before they become disasters. So when the question is asked, "Are there locations in our infrastructure where a single event, such as a fire, could cause significant risk to both primary and backup systems?" there is a system in place to provide the answer. That answer will likely be in the form of a map created by enterprise GIS showing those precise locations.

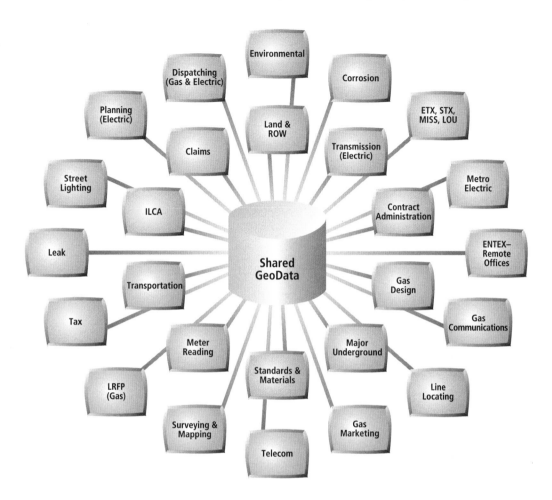

Figure 1.9   Through custom-designed interfaces, the enterprise GIS can be accessed from multiple locations and data can be easily transferred.

Courtesy of CenterPoint Energy

2

Life cycle management and utilities: Planning, designing, engineering with GIS

AnyTown Energy's mapping department had an old automated mapping/facilities management (AM/FM) system that captured work-order information to produce operating maps. The system was not integrated with any of the corporate systems. The twenty mapping technicians had large piles of work-order folders on their desks. Each folder contained the original design sketches produced by the distribution planning department, a list of materials used during construction, and any field notes made by the crews. The mapping technician's job was to incorporate the as-built information from the work-order packages into the AM/FM system. AnyTown Energy had centralized the mapping department in the corporate office building.

AnyTown Energy decentralized the distribution planning department in each of five major service centers. Distribution planners had long lists of new work orders to design. The designs started with a plot from the AM/FM system that showed the area of the work order and the current configuration of the utility system. The planner then manually sketched the information for the construction crews on the AM/FM system plot. The plots showed pole removals, gas valves to add, new poles to add, and wires or pipes to run, among other information. The planners manually wrote a list of the material for the job directly on the print. They also entered the material and a text description of the work in AnyTown Energy's work management system. Clerical people made multiple copies of the work-order design packages. These packages were either faxed or mailed to the construction offices. Distribution planners rarely had time to verify that the AM/FM system information was correct in the field.

Error-prone system

The electrical crew chief received his day's work orders. After twenty years on the job, the chief knew the work-order designs tended to contain a lot of mistakes. As his crew arrived on the job site, the chief took a quick look at the work order to grasp the intent. However, he directed the crew to do the job his way. Some days, he documented major deviations from the design sketches. Usually his field note simply read, "constructed as designed," regardless of whether the job was built exactly as designed. These were the same field notes that eventually landed on the technician's desk in the mapping department.

Whether the work-order field notes were complete, legible, or neither, they were intended to document the differences between what was supposed to be built, as indicated on the work-order design, and what the crews actually built. The more inaccurate or out-of-date the source documents were, the greater the risk that designs would be wrong. So, the crews took on the responsibility to do the work based on actual field conditions. If the deviations were extensive, the crew chief would not be inclined to create detailed field notes, finding the task onerous and time consuming. Marking up work-order sketches on the fender of a line truck was not conducive to completeness and accuracy. Many crew chiefs provided little or no feedback. While it was easy to blame the crews for not properly documenting the field deviations, the real problem was insufficient and inaccurate information and poor work processes.

Accurate data leads to accurate designs. Inaccurate designs lead to greater field deviations. Greater field deviations increase the backlog of work in the mapping department. In this example, planners created the designs while mapping technicians posted the deviations to the source maps. The result was that the people who created the designs didn't get appropriate feedback and the process never improved. The planners blamed the mapping technicians for creating inaccurate source documents, the crews blamed the planners for poor designs, and the mapping technicians blamed the crews for incorrect field notes.

In the meantime, the data quality suffered. To make matters worse, the mapping technicians had to decipher crew chiefs' hand-written notes from months or even years earlier, adding to the time for posting the work orders. As if that wasn't bad enough, since the mapping technician, distribution planner, and crew chief were in different departments, none of them had access to the same information at the same time.

Nonetheless, utilities learn how to deal with this data mismanagement and the inevitable low-operating performance. They still provide service—turning lights back on, plugging leaks, and adding accounts to the system—but waste resources at customers' expense. Utilities would not have to incur costs for false starts, missing material, longer-than-acceptable outage restoration times, and field rework if they had timely and accurate records to begin with.

On the same page

Utilities can dramatically improve this situation with GIS. If AnyTown Energy had adopted an enterprise GIS as part of the overall IT platform, the crew chief would have full access to GIS via a mobile device and could easily update the as-built information. The mapping technician would get immediate digital feedback about the deviations. The distribution planners would have full access to the field notes and any deviations so they would know how to improve the designs.

A utility's infrastructure is constantly changing, adding lines, connecting new customers, and plugging leaks. Engineers plan for increases in capacity for a new part of the city. They replace cast iron mains with plastic ones. Like most enterprises that operate and maintain complex infrastructures, utility companies follow a particular life cycle for the work. The elements of the utility life cycle are: (1) demand or load forecasting, (2) planning, (3) asset management, (4) engineering, (5) surveying and rights procurement, (6) design, (7) construction, and (8) facility documentation.

Demand or load forecasting

Many utilities project a more or less uniform load growth pattern throughout their service territory. This process is called regional load forecasting. The reality is that load growth isn't always uniform throughout large areas, such as a utility's service territory. Loads grow faster in areas where land and zoning permits development, and slower in established areas. The smaller the area of load projection, the better the chance of matching the projected load growth to the infrastructure's capability. Subregional load forecasting—that is, using smaller load forecasting areas—is much more desirable. Utilities have traditionally avoided it because it is costly, time consuming, and requires access to data from many sources outside the utility.

Utilities can use enterprise GIS and the multitude of data sources widely available through the Internet to perform subregional load forecasting simply and economically. They can subscribe to Web services from agencies, such as local planning commissions and

Life cycle management for utilities

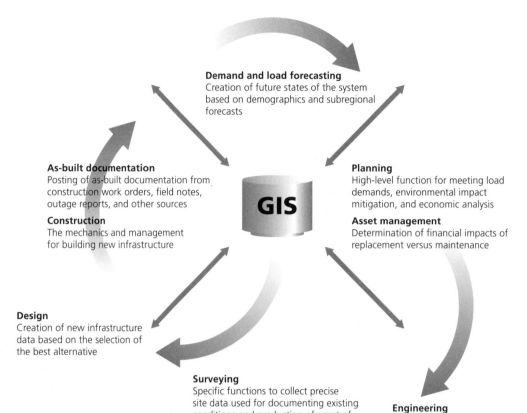

Demand and load forecasting
Creation of future states of the system based on demographics and subregional forecasts

As-built documentation
Posting of as-built documentation from construction work orders, field notes, outage reports, and other sources

Construction
The mechanics and management for building new infrastructure

GIS

Planning
High-level function for meeting load demands, environmental impact mitigation, and economic analysis

Asset management
Determination of financial impacts of replacement versus maintenance

Design
Creation of new infrastructure data based on the selection of the best alternative

Surveying
Specific functions to collect precise site data used for documenting existing conditions and production of grant of location documents

Engineering
Analytical assessment of alternatives, load flow, gas flow, and system configuration

Figure 2.1   Utilities follow a particular life cycle for the work.
Source: ESRI

ministries, for many kinds of current and projected data. Or, they can simply get copies of the data directly. Forecasters can use data sources such as vacant land-use inventory, present and proposed zoning, annexation plans, census data projections, and regional planning studies. These disparate data sources help them determine the future population densities. It also gives greater insight into customer behavior. Forecasters can consolidate and reconcile the various data layers using the powerful spatial processing ability of GIS to get composite views of the reconciled data.

These load forecasts show how the population profile is likely to look one, two, five, and even ten years into the future. Using customer-usage data derived from their customer information and load research systems, utilities create spatial views of customer usage patterns. Utilities can organize pockets of projected load growth into polygons as separate layers within their enterprise GIS. Forecasters can then automatically translate population projections into load projections.

GIS applications and tools: Avista Corporation

Avista Corporation provides natural gas distribution services to more than 298,000 customers in regions of the Pacific Northwest. Avista's facilities management GIS project has developed construction design tools (CDT), models, and applications that make it possible for both gas and electric construction designers to use GIS in their job designs.

The CDT is used by designers to place new facilities on the map. This process produces construction prints to communicate work orders to field crews. It also keeps the GIS data up to date with continuous changes occurring on the system. An added benefit is the standardization of designs.

Avista is further developing the gas compliance tool to track U.S. Department of Transportation requirements spatially. Read-only GIS applications help field workers enhance work processes.

Avista's gas network is modeled so that the pipe, emergency operating plan (EOP), and cathodic systems can be analyzed by sharing the same network. During an emergency, EOP valves that need to be closed can be located easily and all affected customers identified. A cathodic protection system is required on steel pipes to prevent corrosion. The gas model facilitates analyzing the system to ensure all pipes are protected correctly.

From *GIS for Gas Utilities*

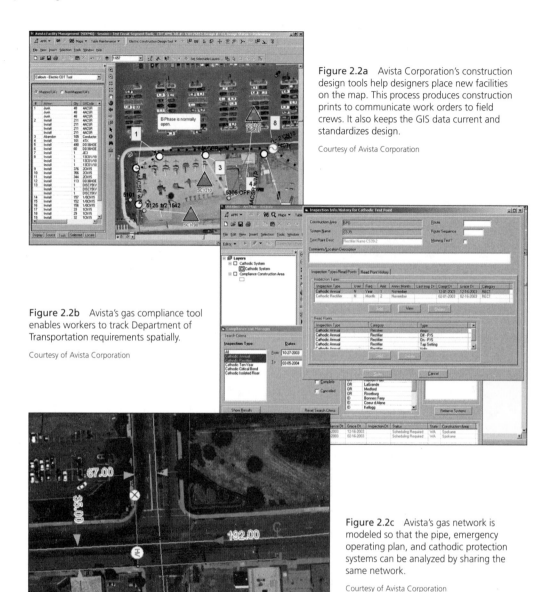

Figure 2.2a Avista Corporation's construction design tools help designers place new facilities on the map. This process produces construction prints to communicate work orders to field crews. It also keeps the GIS data current and standardizes design.

Courtesy of Avista Corporation

Figure 2.2b Avista's gas compliance tool enables workers to track Department of Transportation requirements spatially.

Courtesy of Avista Corporation

Figure 2.2c Avista's gas network is modeled so that the pipe, emergency operating plan, and cathodic protection systems can be analyzed by sharing the same network.

Courtesy of Avista Corporation

Planning

The first objective of the planning process is to project what equipment (such as valves, city gates, transmission conductors, supply transformers, circuit breakers, switches, distribution transformers, fuses, gas mains, conductors, cables) exceed their ratings based on the load projections. The system engineer compares the load projections for a future year based on what the system will look like then. The engineer can use GIS to find all the substation transformers that will exceed their normal rating within the next ten years, display those transformers on a map, and label the year that the transformer will exceed its rating.

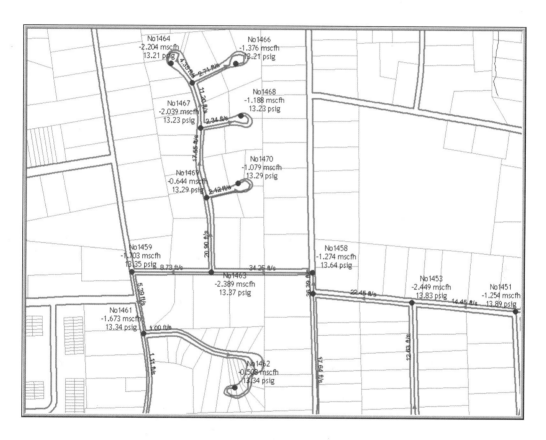

Figure 2.3   Planners get the result of a gas analysis directly into the GIS.

Courtesy of Advantica

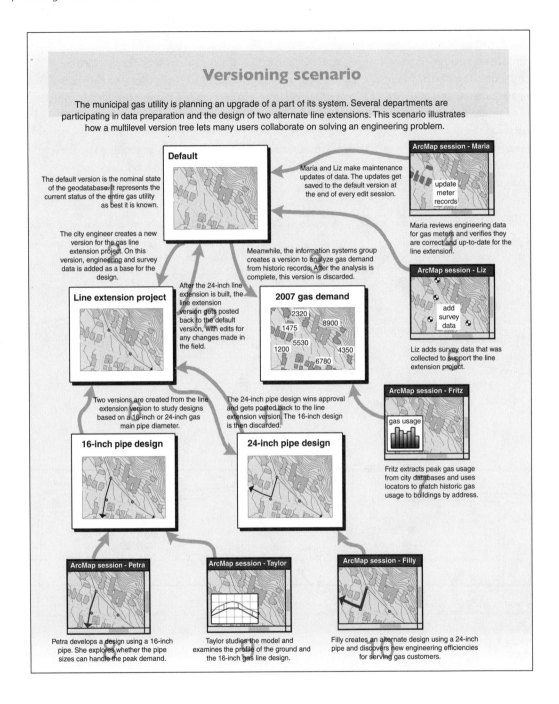

Figure 2.4   This scenario shows how versions can be used to support a modeling environment for utilities that build complex systems.

Reproduced by permission from *Modeling Our World: The ESRI Guide to Geodatabase Design*

The second objective is to determine how best to relieve overloaded equipment. System engineers can propose to reconfigure the network to add new equipment or upgrade existing equipment. They can develop scenarios to determine how the system behaves under both normal and abnormal operating conditions in these future states.

System engineers have historically had an ongoing problem with managing different future states of the utility system. Today's GIS users can solve this by using the concept of versioning. Using GIS, planners have the ability to maintain multiple states or versions of the data. A version is not a copy of the data. Instead, features that are changed from the original are simply noted as belonging to a particular version. Present and future states within the same database can be maintained within the single enterprise GIS. As people make changes to the as-is state, those changes are reflected in all future states. Utilities can view the current system in relation to future and alternative states without having to create multiple copies of the GIS database.

System engineers can run network analysis models from the data maintained directly in the GIS-versioned database. Some examples of network analysis programs are gas pressure and flow analysis, electric load flow, and short-circuit analysis. Automated network analysis tools are fast and efficient; they can perform their calculations in minutes or less. For utilities that have not integrated their planning tools with GIS, the time to prepare the data for analysis can be significant. Further, system engineers tend to capture the data at one point in time. They may not know that the factors that contributed to the analysis can change regularly.

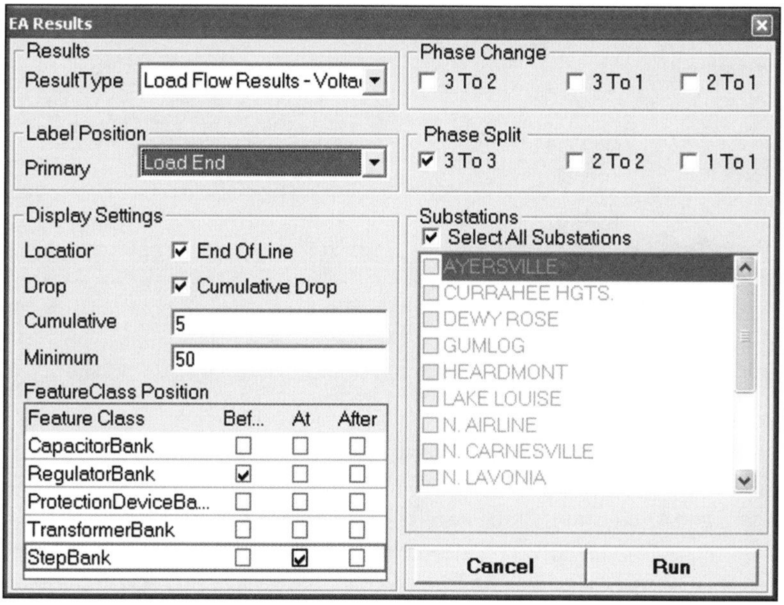

Figure 2.5
Planners use GIS to model the electrical system and create load flows.

Courtesy of Origin GeoSystems

GIS aids long-term planning

To illustrate the problem of not integrating the planning activities within the enterprise GIS, consider the following five-year planning case:

System engineers project loads five years into the future and suggest an upgrade strategy for potentially overloaded circuits. They assemble the data needed to run analysis calculations, including lengths and parameters of conductors and other network characteristics. Then they assemble the data from maps and records. They input the data into stand-alone network analysis tools and examine the results. This may create a number of separate cases, which they store in individual files. Once the particular study is completed, they archive the files.

The following year, the system engineers again refine the five-year plan. They have two choices: they can resurrect the archived files from the previous five-year study cases and try to figure out what has changed, or they can start the process all over again. If they decide to use the previous year's cases, they have to examine every piece of data and compare it to the new as-is data. This is a tedious and error-prone process. So, what would likely happen is that the system engineers would re-input the data from the currently available records. Since the load forecasting data would be a year out of date, they would have to find new data.

The versioning and advanced data management capabilities of GIS greatly simplifies the process. The system engineer creates a version of what the system would look like in five years, along with the load profiles that correspond to that period. Cases are saved as separate versions with very little additional data stored in the database. When the system engineers revisit the five-year planning study the following year, the base data would have updated automatically. The changes made by technicians, planners, and crew chiefs are already in place. The load forecasting data could also be stored data layers in any number of versions.

In one database, enterprise GIS users manage

- the electric and gas infrastructure data as it exists;
- all future proposed states of the infrastructure;
- all contingency states of the infrastructure;
- the present and future states of the service territory land features; and
- load forecasting data by year.

This means that system engineers can frequently look at their long-term plans without the arduous process of data collection and validation. This helps them decide whether to accelerate or decelerate projects. For instance, they could learn that a circuit is old or prone to failure and decide to rebuild it. They could discover that a section of the city is earmarked for redevelopment. They may find an altered boundary on a vegetated wetlands or a zoning change. The system engineer's primary goal is to assess the utility's ability to meet future load requirements. Enterprise GIS users provide easy data maintenance for present and future states of the system. It clearly shows engineers what is happening in the system.

The end result of the planning process is a series of proposed projects visualized as maps. System engineers can also estimate costs as part of the planning process so they can create capital budgets.

Four tools are needed for utility system planning:

1. An inventory and configuration of the gas and electric system, including all the ratings of the equipment. This is contained in the enterprise GIS as-is state.
2. Demand or load projections that include one-, two-, five-, and ten-year projections of area or service territory load based upon historic trends. GIS users can create layers to show where load is projected to grow in stages over specified time intervals.
3. Network analysis tools that are often embedded into the software or are able to seamlessly integrate network information. The results of the analysis are populated and displayed in the GIS.
4. Automated cost estimates that are based on new equipment added to the system and attributes such as length of cables and pipes, based on the data contained in the GIS.

Engineering and design: Alagasco

Alagasco turned to GIS software to improve its asset management. Providing reliable natural gas service in Alabama for 150 years, the utility serves 463,000 customers in 200 communities.

To centralize all accounting and asset management activities, Alagasco initiated two projects, the Enterprise Resource Management Application (ERMA) and the Mapping and Geographic Information System (MAGI). These two systems can be accessed throughout the corporation. This improves engineering analysis, supports asset management activities, and streamlines work-order processing.

The ERMA application works with SAP to handle asset management and project accounting needs and MAGI works with Telvent Miner & Miner's ArcFM and Designer products built on ESRI GIS technology. Telcordia Technologies acted as the systems integrator for the entire project life cycle.

The Designer Work Flow Manager tool is being customized to manage the gas utility's extensive design reporting requirements so that in the future, engineers can

- enter work request information;
- perform a geographic design based on SAP stock code data;
- create a construction plot;
- generate a cost estimate for the design;
- generate a construction package with forms required for design approval; and
- submit a job for design approval.

Some data needs to be accessed by both the MAGI and ERMA systems, such as regulator station data that is stored in SAP for inspection tracking and in GIS for location and critical pressure information. Data integrity rules were established that dictated which system owned which data. For project management, interfaces are being designed to take the design specifications from the Telvent Miner & Miner Work Flow Manager application and create projects and associated job information in SAP. The future integration of these intelligent technologies will leverage the strength of the database to improve the efficiency and effectiveness of work processes throughout the company.

From *GIS for Gas Utilities*

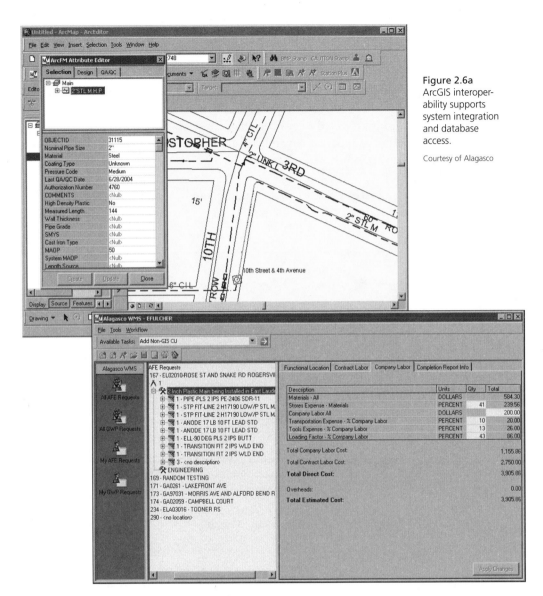

Figure 2.6a
ArcGIS interoperability supports system integration and database access.

Courtesy of Alagasco

Figure 2.6b   GIS supports workflow processes.

Courtesy of Alagasco

Asset management

Asset management is about making the right decisions to repair or replace equipment, assess the risks concerning when to repair or replace, and prioritize all work within the system for budgeting and forecasting. To do this effectively, utilities must

- have a solid inventory of actual assets;
- know where assets are in relation to the environment;
- know the condition of assets; and
- decide what actions they need to take to optimize costs and reliability, often a choice between maintaining or replacing.

Because the vast majority of utilities' assets are spread widely over their service territories, enterprise GIS is the most effective way to monitor asset inventory. Utilities can clearly see their assets' condition by organizing a myriad of attributes along the transmission lines, gas mains, and distribution systems. Utilities also need to know what exists near their facilities. For example, a gas transmission line operator should know about plans to build a facility that could be endangered, such as a nursing home close to the pipeline. Charts, even databases, can't provide the intuition of a GIS.

While GIS in utilities is typically associated with displaying physical devices on a map, utilities can also use it to visualize other attributes of the system. For example, a utility may want to show the age of equipment distributed throughout its service territory. Or it may want to spatially display equipment maintenance costs. Perhaps the utility wants to integrate data about age, reliability history, and maintenance costs. Asset managers can use this data, combined with data about critical facilities, to make wiser decisions about replacement than if they viewed the data alone.

Using enterprise GIS, the asset managers see the plans of the system engineers. Likewise, the system engineers can view the plans of the asset managers. This results in better collaboration and coordination of projects.

Engineering

Utilities create projects from

- the planning process that looks at future load forecasts in relation to the capability of the current system;
- the asset management process that looks at the life cycle costs of maintaining versus replacing equipment;
- new customers connecting to the system;
- reliability-related projects not forecast; and
- natural disasters and their aftermath.

Once planners, asset managers, and system engineers make a case that the system needs to be modified, design engineers determine how to upgrade a circuit, add a new gas main, or locate a distributed generator. They make decisions ranging from what kind of conductor or material to use, to whether parts of the system should be built underground or overhead. They may need to decide how to route a new circuit, determine what parts of a circuit require new protection, or how the gas main is to operate as a backup to another main. Like the planning engineers, design engineers perform network analysis studies to ensure proper pressure and voltage drop under normal and emergency conditions; corrosion and short-circuit studies to make sure the system is adequately protected against fault currents; and fuse coordination studies to ensure the absolute minimum disruption occurs during a fault. Using GIS, design engineers can maintain many versions of the system without having to maintain separate copies of the utility system data. GIS users not only manage many alternatives to a specific engineering project, but they can manage all the engineering projects and their alternatives within a single GIS database.

Enterprise GIS allows design engineers to see what the planning and asset management groups propose. This provides insight into how their solutions will coordinate with the company's plans. Engineers also can leverage the spatial analytical functionality of GIS to automate many of the engineering functions. Examples include automatic placement of poles to minimize costs, shortest path routing of cables through an underground conduit system, and automatic design of subdivision electric and gas systems. This allows engineers to run more scenarios to minimize costs and increase reliability. Using accurate data and automated tools substantially lowers capital costs.

Figure 2.7   Avista Corporation uses GIS to generate analysis models.

Courtesy of Avista Corporation

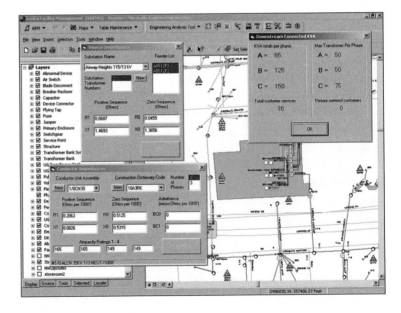

Surveying and rights procurement

Many municipalities require utilities to prepare petitioning plans to grant rights for placing poles, towers, mains, and any other equipment installed in public areas. Since granting location has to be accurate, utilities hire surveyors to create the plans. Then they submit these plans for approval by the public works commission or municipal council. Once approved, the plans become legal documents granting location. If the utility needs equipment on private property, it has to obtain licenses or easements. The utility must have precise surveys for the legal description of the easement. Design engineers may require test borings to determine if there are underground obstructions that are not marked on reference documents. Surveyors need to capture the locations of any obstructions.

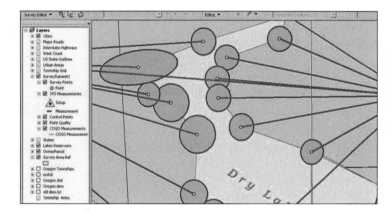

Figure 2.8   The ESRI Survey Analyst extension manages error ellipses of actual locations based on survey instruments.

Source: ESRI

GIS users can transform the classic metes and bounds of survey measurement into typical data processed in the software. Design engineers can then look to GIS for a complete picture of all the data captured by the surveyor. By capturing field information, such as test borings, utilities will preserve that data for future projects that occur in the area.

GIS users play a major role in the preparation of the petition plans, the management of the survey data, and the final legal documentation. The petition plans are output products produced by GIS users, with special emphasis on the proposed location of the electrical or gas facilities. The GIS integrates smoothly with document management systems. For example, it can create links between the location of the facility, a pole, and the legal grant-of-location document. Conversely, by selecting the grant-of-location document in the document management system, the facility can be located within the GIS.

Utilities must obtain permits to work in public areas that often require them to describe the requested work on map-based sketches. GIS users can create the permit application, track its progress, and manage the permit process during construction. Utilities can then see the permit's progress in relation to all the other activities within the geographic region.

Using enterprise GIS, there is a significant opportunity for utilities and municipalities to work together to automate much of the information exchange that's involved in the granting of rights and permits.

Design

Once the engineering projects have been determined, rights to land and easements granted, and the route and specific parameters of the new construction developed, the utility must then prepare design documents for the building contractor.

Many utilities do not design their facilities using GIS. Instead, planners and designers manually sketch the designs on top of GIS plots. Some utilities export the GIS as-is data into a CAD system and use the CAD design tools to create the design. In both cases, the designs become stand-alone files or paper documents. When the construction is completed, the people in the mapping group have to reenter the design sketch information along with the as-built changes into the system. They also have to reconcile any differences in the as-is state that may have occurred in the design area since the GIS plots were made or the data was exported to CAD.

If the planners or designers used GIS to produce the designs, the designs could be immediately reconciled with any changes that may have occurred in the area of the design, such as a pole relocation for a street widening project by the city. They could reissue the designs with the new pole locations automatically updated. The crew chief confirms that the poles are in the right position, and the GIS technician's work is simply to reconcile and post the design into the as-is version of the GIS database. Users of modern GIS can apply the software's capability and graphic manipulation features to create electric and gas distribution construction documents easily. Performing the design within GIS saves the awkward effort of exporting data from one system into another. Since GIS users manage many versions of the system, it becomes a relatively simple matter to keep all the designs and their design state (such as proposed, in review, awaiting construction, and construction completed) as separate versions within a single GIS database.

Integration with work and material management subsystems of enterprise resource planning (ERP) or stand-alone work and material management systems is becoming more common. As planners and designers specify construction material within the GIS design function, the software can estimate material costs. Once the planners and designers approve the designs, they can integrate them with the materials management systems. This allows for automatic material reservation, inventory management, and material requisitioning. Labor estimates and work durations for each component of the project provide input into the work scheduling, crew management, and dispatching systems of the work management subsystems.

GIS creates the possibility of field design. In this workflow, planners and designers use mobile devices containing the GIS data to create the designs directly in the field. They can create a version and download the GIS data at the beginning of their shift and then edit the information in the field to show the proposed new design. They can upload the data at the end of their shift. Using versioning technology, they can synchronize the data to the versions. If the data changes while the mobile device was disconnected, the GIS can detect and reconcile any differences. Alternatively, field devices can communicate directly with GIS using wireless technology.

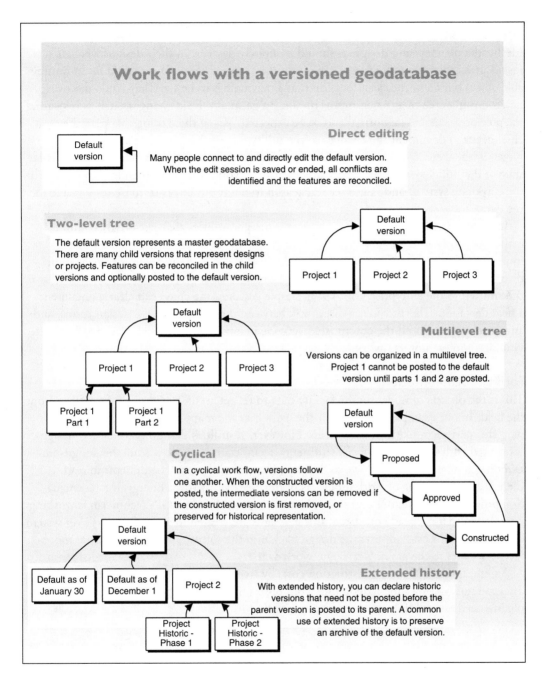

Figure 2.9 This chart summarizes the basic workflows supported by versioning.

Construction

Ideally, the planners and designers should accurately describe in their designs what to install. Even then, there are some things that they cannot know. There could be an immovable object buried in the exact location that a new pole is to be set. They could discover hazardous material in a trench meant to house a gas main. Field changes, such as relocating the pole or gas main, are normal and to be expected. When these things happen, the crew chief needs to document the changes so the utility records are complete and accurate. If, however, the crews consistently discover that the designs do not accurately reflect the as-is state of the utility system, the crews face additional work. The crews then lose confidence in the corporate systems and fail to see any reason to point out errors to those responsible for the data.

In addition to using mobile technology for design, utilities are increasingly communicating the work-order designs directly to the field crews. The construction crew can immediately note the differences found in the field and document them for verification directly in the system. Crew chiefs can create a redline layer on the field device, which is transmitted to the enterprise GIS. Using simple gestures, the crews can clearly document a field deviation. This provides a direct link between the field crews, the design teams, and anyone else throughout the enterprise. Everyone involved in the process then has complete visibility into each other's work.

Facility documentation

This is the process of updating the facility data to reflect accurate as-built information from the field. In our example above, this is the work that the mapping technician does every day. This may seem like a trivial process. However, at utilities that don't have their designs integrated with GIS like at AnyTown Energy, technicians have to recreate the designs into mapping systems. They also have to decipher field notes that may be difficult to read. If there is a large backlog of work orders, as in the case of AnyTown Energy, the reconciliation process can be onerous and error prone. It is possible that a GIS technician is working on a design that is already outdated. If the designs are created in a stand-alone CAD system, then when a GIS user imports the design back into the software it could overwrite more recent updates to the gas or electric network data.

An enterprise GIS saves construction costs by freeing up the field crews to do their work. They are not wasting time redesigning work orders, looking for the right materials, or completing needless and time-consuming paperwork.

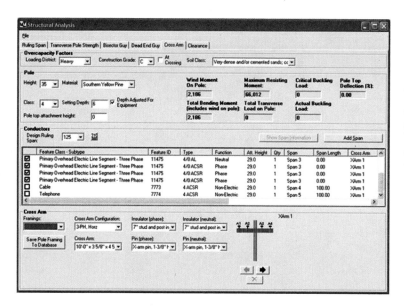

Figure 2.10 This GIS application from Telvent Miner & Miner allows designers to create a structural pole design from within the GIS.

Courtesy of Telvent Miner & Miner

Benefits of the work management life cycle

At any given time at a utility, there will be dozens, perhaps hundreds, of projects going on simultaneously in various states of load forecasting, planning, asset management, engineering, surveying, design, construction, and facility documentation. Enterprise GIS, integrated with corporate systems, SCADA, crew dispatch, and customer systems, helps with decision-making, provides better coordination and communication, and lowers costs.

Enterprise GIS enhanced with field devices improves the entire process by
- combining the load forecasting and planning processes in a single GIS view;
- allowing multiple planning scenarios to exist within the same database;
- easing visualization of projected loads to current system capability;
- providing one consolidated view of all active projects in their varying stages of development;
- building a framework for engineering decision making based on data from within and outside the utility, using location as the common denominator;
- creating a means of integrating survey data directly into the engineering and design process;
- allowing engineers, planners, crew chiefs, and many others to view each other's work; and
- lowering the number of field changes by creating a self-healing process to improve data quality.

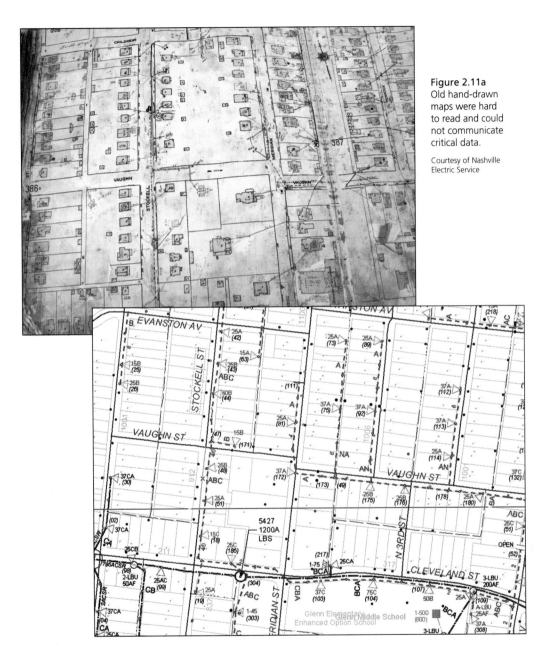

Figure 2.11a
Old hand-drawn
maps were hard
to read and could
not communicate
critical data.

Courtesy of Nashville
Electric Service

Figure 2.11b Same map captured by GIS. Data is accessible
throughout the enterprise.

Courtesy of Nashville Electric Service

3
Power generation: Finding suitable plant sites

"How could you argue against producing electricity from Mother Nature's abundant wind supply?" asked an AnyTown Energy representative, who was proposing a renewable energy project to the city council. "It's free. It doesn't produce any greenhouse gases. It is the perfect solution to the world's energy crisis."

"Imagine a string of ugly, 100-foot towers blocking our view of the landscape," countered an opponent.

"Imagine clean air," said the proponent.

One advocate strapped a tall model turbine on his back. Another sang the chorus from Bob Dylan's "Blowin' in the Wind."

"I'm in favor of wind energy," said a local politician, "but not at this location."

"So where, then?" hollered the proponent.

As this scenario illustrates, finding locations for wind turbines, or other types of power for that matter, can be fraught with difficulties.

GIS helps find the place

Generation planners use several factors to determine the cost to produce electricity in a new plant. They look at land and construction costs, operating and maintenance costs, and fuel costs. They take into account the cost of fuel transportation and electric transmission. They consider how many employees to hire and if there are enough workers in the vicinity of the new plant. Finally, the planners have to think about the impact of the power plant on the community.

Land availability and suitability dominate GIS spatial analysis, making it the ideal platform to help planners locate a power plant site. With the software's 3D visualization capabilities, planners can gauge the plant's visual and audible impact. GIS can display the proximity of population centers, fuel sources, transportation networks, and transmission lines to possible locations.

In the example above, had the wind farm planners used GIS, they would have found many options to consider and could have arrived at a suitable site not so politically charged.

Utilities can search many of the private and public GIS Internet sites that list land for sale. Generation planners can consolidate a host of available data sources in GIS, including data about land the utility already owns. This gives planners, executives, and community leaders a realistic view of the possibilities for finding a new plant location. They can easily view all the available land in relation to the utility's facilities and the growth patterns of their customers. This initial view allows utility planners to narrow the field of available sites to a handful of reasonable alternatives.

Figure 3.1 GIS can model solar radiation for optimal siting of a solar electric system.

Source: ESRI

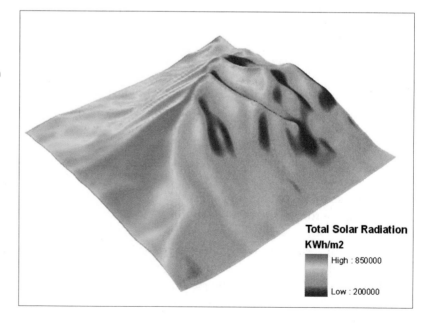

**Total Solar Radiation
KWh/m2**

High : 850000

Low : 200000

With GIS, planners can analyze all this information in a matter of hours. Without GIS, planners have to do much more research to find the available land. It could take weeks or months just to consolidate the data. By then, the right piece of land may not be available.

Assessing land suitability

Available land may be rocky, heavily sloped, earthquake prone, polluted, or have some other factor that might limit its use for a power plant. Planners use GIS to capture features that potentially impact land suitability. In this way they can compare one parcel against another on a variety of characteristics. For example, one site may be near a vegetated wetland, while another may have soils that are not suitable for a power plant. Analysts can also build terrain models in GIS to provide insight into the contours of the available sites and the surrounding areas. They may discover that mountains surround a flat piece of land, causing problems with access. Yet another factor planners take into consideration is the impact on the air and water quality. Depending on the type of plant to be built, this may be a significant factor in determining site suitability.

As noted at the beginning of this chapter, not everyone welcomes a power plant in his or her community. Utilities can assess the location for possible negative impact on the community early in the planning process. Site planners can use GIS to create a three-dimensional rendering of the plant, place it within the proposed site, and view it from a number of different angles. They can determine the visual impact on the landscape and search the surrounding area for population centers, popular recreation sites, or other sensitive locations. They can model the existing vegetation and forestry as well. A large plant would certainly alter the landscape, which in turn may have negative social impacts.

Planners can combine the physical and social suitability in GIS. The result is a map that illustrates new knowledge about all the available sites to provide enhanced decision making.

Considering the proximity

Every power plant needs to be located near resources to deliver the electricity. If everything else about the site is ideal except its distance from transmission, then the cost of delivering the power may be prohibitive. Nuclear plants must have an adequate roadway network to transport sensitive fuel. Hydroelectric plants must be on waterways. Natural gas plants must be near pipelines. Coal plants must be near trucks, trains, and boats. Plant operations must have access to qualified people to work in the plants. Planners use GIS to locate plants close to resources needed for plant operations.

Utilities seek locations where they can adequately protect the plant from vandalism or terrorism. Operators must consider if the proposed plant site is near high-crime areas. They have to be aware if there has been known terrorist activity near the proposed site. They also have to consider escape routes for their employees. In case a catastrophic or even minor incident happens, planners need to know the proximity of the proposed plant to the nearest police station or hospital.

Figure 3.2   GIS offers three-dimensional visualization of multiple datasets. This map shows an automatic overlay of vector data on raster data.

Courtesy of City of Riverside

Sites for plants with special considerations

Coal-fired plants

The major spatial issue in finding a good location for a coal-fired generating plant is its proximity to coal. If it is not close to a major source, then the plant must be near a transportation network adequate to deliver large volumes of coal. Operators can use GIS to view coal sourcing options near the site.

However, not all coal is the same. Some coal has higher sulfur content, heating potential, and ash makeup. High-sulfur coal is more expensive to clean than low-sulfur coal. So the spatial analysis for coal plants includes analyzing the closest, most economical source of the right kind of coal. Two major cost components of a coal-fired plant are the coal handling and pollution-control facilities. If the coal plant is close to a source with high-sulfur content, the operator will have to consider the higher cost of pollution-control equipment. Using GIS to model various scenarios, operators can distill an enormous number of factors to just a few.

Hydroelectric plants

Finding a good location for a hydroelectric power plant naturally involves finding a fast-flowing waterway. That's the easy part. These plants can have enormous environmental impact on wildlife, watershed, and neighboring communities. Hydro plant operators use GIS to visualize and minimize those impacts. GIS is also an essential tool used to relicense existing plants. In this process, hydroelectric plant operators use GIS to monitor the ongoing impact of the plant on the surroundings and communicate that impact to the licensing authorities.

Wind power plants

Even though wind energy is environmentally friendly, it has some serious drawbacks. Wind is variable. So, unlike coal, oil, gas, or nuclear base-load power plants, utilities cannot count on the energy all the time. Wind farms are expensive to build and difficult to properly locate. They can harm birds. They are loud. They can be visually obtrusive. To justify the cost of wind turbines, the atmospheric conditions must be strong and constant.

Figure 3.3   GIS helps energy companies find suitable locations for wind turbines such as these.

Photo by Comstock Images—Industrial Strength/Jupiterimages

Site selection and evaluation: North Sea Wind Park

Nuon, one of the largest energy companies in the Netherlands, planned to build wind parks on the continental shelf of the Dutch North Sea. The company used GIS to assist in its quest for suitable locations. A myriad of factors complicated the actual selection process, ranging from density of shipping traffic and the proximity of drilling rigs to bird migration patterns and military restrictions.

Each factor had its own weight in the decision-making process. Superimposing the data that had been charted on separate maps helped in finding suitable locations. On an interactive and multilayered map, the weight of each factor could be adjusted and a sensitivity analysis could be executed for all concerned parties.

From *GIS Solutions for Power Generation and Transmission Services*

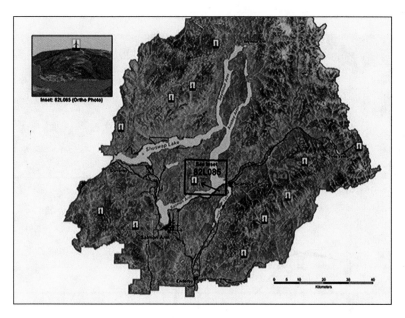

Figure 3.4 This wind turbine placement model takes into account wind patterns, environmental impact, elevation, and transmission lines.

Courtesy of Linda Deker, Salmon Arm Forest District

Site selection and evaluation: Salmon Arm Forest District

Accurate wind turbine placement requires geographic and environmental analysis that includes multiple variables that can be computed and displayed with GIS. GEM Mapping and Design developed a wind tower site analysis model that was used to determine the most ideal locations for establishing wind turbines in the Salmon Arm Forest District of British Columbia, Canada.

The analysis targeted areas with fairly steady wind patterns that presented minimal impact on the environment and neighboring communities. The determination of the best turbine locations was based on the following criteria: close to transmission lines and existing roads, moderate elevation, no wetlands, and no mature tree stands.

ArcView, ArcInfo, and ArcGIS 3D Analyst were used for the project. A 5-meter-resolution, colored orthophoto was surface draped over the digital terrain model of a 1:20,000-TRIM map sheet to show a close-up of an ideal location. A 15-meter-resolution color satellite image was used for the entire district. Programs were written to create the triangulated irregular network grid, draw relationships for the tree heights database information, and create the buffers and union coverages for the entire district. This project covered approximately 65 map sheets.

From *GIS Solutions for Power Generation and Transmission Services*

Wind farm planners can use GIS to spot the most favorable source of wind energy. Planners also need to incorporate into the analysis the location of sensitive bird habitat. A viable wind farm needs wide expanses of land. To be effective, wind turbine towers should be spaced fairly far apart. Rotor blades can be more than 60 feet long. A 400-megawatt (MW) wind farm could have up to 200 wind turbines spaced 90 to 120 feet apart. So planning a wind farm, or even a single wind turbine, is a complex spatial problem that GIS can help solve.

Solar power plants

Solar energy has the smallest environmental impact of all the common sources of energy. It is silent and completely clean. However, building a solar generator is very expensive. It's unlikely that utilities can afford to build large-scale central station solar generating facilities anytime soon.

Until costs decrease and power densities increase, distributed solar generating systems are a more likely application of the technology. Utilities focus on finding the many locations where solar energy plants can supplement the total electric production within a region. Examples include areas where the cost of increasing the electric transmission or distribution capacity is prohibitively high, areas with significant new construction (opportunities to install solar panels on roofs), remote areas, areas with poor reliability, and sparse outposts.

Figure 3.5a   Residential property powered by solar energy.

Photo by Bill Meehan

Figure 3.5b   The inverter converts the direct current to synchronize with the local electric grid.

Photo by Bill Meehan

With GIS, users can show solar densities that exist throughout the region at any given time. They can combine the solar potential and the energy demands to find the optimal and most economical location to use solar energy.

Suppose a utility needs to provide 25 megawatts of power to a new, combined residential/commercial development and the distribution system is only able to provide 10 megawatts. The utility could arrange with the developer to install solar energy roofing tiles and share the cost of the tiles with the developer. Since many countries offer substantial subsidies for solar energy, the actual cost of the solar systems could be much lower than the installation cost. While the solar energy produced by these solar roof tiles is probably not adequate to supply all the electricity for the building, it would supplement the energy supply when customer usage is highest during hot, sunny weather. So in this particular example, the application of solar energy may be economical. Once installed, the solar systems would generate local electricity while not placing demands on the already stretched distribution systems. In effect, the solar systems reduce the peak demand within the application region.

Using GIS, utilities bring three disparate data sources together:

1. The locations of significant new or potential development with sufficient rooftop space to allow adequate solar generation
2. Electrical demand profiles and load projections by area showing utility distribution deficiencies
3. Solar energy potential

GIS users can produce a visual analysis of polygons or surfaces that show the relative merit of a particular region for the application of solar energy. The spatial analysis function of GIS can assess economic advantages of solar energy that otherwise may be overlooked.

Nuclear plants

Finding the best location for a nuclear power plant has all the complexities of locating a coal plant with added public safety sensitivities. Population densities and evacuation routing are significant factors. GIS users can handle this problem through routing and logistics extensions.

While looking for the best location, utilities need to consider evacuation plans should an accident occur. This involves a complete spatial analysis of the surrounding communities. Utilities need to determine optimal routes for emergency vehicles. They must examine possible contamination areas and create evacuation scenarios. Utilities must update evacuation plans regularly. Creating evacuation scenarios in GIS provides an ongoing framework for testing the plans against real-life conditions.

Geothermal power plants

Geothermal plants produce electricity by extracting heat from deep within the earth. The plant converts the heat to electricity by a variety of means, but commonly by conventional turbines. The heat from the earth's core is essentially limitless so the United States and other governments consider geothermal energy production renewable. While there are ample geothermal resources worldwide, getting to them is a considerable challenge. GIS is an essential tool to guide developers to the optimum location for a geothermal plant. The effectiveness of the plant depends on the underground structures that permit heat to flow to the surface. In some cases there are clues, such as geysers, that tell explorers structures are nearby. Mapping this activity in GIS can provide some insight into possible development sites.

GIS is a valuable tool to map the geological aspects of the earth to find ideal geothermal plant locations. Oil producers use a similar process to find locations to drill wells. GIS can assess the economics of various sites. In addition to finding the right geology for a geothermal plant, the spatial assessment takes in factors such as groundwater protection, proximity to transmission, transportation, and labor sources. Since geothermal plants are often near tourist attractions, like geysers, they are difficult to permit. GIS can be an ideal tool to help developers with the permitting process.

Operating the plant

As more wind farms and solar systems are installed, utilities will use GIS to help manage the facilities, help forecast daily and long-range wind energy and solar densities for dispatching and capability planning, as well has help with asset management as facilities age.

Once power plants are built, operations continue and GIS helps operators deal with emissions, noise, security breaches, spills, and other environmental impacts. Operators can also use GIS for inspection, maintenance, asset management, crew dispatching, mapping the location of underground facilities for safe digging, and security monitoring.

GIS users can provide a road map of sorts that pulls disparate information together using location as the most intuitive way to view the complexities and dependencies within the power plant.

Finding and building infrastructure to deliver new sources of energy will continue to challenge utilities throughout the world. Some regions may have enormous natural supplies underground, but no means to produce or deliver it. Other regions have huge demands and significant environmental issues. Some regions have political turmoil that limits development of resources. Still others have activists who block certain kinds of energy development. Some areas may be rich with energy resources that government regulations protect. Some areas have great wind or solar potential.

Using GIS provides a way to model the world of electric power generation to give utilities a way to make the best decisions and communicate those decisions toward a common understanding.

Asset management: Great River Energy

Great River Energy, based in Elk River, Minnesota, provides electricity and related services to twenty-eight member distribution cooperatives located in Minnesota and Wisconsin. Great River mapped its transmission facilities with the help of ArcGIS software. In addition, the generation department used ArcGIS for tracking equipment maintenance history in generating facilities.

The ESRI software was used to help Great River track failure rates for heat shield tiles in combustion turbine generators. United Services Group, a department of Great River Energy, developed this application by recreating the manufacturer's drawings of the heat shield tile locations. The tile failure data was then moved to an ArcGIS personal geodatabase and published as an ArcReader document.

By using ArcReader as a visual tool to present multiple years' worth of inspection data, Great River Energy could establish trends in failure rates of the tiles inside the combustion turbine. This graphic information was then used to assist with decisions on modifications to the turbine to reduce the cost of maintenance.

From *GIS Solutions for Power Generation and Transmission Services*

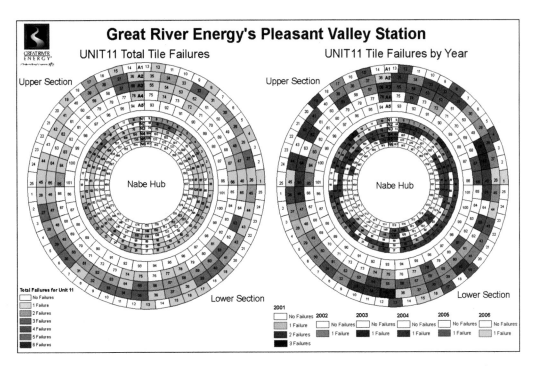

Figure 3.6   GIS is used to map the heat-producing portion of a generating station and represents the location of each heat tile. Color coding is based on maintenance activities. The map serves to highlight problematic areas and suggest resolution activities such as tile replacement of a different strength.

Courtesy of Great River Energy

4

Electric transmission: Easing high-tension decisions with GIS

The trouble with New York City in the summer is not so much the heat, but the humidity, and this was a typically steamy afternoon. The buildings and the concrete seemed to absorb the heat and the dampness. The city used thousands of megawatts of electricity that afternoon just to keep the air conditioners running. Then the lights went out.

The air conditioners stopped cooling the thick, Manhattan air. Stalled elevators trapped sweaty, skyscraper employees. Traffic signals were out, causing chaos among angry cabbies. This wasn't a rolling blackout. This wasn't an energy shortage. This was the Great Blackout of August 14, 2003 that impacted an estimated fifty million people and involved nearly 62,000 megawatts of electric load in the Midwest and Northeastern United States and Ontario, Canada.

It started with a couple of trees near Cleveland, Ohio. A heavily loaded and badly sagging 345-kilovolt transmission line, the Stuart-Atlanta Line, came in contact with two relatively small ailanthus trees, one with a diameter of about 2 inches, the other about 6 inches. The line tripped out. Heavy sagging occurred on other transmission lines due to the additional load caused by the loss of the Stuart-Atlanta line. Those lines came in contact with the trees and tripped out. This caused a cascading tripping of transmission and generation that crippled much of the Northeastern United States and Canada for many, many hours. Reasons for the blackout go much deeper than small trees growing into a transmission line, but tree contact was the trigger event.

Figure 4.1   Workers do a high-wire act to service high-voltage transmission lines. GIS helps analyze the specialized information needs associated with maintaining and repairing these systems.

Photo by Photolink/PhotoDisc/Getty Images

This blackout and other transmission-related outage events throughout the world underscore the importance the transmission system plays in a reliable electricity supply.

Transmission is many things

Electric transmission is a physical system consisting of structures, high-voltage equipment, and wires that the utility manages. It is a business that generates revenue, incurs costs, and embodies business processes, such as asset and risk management, engineering, design, and maintenance. At any given time, electric transmission operators run complex projects and the most common element is location.

From a consumer's perspective, the transmission grid connects the power plants to the bulk distribution supply substations. The grid rarely fails but when it does, the impact can be catastrophic, as the 2003 blackout illustrated. Besides blackouts, tree contact with transmission lines can also cause wildfires, which can jeopardize the transmission system and destroy property.

A few utilities make a digital model of their transmission system as part of an overall enterprise GIS. One of the most significant benefits of this practice is the added assistance in managing the vegetation that grows near overhead transmission lines. Utilities, such as our fictional AnyTown Energy, that maintain transmission system data in manual strip plans are unable to provide the data contained in those plans to their IT systems.

Utilities have been modeling transmission systems for decades. One of the earliest electronic simulators, an analog network analyzer, calculated load flows on transmission systems. After the first widespread blackout in the United States in 1965, operators used digital computers to help solve the complex problem of power system stability. By the 2003 blackout, these analysis tools were in common use in control computers, power pools, and system operations. The data required to run these simulators generally comes from schematic representations of the transmission systems. Most simulators do not display their results geographically as GIS does. This is changing. Probably due in part to the 2003 blackout and the widespread use of the transmission system as an open access vehicle for deregulated generation, utilities now recognize the importance of viewing the transmission system geographically.

Modeling a transmission system in an enterprise GIS allows users to view the system from both operating schematic and physical geographic perspectives. The schematic view is powerful for a complex interconnected grid. Operators can easily see the power-flow paths and switching alternatives. However, seeing that same view geographically adds a new dimension—the transmission system in relation to its physical surroundings. For example, it may show where trees need pruning. While the schematic view is effective to study transmission line flows, it doesn't show potential hazards to the lines, such as its proximity to a wildfire area, an earthquake fault line, a major natural gas pipeline, or a major waterway.

Even more helpful is the ability to create an enterprise view of the transmission system. This means that everyone who has an interest in the transmission system within the enterprise can access all the relevant information about it within a single view. It should be possible with enterprise GIS for anyone working with transmission to visualize the system and collect the results of

- helicopter inspection surveys of transmission line equipment;
- infrared surveys showing hot spots;
- encroachment in the right-of-way, such as swimming pools, abandoned cars, and metal sheds;
- lightning strike assessments;
- salt or smog contamination results;
- grounding surveys; and
- access points along the transmission line right-of-way.

Anyone within the utility could view recent maintenance activity, earthquake activity, areas where trees grow fast or slow, areas of higher-than-normal rainfall (which makes fast-growing trees grow faster), and areas of significant environmental sensitivity and its proximity to oil-filled transmission equipment. It also is important to know where transmission facilities may transverse sacred burial ground of indigenous people.

The geographic view highlights common points of failure, such as where transmission lines cross highways, railways, and waterways, or where critical transmission lines are near each other. It's important to know the legal attributes of the land (easements, licenses, leases, and their expiration) that lie within the transmission right-of-way, as is discussed further in the chapter.

With effective use of GIS, users can communicate to operators the accurate condition and threat to the security of its transmission system.

Network viewing: Georgia Transmission Corporation

At Georgia Transmission Corporation (GTC), using GIS-based Web applications is part of the daily routine for employees throughout the company. GTC is a not-for-profit cooperative owned by and serving thirty-nine electric membership corporations in Georgia.

Because GTC has been using GIS for several years, it has accumulated a wealth of geographic data for the state of Georgia, including orthophotography, parcel data, and systems data. The company uses Web-based applications that enable it to make this data more easily accessible to a greater number of company employees.

By implementing an ArcIMS Web application called GTCView, GTC integrates its maps, databases, and image files, which are located in separate areas of the company, into a single, common interface.

One of the goals in designing GTCView was to take information and characteristics about the location of facilities and integrate them with other attribute databases. GTCView links four relational databases for GIS use. Its primary feature is an interactive map from which the user can make textual queries and access relational databases, allowing for map design.

If the planning department wants to determine the load need for a new area, it can access databases through GTCView. The user enters the location of the new area and performs a distance query such as the location of all 115-kilovolt transmission lines within 50 miles of the site. GIS produces both a map and a list of those transmission lines.

GTC has a database of video images of transmission lines photographed from aircraft flyovers and linked to GPS. Using the GTCView application, a company employee selects a transmission line and clicks a video camera icon to watch video of the line. The user can also click directly on a tower and see a photo of the structure. The tool extends the benefit of the data-gathering investment.

The Web-based application allows the user to create custom maps without a cartographer. The symbology is available and easy to use, a map template sets the stage, and the employee creates the map.

From *GIS Solutions for Power Generation and Transmission Services*

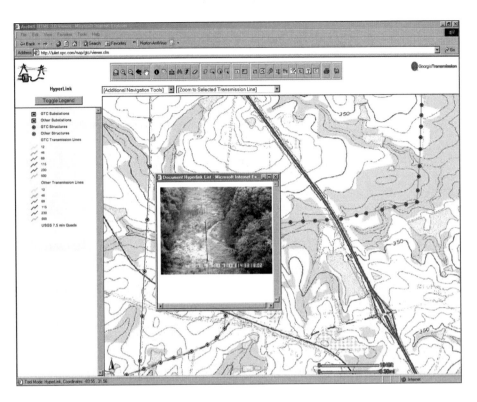

Figure 4.2   Georgia Transmission Corporation integrates its maps, databases, and image files—located in separate areas of the company—into a single, common interface by using an ArcIMS Web application called GTCView.

Courtesy of Georgia Transmission Corporation and Photo Science

Manage the land

A patchwork quilt of land parcels with a variety of shapes, ownerships, and easements describe transmission rights-of-way. Rarely do utilities own all of the land within the right-of-way. Each easement may have different rights. The utility may have perpetual rights or it may have licenses with expirations. It's up to the utility to know of any special requirements of the easement. For example, suppose an easement for a parcel within the right-of-way grants the utility only the right to install power delivery equipment. The utility installs fiber-optic cable encased in its ground wire for its relay and control equipment, which the easement allows. Then the utility grants a wireless carrier the right to use one of the spare fiber strands for commercial phone service. All the owners of each parcel must grant an amendment or the utility cannot legally use the fiber strand for anything other than power delivery. If a license expires on a parcel of land, it is up to the utility to renegotiate the rights to use the land. Theoretically, the owner of the parcel could require the utility to vacate the parcel. While this is an unlikely event, it could certainly create an embarrassing situation for the utility and result in unforeseen costs.

Flight tracking: Basin Electric Power Cooperative

Basin Electric Power Cooperative uses small aircraft to fly over its transmission lines and generation facilities to capture data. Based in North Dakota, Basin Electric is a regional wholesale cooperative with 120 member systems that provide service to 1.8 million consumers in nine states. Small aircraft have proven useful for gathering and maintaining data about this extensive power network.

Onboard telmatic technology is used to transmit GPS coordinates to a server for recording the flight path of the aircraft. Telematics incorporates computers and wireless telecommunications technologies to create information solutions. Basin Electric's flight-tracking solution integration includes GPS, GIS, transceivers, and server applications.

For several years, Basin Electric had been using ArcInfo, ArcSDE, ArcIMS, and other ESRI software technology, so it had the foundation to add flight-tracking capabilities. The application integrates ESRI software with SkyWave Mobile Communication GPS technology and an interactive Web site so that technicians can map aircraft in real time. The aircraft is equipped with SkyWave DMR-200 satellite transceivers that have low-elevation antennae. The DMR-200 is integrated with a GPS receiver. The internal GPS is used to generate aircraft position, altitude, airspeed, and direction of flight. The terminal is hooked into a navigational GPS formed by twenty-four satellites.

The transceiver sends a signal to the satellite which sends data about latitude and longitude, speed, and direction to the SkyWave model Web server. The system's reporting function relays latitude and longitude data at two- to ten-minute intervals. The data is put into Microsoft SQL Server and then automatically loaded into the geodatabase managed by ArcSDE. Airplane data is geoprocessed in ArcInfo, then displayed on a Web-based map that employees can access. The application refreshes data and redraws the map at 30-second intervals. An airplane symbol shows the plane's direction and time.

Dispatch can add notes and see other information related to the asset data such as photos, conductors, and maintenance histories. The ArcIMS Image Map Service uses ArcSDE to reference the feature class file containing aircraft locations. An HTML viewer can select an aircraft feature and add comments. The comments trigger an automated process that updates the business table of the ArcSDE feature class. The user can also specify start and end dates and map the history of the aircraft's positions.

GIS provides the utility's service teams with a parts lists, right-of-way data, parcel information, and access road locations. Field workers can print a map of a specific corridor and use GIS to create a route map to a selected asset. Besides providing asset management data, the fight-tracking application also supports the cooperative's safety policies, provides data for Federal Aviation Administration audits, and assists incident investigations.

From *Energy Currents*, summer 2005

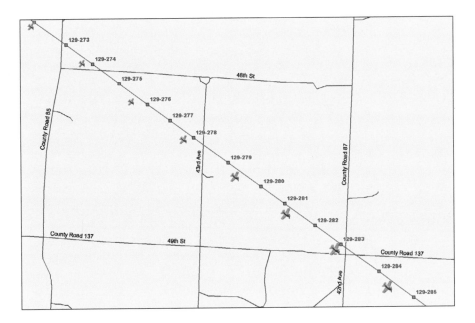

Figure 4.3 Flight map tracks aircraft during aerial inspections of Basin Electric Power Cooperative's transmission and generation facilities. The system integrates GPS, GIS, transceivers, and server applications.

Courtesy of Basin Electric Power Cooperative

Asset management: Southern Company

Southern Company is one of the largest utility companies in the United States and is a leading generator of electricity. Its four individual operating companies have transmission line inspection crews that are independent of one another. Each operating company had different inspection requirements. Although the operating companies have used the same inspection contractor, corporate use of the contractor had not been centrally planned. This created personnel coverage gaps for the contractor, which resulted in inspector turnover and increased time spent on training.

The company identified four types of operations that would ultimately be incorporated into a Southern Company Transmission Line Inspection System (TLIS): ground line treatment, aerial patrol, climbing, and general navigation. The first phase of the project addressed ground line treatment requirements.

ArcView software loaded on mobile laptops provided a tool for ground line, climbing, aerial, and navigation inspection tasks. The field data was collected, processed, and uploaded in TLIS. ArcView was combined with GPS so field workers could capture location data about company assets and log access road locations. The mobile application also displayed documentation associated with current inspection work orders.

TLIS allows inspection contractors to quickly gather information in the field using ruggedized computers. Once inspection data is collected in the field, the contractor is able to package the data and transfer it to the appropriate Southern Company resource. By using the IT-developed transmission line management system application, the Southern Company resource group is able to integrate the collected data into the system asset database.

Inspection contractors and Southern Company personnel are able to more effectively and efficiently perform their inspections in the field and use this information to make the asset database more complete and reliable.

Southern Company's enterprise approach to GIS enables its four operating companies that serve millions of customers—Alabama Power, Mississippi Power, Georgia Power, and Gulf Power—to improve customer service, minimize costs, and improve efficiencies.

The E-GIS solution consisted of an ArcGIS platform based on ArcSDE. Also in use are Telvent Miner & Miner's ArcFM toolset, ArcIMS, and ArcGIS Server. E-GIS was set up to centralize assets for distribution, transmission, and land records across the enterprise. It also provides consistent, high-quality data to other systems such as feeding data to the outage management systems at the operating companies to ensure optimum response to hurricanes and other disasters.

The ArcGIS platform serves as an enabling technology for addressing future Southern Company business needs. The E-GIS project positions Southern Company to optimize business processes and decisions.

From *GIS Solutions for Power Generation and Transmission Services*

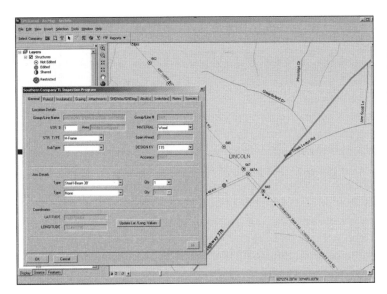

Figure 4.4   Southern Company's transmission line inspection system collects asset data and provides detailed information such as coordinates and arm details.

Courtesy of Southern Company

Utilities can use GIS to manage the legal wrangling of land rights along a transmission corridor. A GIS user can answer the query, "Show me all the parcels in Right-of-Way 9 whose licenses are due to expire in one year," or "Show me all the easement documents for the section of right-of-way from station 1+10 to station 2+200." The utility can determine where they have the legal right to gain access to a right-of-way. Even though a utility may be entitled to access a piece of land based on an easement, regulations such as wetland protection laws may supersede the rights granted by the easement. Some laws prevent heavy vehicles, such as bucket trucks, from driving through a protected area. Conservation commissions may fine a utility and require it to replicate or repair the wetland area. Laws protect wildlife habitat in certain areas. Utilities have to know whether these areas are in or near their rights-of-way.

It is critical to have a solid understanding of the transmission line assets in relation to the environment. Should there be a downed transmission wire, it is not enough to just know where the problem is. The utility must know how to get to the location of the problem and which areas to avoid. Integration of the land information within the enterprise GIS significantly reduces the research required to determine rights and land ownership. A GIS user can manage land parcels, easements, vegetated wetland, protected habitat regions, regions of environmental sensitivity, and a host of other land attributes. All this can be done while modeling the hard assets of the transmission system.

Right-of-way access

Crews, inspectors, and maintenance personnel need access to the transmission facilities. The point of access is often an alley or dirt road leading from a paved roadway into the right-of-way. Since utilities do not have the right to travel across private property, they have to rely on explicit easements along the path into the right-of-way. Often these dirt roads become blocked with debris or overgrown vegetation and are difficult to find. Maintenance departments use GIS to inventory access points, direct repair crews to the closest access point, and help include access points into the maintenance programs. Asset managers use GIS for access planning and to model different access scenarios.

High-voltage transmission lines must have proper clearance of trees, fences, buildings, sheds, swimming pools, roadways, or any natural or human-made structures. The system must conform to the land and the surroundings. So a critical component of transmission line design is the integration of the tower and line design with the land and all its features. For example, engineers often need to route transmission lines over hilly terrain and must coordinate the changes in the terrain with the line and tower designs. Grounding schemes must be coordinated with the terrain and soil characteristics. GIS is an ideal tool for engineers to pull all the disparate features of overhead transmission line design together in one view.

Perhaps a greater challenge is the design of high-voltage underground transmission, which is becoming increasingly common in urban settings. Underground transmission is significantly more expensive to build than overhead lines and poses more of an engineering challenge since there is no natural way of cooling. So, some underground transmission lines consist of conductors contained within metal pipes. Pressurized and circulating oil cools the high-voltage transmission cables. The oil flows through heat exchangers constructed strategically along the line. Utilities use GIS to optimally locate the heat exchangers for maximum cooling efficiency. Operators also need to know how close the line is to rivers, streams, and other water supplies should a rupture occur.

Manage routing needs

When planning an acceptable path for any new line, cost is the primary consideration. The type of line—whether overhead or underground, steel or wood construction—and distance determine the cost. Suppose the shortest path would require an underground line, but the cost is prohibitive and the neighborhood opposes an overhead line. The utility could choose a line that goes through uninhabited land, but that might create problems of access and maintenance. A GIS user can perform an optimal routing algorithm that creates solutions based on economic, demographic, political, engineering, visual, and environmental factors. Then, the GIS user can determine the best path based upon all the factors.

Transmission system planners continually monitor the utility's ability to meet the projected power load. They study electric load flow, short circuit, and stability of the system using the existing network model as a starting point. They then project the load five, ten, and twenty years into the future. They add proposed facilities to the model. The data collection and assembly process can be time-consuming, tedious, and subject to error. Utilities that have modeled their transmission system network in GIS can directly import existing network models into the analysis tools in the software. Planners can propose different future scenarios, creating multiple versions from the existing network without having to duplicate the data. They can also see where loads are developing and assess where to place transmission lines. This improves the process efficiency and provides a single source of existing network data for all studies. When the existing network information is changed, all of the future cases will update as well.

Assess transmission congestion

Congestion occurs when there is inadequate transmission capability in a region to take advantage of lower-cost generation. There may be inexpensive generation available outside the region, but not enough transmission capacity to deliver the power to a particular region. So, higher-cost generation has to be run in order to meet the load. This is good for the generation owners, but not for the consumers.

Transmission planners can use GIS to visualize the impact of congestion on the region. A schematic view would never give an operator a complete picture of exactly where congestion occurs geographically. The GIS view helps utilities decide how to respond to the short-term impacts of congestion. They may step-up their campaign for demand-side management within the congested region, look to install distributed generation, or perhaps even install local temporary generation at strategic sites within the region.

Right-of-way: Eskom, South Africa

The Republic of South Africa's government utility, Eskom, is the seventh largest electric company in the world in terms of generating capacity and sales. It provides more than 98 percent of South Africa's electricity requirements and more than 50 percent of the electricity produced in Africa. Eskom is involved in the generation, transmission, and distribution of electricity.

Eskom's transmission division maintains a transmission spatial information system (TxSIS) that is built on ArcGIS software and supports GIS across the enterprise. TxSIS provides support for strategic maintenance planning, line fault investigations, and real-time system operations. The geodatabase is managed with ArcSDE spatial data engine software. The system includes an Internet mapping service on the TxSIS intranet site accessed by about two hundred transmission users each month. ArcIMS software distributes online maps that show the transmission network relative to its natural, physical, and legal environment, and other technical transmission information.

GIS manages the administrative process of obtaining servitude (right-of-way) rights for new transmission line projects. This includes the total process, from notification management for public input during environmental assessments for a new line project, to right-of-way negotiations with landowners. TxSIS generates instructions to the contractors involved in the line construction as communicated by the landowners. GIS dramatically cuts the time required for obtaining servitude rights and also is used to track progress with the legal registration of the right-of-way. GIS also is used in the performance management of employees involved in the registration process.

Line faults in South Africa are primarily caused by birds, lightning, and fires and all are tracked with GIS. Annual raptor nest surveys are used to track trends, monitor risk, and evaluate the effectiveness of nest relocation initiatives and bird guard installations. GIS processes real-time lightning information, weather forecasts, and real-time weather data.

The integrated system shows where lightning is prevalent along sections of transmission lines and how maintenance efforts can best be directed for improving the network. Fire location data is automatically derived from satellite services and this data can produce a fire incident map for posting on the Web.

From *GIS Solutions for Power Generation and Transmission Services*

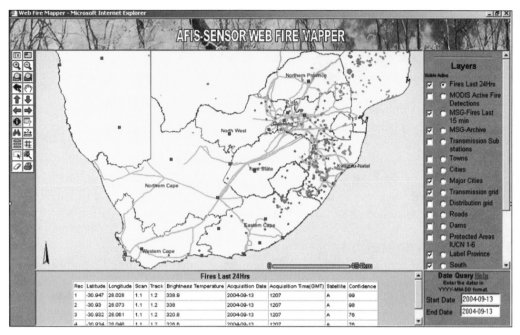

Figure 4.5   Fire information is served on a GIS-enabled Web site.

Courtesy of Eskom

Transmission asset management

Utilities must decide whether to maintain or replace their assets to deliver adequate service. A detailed and coordinated inspection program is the most effective way to monitor asset conditions. Inspection information must be associated correctly with the proper components of the transmission lines. Transmission inspection tasks include ground and aerial patrols, digital photography and videography, infrared surveys, and satellite imagery. This material can all be stored within the GIS database. The GIS user pulls these disparate sources of data together to provide a clear and often stunning visualization of the transmission line condition. By adding maintenance and reliability history into the analysis, asset managers can properly assess the risk of component failures.

Transmission lines often share rights-of-way or portions of rights-of-way. Asset managers can determine where an incident on one transmission line could impact an adjacent line. Field crews can communicate conditions of the line and other features directly into the office via their mobile devices. Thus, decision makers in the field and in the office know the condition of the line at virtually the same time. Compare this workflow with AnyTown Energy's. Since AnyTown could not coordinate transmission geographic data with inspection information, field crews relied on their knowledge of the transmission system and patrols.

Once transmission line operators collect the information on the condition of lines, they can make informed, cost-effective decisions about how best to invest in the upkeep of the lines. While GIS alone does not provide the tools for comprehensive reliability-centered maintenance, it can provide a complete visualization of the factors that will help make a sound decision.

With GIS, asset managers can see patterns to organize repairs efficiently. Effective maintenance work means going to the site once, with the appropriate equipment to fix all the problems at that location. By not having all the asset and condition data coordinated logically by location, crews could travel miles into the woods to fix one problem while unaware of another problem nearby. It would be costly and embarrassing to have a line fail shortly after a maintenance crew was in the area. Since transmission systems often span long distances, travel costs can be significant. GIS users can help optimize crew routing.

Controlling vegetation

To understand how vegetation impacts the transmission equipment, utility arborists use GIS to model the types and growth patterns of the vegetation within rights-of-way. The utility can perform vegetation inventories as well. They can assign specific work tasks with scheduled frequencies. For example, utilities may have scheduled intensive right-of-way clearing based strictly on four- or five-year clearing cycles without regard to other factors that impact the vegetation. With detailed GIS modeling, arborists can schedule vegetation management tasks based on an intelligent assessment of exactly what part of the right-of-way needs management and what doesn't. They can assign crews with accompanying GIS-developed maps showing exactly where and where not to trim, or where to plant low-growing brush. GIS has additional functions such as tree valuations and assessments, future work planning, budget management, stand collection, and unlimited custom reporting. Arborists can base the frequency of tree trimming on the specific variety of trees detailed within geographic areas.

GIS users can assess areas of significant deviations of rainfall in certain parts of the transmission system that would impact tree-growth rates. Based on these spatial models, arborists can optimize the work. They can cut back on vegetation management in those areas that have less-than-expected rainfall and increase the maintenance in areas with greater-than-expected rainfall.

Utilities often need to record animal species within the right-of-way. The utility arborists can include endangered species sensitivity factors within the GIS database. GIS users can create layers of information about the assets and vegetation as well as characteristics of the land and the habitat to produce a comprehensive utility vegetation management program. This goes much further than the outdated practice of simply trimming the trees in the right-of-way every four or five years without regard to the overall effectiveness or environmental impact. Since vegetation management is environmentally and politically sensitive, utilities find it invaluable to have ready access to spatial data about vegetation in relationship to the transmission assets and surrounding land features.

Utilities spend an enormous amount of money on vegetation management. GIS provides the tools to do it right. Solid vegetation management allows utilities to properly assess the methods and the effectiveness of the contractors doing the work on their behalf. The addition of routing services and GIS-based maintenance records can help inspectors record confirmed tree-trimming activities or note where vegetation abatement needs to be readdressed.

Reporting to regulators

Regulators and oversight agencies must ensure that utilities are making the best effort to perform their duties. When things do go wrong, such as a blackout or a serious injury or fatality, it is the regulator's responsibility to investigate the incident to protect the public. The regulator should assure the public that the utility is not guilty of mismanagement or negligence if the facts support that conclusion. If the utility is negligent, regulators can impose expensive fines and the utility's public image suffers.

Figure 4.6 Vegetation management is an important and costly responsibility and GIS provides utilities with the tools to do it right.

Photo by Skip Nall/PhotoDisc/Getty Images

Vegetation management: New York Power Authority

The New York Power Authority (NYPA) vegetation management program maintains approximately 16,000 acres of right-of-way. The program's principal goal is to provide safe and reliable electric power transmission in an economical and environmentally compatible manner.

NYPA is the largest state-owned power organization in the United States and one of the largest producers of electricity in the state of New York. The power is produced at 17 generating facilities and distributed by approximately 1,400 circuit miles of high-voltage transmission lines.

The authority has designed an integrated vegetation management ArcGIS application. The enterprise-wide right-of-way application is linked to the land management, equipment maintenance, and environmental and engineering data, which is necessary to manage the authority's facilities and to comply with regulations.

NYPA partnered with the URS Corporation of Buffalo, New York, to develop a GIS-integrated vegetation management (IVM) application that provides easy access to data. The IVM has a simple interface and can perform relatively complex tasks such as creating treatment plans that ensure compliance with regulatory mandates and landowner agreements.

Using ArcSDE, NYPA maintains all vector and tabular data at its central data center. The center provides all parties with access to the most current information. Image data (digital orthophotos and document scans) are maintained on local servers at each NYPA site.

From *GIS Solutions for Power Generation and Transmission Services*

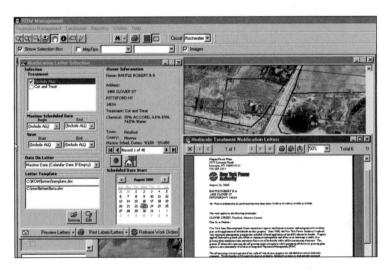

Figure 4.7 New York Power Authority's notification system is integrated with GIS. The user defines the vegetation treatment area and herbicide treatment notification letters are automatically printed and sent to landowners in the target area.

Courtesy of New York Power Authority

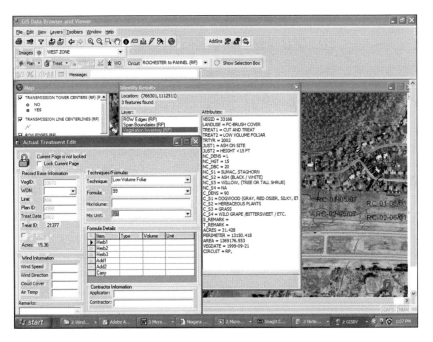

Figure 4.8 GIS provides access to geographic data so integrated vegetation management techniques can be examined, taking into account conditions such as wetlands, landowner issues and agreements, site access, regulatory commitments, and security.

Courtesy of New York Power Authority

The utility's best defense against an accident or incident investigation is ready access to thorough records. GIS users can coordinate the events, condition, history, inspection reports, environmental assessment reports, training records, surveys, and testing results. The lack of coordinated records casts doubt on the utility's control over its work and employees.

Transmission includes not only overhead lines, poles, and towers, but also large electric switching stations that can switch and isolate parts of the system. Much of the equipment within these stations contains insulating fluids. Most stations have containment systems should a leak occur. However, a major rupture and oil spill could contaminate wetlands, rivers, and streams nearby. GIS users can model the contours of the land leading from the station to sensitive areas. Through GIS, users can design facilities to prevent the spread of the hazardous fluids. Further, the transmission operator can use GIS to create a damage control plan should a spill occur.

Transmission lines produce an electric and magnetic field (EMF) around the conductors. Transmission operators must have a solid understanding of the full extent of EMF in relation to the surrounding population. Lines can crackle or buzz when the air surrounding high-voltage conductors becomes moist. Using GIS and a spatial analysis, utility technicians can model the noise levels. If the noise is bad enough, they can construct noise mitigation barriers.

In addition, since the visual impacts are significant, it is important for the utility to identify and present these impacts to the community. Using GIS to communicate site selection to interested parties can often improve the frequently contentious permitting process. GIS can make the information more accessible to the public.

A switching station must have the ability to communicate to the other components of the transmission system. Utility communication engineers geographically model microwave systems, cell towers, radio, and fiber-optic systems using GIS. They assess factors such as line of sight, spacing of amplification systems, and placement of communication systems.

Assess natural factors

The transmission equipment must accommodate natural events, such as lightning strokes, salt spray, dust contamination, and earthquakes. With GIS, users can model these factors.

Lightning can have a devastating impact on an electrical transmission system. It can damage the system with a direct hit to the structures, cause wildfires in areas near transmission lines, and cause harmful transients to propagate along the transmission lines causing flashovers and faults. GIS users can track the locations of historical, recent, and real-time

Figure 4.9 Lightning can damage an electrical transmission system with a direct hit to the structures. GIS can track the location of lightning strike activity.

Photo by Comstock Images—Industrial Strength/Jupiterimages

lightning strike activity. This information is useful for planning, engineering, and operations. A spatially enabled lightning strike analysis can help utilities find the best location for the line to minimize exposure to lightning.

Siting a transmission switching station

Selecting the location of a large power plant can be a daunting task. Finding the best location for a transmission switching station can also be a significant challenge. Switching stations are large, visually imposing buildings that contain oil-filled equipment. They are dangerous and can be noisy. Neighborhood and environmental groups may try to block the utility from building a transmission switching station. Chain-link fences and barbed wire surround the sites. "Danger High Voltage" signs hang ominously.

Often there is local opposition to the construction of a transmission switching station because it doesn't directly benefit the surrounding region. Instead, the station benefits the entire network. So, dealing with local concerns requires particular care. Utility public relations managers can use GIS to illustrate the long-term benefit to abutters and interveners. The GIS-created maps communicate to the public, regulators, and the local planning authorities, the visual and audible impact on the surrounding region. GIS-created maps can show the exact positioning and landscaping of the station. Utilities face similar issues when finding locations for transmission substations as they do when choosing a site for a power plant. They have to consider factors such as aesthetics, future development of the area, and the potential for natural disasters.

Transmission switching stations are critical for the operation of the grid. GIS users can model the effectiveness of security, assess threats, and form response plans should an emergency occur. Since utilities don't often staff these switching stations, GIS users can provide the analysis for routing emergency workers to the scene effectively, depending on the type of emergency.

Protecting the system

High-voltage switching and lightning strikes cause disruptive transients on the transmission lines. Transmission line engineers need to design the line insulation to withstand the stress that these short duration but high-voltage surges impose on the system. Power system grounding plays a critical role in the mitigation of these transients. Engineers must perform a transient analysis whenever the transmission system undergoes a change in configuration to ensure that the insulation and the grounding continue to provide adequate protection against damaging transients. This analysis is complex and requires sophisticated modeling of the system's physical configuration. Accurate and timely data about the condition of the system is critical for the analysis to be meaningful.

Utilities can take advantage of the asset management data to provide the core data infrastructure for transient analysis. These analyses might be too theoretical and not take into account the present condition of the transmission system as captured in the GIS. It is especially important to keep an accurate picture of the grounding network, since weaknesses in this system could contribute to unnecessary transmission line failure. The GIS should model both the above grounding system as well as the buried grounding systems, including the substation grounding grids, ground rods, and counterpoises. Having up-to-date field inspection data provides practical applications for transient network analysis.

Managing the grid

Utilities are familiar with the schematic representation of the transmission system. Nearly every transmission control center has a large board displaying the grid, complete with switching points and switching substation schematics, lights, and special graphics. The utility has these boards custom built around their unique transmission system, and they are quite expensive. When the utility adds a new station or transmission line, they must reconstruct and rewire the board to reflect the change. These boards often span entire control rooms.

Geographic representations of the transmission system are far less common. One reason is that it is impractical to build a similar control board that models the system geographically, given that transmission lines span many miles. The technology of large computer-generated displays and projectors now make it possible to replace the hard-wired control board with computer-generated graphics. This eliminates the effort required to rebuild the board every time the system changes. When utilities switch to the concept of a computer-generated control board, then a large-scale projected GIS representation of the transmission system becomes extremely practical and effective for operating the grid.

Once the system is represented both schematically, for ease of switching and visualization of flows; and geographically, for ease of pinpointing problems—operators in the transmission grid control area can better manage the minute-to-minute operations of the grid. When a fault occurs on a transmission line, utilities can use telemetered relay protection information to accurately determine the exact location where the fault occurred. As utilities have discovered, a loss of even a single transmission line could trigger a cascade with catastrophic consequences. Since it's important to keep a close eye on the transmission system, using GIS in the transmission control room could speed response.

Utilities need to understand exactly where all the components of this complex and critical system are located. They need to keep track of the condition of the assets that make up the transmission system. And they have to understand how the system interacts with the surrounding environment to make sure that the events of August 2003 don't happen again.

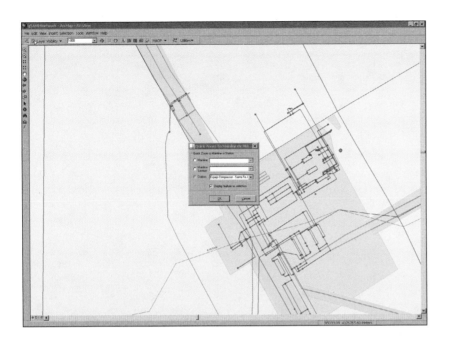

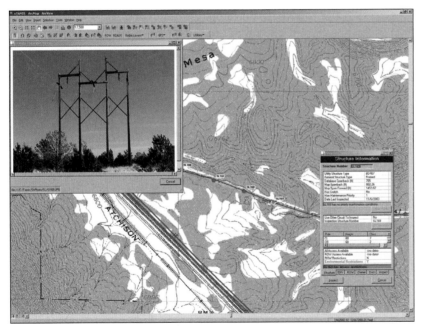

Figure 4.10 Public Service Company of New Mexico uses eTAMIS, a software application for online mapping. Included in eTAMIS are real-time routing, online analysis of structure information, and a fault location tool.

Courtesy of Public Service Company of New Mexico

5
Electric distribution: Improving systems, cutting costs

Practically every week, AnyTown Energy discovered yet another lightning arrestor had failed. The arrestors failed when there was lightning and when there wasn't, so AnyTown Energy couldn't detect a pattern. After considerable research, a standards engineer discovered that two years earlier, the utility had ordered a batch of lightning arrestors with the incorrect ratings. The simple solution would be to replace them with properly rated arrestors. However, no one recorded where they were installed. The only way to find them would be to examine every work order that involved lightning arrestors. It could take months to pile through the old records. AnyTown Energy decided to replace the lightning arrestors as they failed. Of course, this would mean that the overall reliability of their electric distribution system would suffer. If AnyTown Energy had a GIS and recorded simple attributes in it, such as the year installed or manufacturer, the utility could have easily mapped the location of each defective lightning arrestor and coordinated replacements with an ongoing maintenance function.

Or consider this scenario:

An underground system technician at AnyTown Energy poured through manual underground conduit plans until she finally found an empty path to run a cable for a new music store. She notified the field inspector to visit each manhole to verify the route. He sent her a reply that the selected route looked fine. It took her several weeks to complete the design. The technician issued the work order for construction and notified the customer that the service would be available in three weeks.

When the construction workers arrived to install the cable at one of the manholes, they discovered a new cable in one of the conduits the technician earmarked for the music store. As it turned out, another technician planned to run service from the very same transformer vault to a new fast food restaurant. A different inspector verified the route two weeks earlier. Consequently, the technician had to completely redesign the music store project. There were no empty conduits anywhere in the district. She had no option but to order a new duct bank, which meant designing the system, researching other utilities buried in the street, getting a city permit, and hiring an outside contractor to dig up the street and install the new duct bank. This delayed the project by six weeks with escalating costs.

If the technician had modeled the underground duct banks in a GIS, she could have found the shortest path in seconds and then reserved the conduits for her job. Other people looking for underground routes in the same area would be able to see all the projects going on simultaneously. Even if the utility still had to build a duct bank, that would have been known well before making any customer commitments.

Implementing GIS in electric distribution

The two preceding hypotheticals illustrate how GIS is an indispensable tool in electric distribution.

The electric distribution system is ubiquitous. Even in remote areas of third-world nations, people can see distribution circuits winding their way on poles into villages.

Thus GIS is a natural tool for modeling the distribution system since nearly every street, highway, and even dirt road has some kind of electrical distribution line installed on it. GIS also plays a large role in finding the best location for a distribution substation. A number of spatial factors are involved, such as distance to a convenient tap point on a transmission line, distance to the concentration of electric loads, and proximity to environmentally sensitive areas. Substations are visually intrusive, so how the utility describes substation plans to a wary public requires careful presentation and visualization. GIS is a natural tool for addressing neighborhood concerns.

Utilities often use GIS to manage the millions of miles of overhead and underground circuits that make up the electric distribution system. GIS models the location of the poles, wires, guy wires, underground cables, overhead and underground distribution transformers, and switches in all their detail.

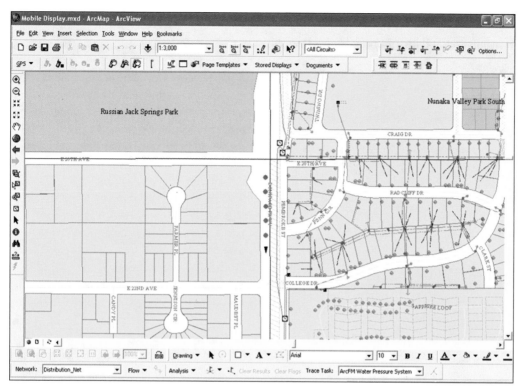

Figure 5.1   The Chugach GIS mobile system provides the field
worker with a street map that shows the GPS location of the truck
and the location of the service site.

Courtesy of Chugach Electric

Transmission and distribution: Hydro One Networks

Hydro One Networks Inc. owns and maintains Ontario, Canada's electricity transmission system, delivering power to homes and businesses. Hydro One does not generate electricity but transmits and delivers it to customers, safely and reliably. Hydro One is responsible for 97 percent of Ontario's electricity transmission system and approximately one-third of the province's distribution system. Using ESRI software, the company has implemented a variety of GIS applications to serve the needs of the staff and serve its clients with greater efficiency.

GIS is an integral part of the information management strategy and has been integrated into other business processes, leveraging the technology and data being managed and derived from various applications.

Hydro One replaced its cost-estimating practice with Telvent Miner & Miner's product, ArcFM Designer, which offered greater business benefits. The ArcFM Designer application provides an integrated solution for developing designs in the office and the field. It also presents more accurate cost estimates to customers and streamlines the process for service connections. Design conducted within the GIS environment allows for a single data input without the need to replicate the data in a CAD environment.

Data capture is enhanced with integrated GPS tools developed specifically for Hydro One end users. The data is managed in an enterprise-wide distribution data model. As data is captured, it is automatically documented as part of the network. The innovative, leading edge application supports approximately 30,000 designs per year and reduces the up-front effort for capturing data, reduces data redundancy, and improves data accuracy. It will support other business applications for Hydro One's distribution network, including outage management and vegetation management, creating significant benefits.

From *Energy Currents,* fall 2005

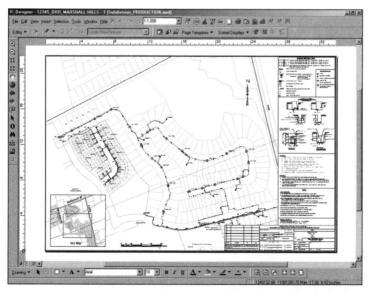

Figure 5.2   Page template in ArcFM Designer is used to produce engineering drawing for design.

Courtesy of Hydro One Networks Inc

Show and tell with GIS

GIS users can find answers to many common queries, including:
- find pole 123/10
- show the extent of circuit 346-21
- show all the poles that are 10 meters or less in height along this street
- show all the poles installed since August 2006
- find all the Ace lightning arrestors that were installed between April 2002 and May 2004
- find all transformers that will be within 90 percent of their ratings in August
- show the transformers that have no primary fuses
- show all the manual line switches that have not been exercised in one year
- show all the fuses that are connected to circuit ABC

Textbox 1

Linking customers to the distribution system

The electric distribution system directly links to end-use customers. So it's essential for utilities to associate customers to events that occur in the distribution system. For example, suppose a distribution circuit trips out momentarily due to an unfortunate squirrel serving as a conductive path across an overhead transformer's terminals. Customers will notice an interruption in their power. While it may only last a few seconds, it can cause damage to sensitive equipment. A momentary interruption may result in an author losing several pages of work or a sports fan missing an important game on television because the video reset. The issue for utilities is to associate that problem on the distribution system with the customer.

As customer demands grow year after year, utilities may find that their distribution transformers and other equipment become overloaded. That's when they fail. Yet, if the utility had an enterprise GIS linked to the customer data, it could proactively display transformers (or other equipment) nearing their limit. A GIS linked to the customer billing system can proactively display areas where transformers are approaching their limit.

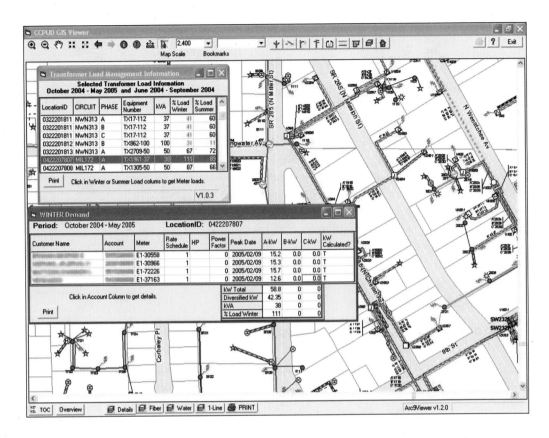

Figure 5.3   The Transformer Load Management tool allows users to assess overloading and underloading of transformers.

Courtesy of Chelan Public Utility District

Managing overhead systems

The majority of electric distribution systems is simple overhead construction. Overhead systems are inexpensive to construct and easy to operate. They are also relatively simple to model in a GIS. Since everything is visible, it is easy for the utility to detect failures. However, overhead systems are subject to all kinds of hazards such as errant motorists crashing into poles, lightning and wind-felled or overgrown trees, and heavy snow and ice.

Utilities model both the structural and electric facilities within the GIS. The structural components of overhead distribution systems consist entirely of poles, guy wires, supports and conduits, or risers. Risers attach to poles to make the transition from overhead to underground systems. Electrical current-carrying devices, such as switches, lightning arrestors, and transformers, are mounted on the poles.

GIS users typically put poles on separate layers. So a common query would be: Show the route of overhead circuit XYZ. The result would be a series of poles shown on a map. Another query would be: Show all the circuits that are attached to pole 123/4.

Circuits are often a combination of overhead and underground segments. A route query might include a series of overhead poles, followed by a riser, followed by a series of manholes, duct banks, or pad-mounted structures.

Asset management: Shanghai Municipal Electric Power Company

Shanghai Municipal Electric Power Company (SMEPC) turned to ESRI software as the exclusive platform for its enterprise GIS solution. SMEPC is one of the largest electric utilities in China, operating in a service area of 2,448 square miles throughout the city of Shanghai and serving nearly 4.3 million customers.

In 1997, some branch agencies of SMEPC began building GIS applications to manage the electrical network infrastructures. However, the applications were built upon different GIS platforms and with incompatible data formats. As a result, SMEPC decided to develop an enterprise GIS solution that could integrate all of its existing asset management information systems.

SMEPC's enterprise GIS was developed by ESRI China (Bejing) Ltd. The system-wide GIS was implemented throughout the company headquarters and its twenty-one branch offices via the Internet. The GIS applications included distribution management, transmission management, power control, cable management, communication management, customer service, and dispatching.

The GIS interfaced with the company's enterprise resource planning (ERP) software, and workers in the field were equipped to get real-time spatial information with mobile GIS via a general packet radio service.

From *Energy Currents,* summer 2004

5.4a

Figures 5.4a, b Shanghai is China's most productive industrial center, busiest port, and home to approximately twelve million people. This infared satellite image of Shanghai (facing page) was captured by NASA. Shanghai Municipal Electric Power Company uses GIS technology to manage the electrical network infrastructures and other functions.

Courtesy of Shanghai Municipal Electric Power Company

Running underground systems

Underground electric systems consist of two parts: the structures that hold the electrical devices and the devices themselves. It is common to model each of these systems separately—for example, on two different layers—but relate the electrical devices to the structures that they belong to.

The underground structure network systems involve complex designs, such as the construction of transport structures of electrical cables within new or existing city streets. The underground structure network system consists of

- pipes or conduits of various sizes that contain the electric distribution cables and often other cables, such as associated fiber-optics cable used for control;
- duct banks that are concrete structures for groups of conduits. For example, a duct bank may have a run of eight conduits in two rows of four between two manholes, so it's important to know the position of a conduit within a duct bank;

- manholes, which are underground rooms of various sizes where the duct banks terminate. Manholes house switches, transformers, and racks of cables;
- vaults, which are underground rooms like manholes, only bigger. As with manholes, duct banks terminate in vaults. Vaults contain larger underground equipment such as large power transformers, switches, and bus bars. Often small substations are inside vaults; and
- building vaults that are contained within larger buildings or plants. Underground duct banks terminate from the street into the building vaults. Vaults, also known as electrical rooms, could be on various floors throughout high-rise office buildings.

Within a city, there may be an extensive underground transport system that includes service pipes, concrete encased duct banks, manholes, and vaults. The connectivity of these pieces allows the utility to route cables from one building to another by examining available conduit. The routing technology is essentially the same technology that allows navigation systems to find the best route from your house to your favorite restaurant. Since AnyTown Energy lacked a GIS, the underground technician could not take advantage of this technology. Instead, she had to manually lay out the conduit plans one by one to find a route for a power cable to a new customer.

Utilities can design the layout, routing, and specifications of the underground system in GIS. In effect, the underground structure system consisting of duct banks, manholes, vaults, and service pipes becomes a fully connected network in the GIS. It has both a geographic representation, that is, each duct bank and conduit can be located in its exact position under the street, and a schematic or connected representation. Modeling an underground transport system in a GIS can prevent situations like those described in the beginning of this chapter. The underground technician can find the shortest path for a cable as well as where abandoned cables still occupy a conduit or where there may be damaged or collapsed conduits. Knowing this data during the design allows the technician to better assess how best to meet a customer demand.

Another type of underground construction, underground residential distribution (URD), consists of above-ground cabinets that house electrical equipment, such as transformers and switches, connected by a buried conduit. The cabinets are mounted on fiberglass structures called pads, which are small underground compartments that facilitate the routing of cables from the underground conduits into the above-ground cabinets. In a similar manner as with conduit/manhole systems described above, by creating a connected system that includes pad structures in GIS, engineers can find the shortest or best routes for cables.

Once engineers model the network structure system or URD systems in GIS, they can determine which cables occupy the conduits. They can relate devices such as transformers and switches to the manholes or pad-mounted structures. In effect, the underground systems as modeled in GIS consist of two related connected systems: noncurrent carrying structural system (manholes, duct banks, conduits, and pad-mounted enclosures) and current carrying devices (cables, transformers, and switches).

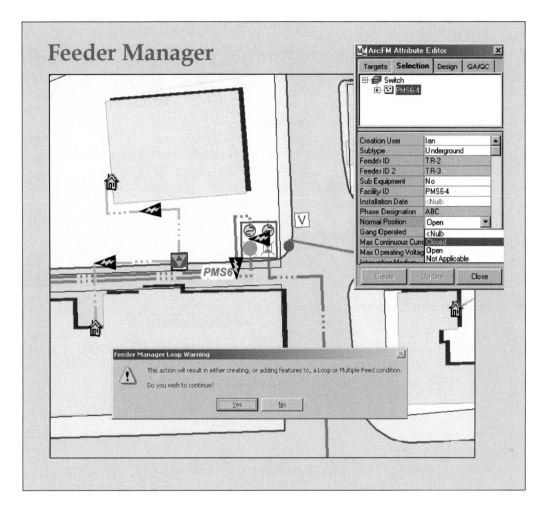

Figure 5.5   Telvent Miner & Miner's Feeder Manager directs every aspect of Truckee Donner's electric utility model. It determines flow direction and connectivity and enforces network business rules. Feeder management is essential for any integrated GIS outage management program to operate.

Map by Steve Murphy, courtesy of Truckee Donner Public Utility District

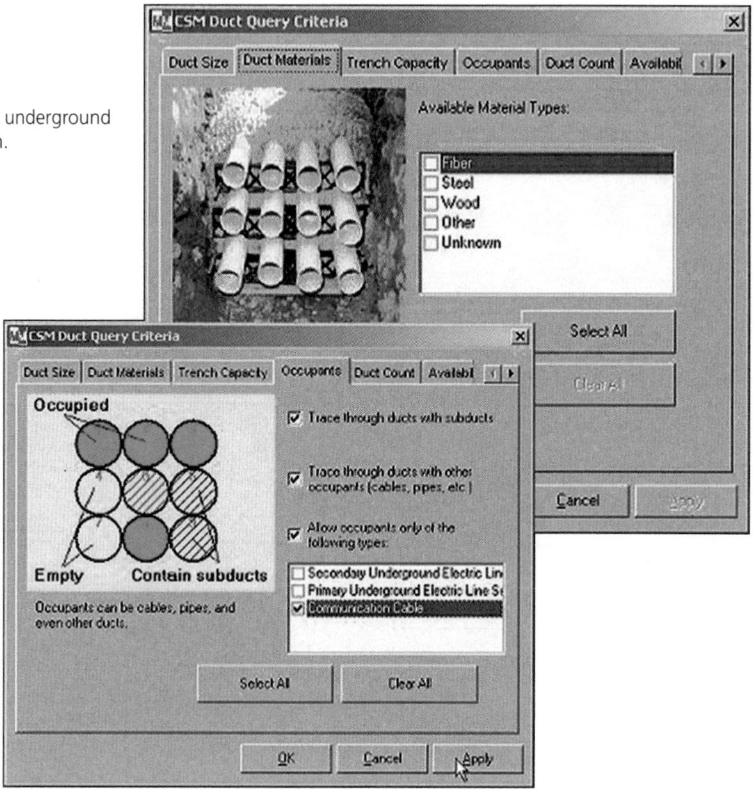

Figure 5.6 GIS helps manage underground conduits for electric distribution.

Courtesy of Telvent Miner & Miner

As detailed in chapter 1, our fictional AnyTown Energy had a devastating fire in a get-away manhole. While the fire was caused by a combination of heavily loaded cables and a steam line, the utility could not see what cables were run in that manhole. AnyTown Energy also had no idea that the main power cables and the primary backup cables ran side by side in the same structure. By capturing the network structure of the conduits, duct banks, and manholes, utilities can query the GIS to discover if there are locations within the system where both primary and backup cables share a common manhole. As luck often has it, it is those locations where problems tend to occur.

GIS users can find the underground structural path of any specific circuit. Then they can show the result in a map with the route of a specific circuit through various underground structures. For example, circuit XYZ starts at Station A, through duct bank 57, conduit 3 to manhole 8853 to duct bank 26, conduit 6 to manhole 8854, and so on. Another application could be to find all the cables in duct bank 57. The resulting map would show all the circuits and their position in a specific duct bank.

Enterprise GIS in operations and maintenance

If there is a difference between what the operating records display and what is actually installed in the field, the operations people may have to resort to field visits to verify what actually exists. If this occurs during an electrical outage, valuable restoration time is lost. Further, if there is no easy way to capture the results of the field visit, the utility may end up visiting the same site over and over again.

Maintenance and inspection

Inspection is the physical process of efficiently capturing the condition of the system. A GIS helps utilities organize the inspection information spatially. Just knowing that ten lightning arrestors have visible cracks in the insulation only tells part of the story. Knowing where they are in relation to the rest of the system is far more telling. Utilities then can relate the lightning arrestors with other events and factors to more fully determine what to do about them. The distribution equipment also tends to be closer to population centers, which means that utilities must cope with a different set of variables, such as traffic. Using GIS for inspection allows utilities to better see the big picture.

Multiservices: Truckee Donner Public Utility District

Truckee Donner Public Utility District (PUD) supplies electric and water service to the town of Truckee, located in the central Sierra Nevada Mountains of Northern California. The district's geodatabase model provided a central, versioned, spatial data repository. It also offered flexibility for integrating other platforms with advanced modeling capabilities.

Telvent Miner & Miner's product, ArcFM Secondary Circuit Analysis tools, helped engineering staff members determine the optimal transformer size based on the number of customers and the size of the businesses served by that transformer. It also helped staff members determine if any transformers were overburdened.

The ESRI ArcGIS Schematics extension used electrical network data to generate one-line schematic diagrams of electric circuits. Telvent Miner & Miner's Feeder Manager directed every aspect of Truckee Donner's electric utility model. It determined flow direction and connectivity and enforced network business rules.

Truckee Donner maintained more than 6,000 distribution and secondary poles. Its electric model contained pole and attachment information, allowing engineering staff to analyze the structural integrity and guy placement for each pole. The utility also modeled the phase configuration on the cables attached to poles.

Advantica SynerGEE provided an electric network analysis tool helpful in circuit analysis and switching scenarios. The GIS model allowed data to be exported quickly and easily to the SynerGEE tool, negating the need to maintain duplicate data.

From *GIS for Municipalities and Cooperatives*

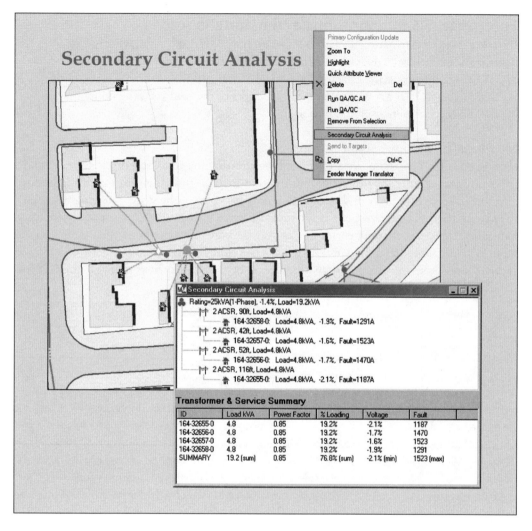

Figure 5.7 Telvent Miner & Miner's ArcFM Secondary Circuit Analysis tools help engineering staff members determine the optimal transformer size based on the number of customers and size of the businesses served by that transformer. It also helps staff members determine transformers that may be overburdened.

Courtesy of Truckee Donner Public Utility District

Since the utility uses the GIS to capture and assess the condition of the system, it is a natural tool for managing the maintenance of the equipment. Utilities typically use GIS in conjunction with a work management system for maintenance. Since maintenance on the distribution system involves so much equipment, all spatially distributed throughout the service territory, the GIS can help to organize the maintenance to minimize travel time and crew workload. The GIS can also help utilities prioritize maintenance activities based on the overall risk of the system. If, for example, a specific area of the system is particularly susceptible to lightning strikes and has a group of lightning arrestors that show signs of failure or are simply in need of cleaning, then those lightning arrestors should be attended to first.

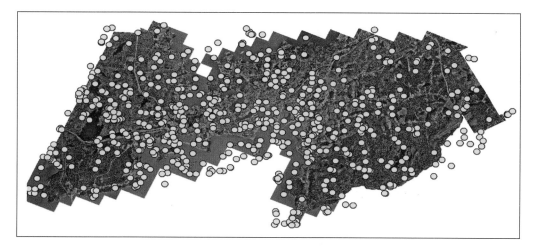

Figure 5.8   Saint John Energy of New Brunswick, Canada, uses GIS to show lightning strikes. This shows strikes between 1:22 and 3:18 a.m. on August 8, 2006.

Courtesy of Saint John Energy

Since the distribution system is so dispersed, inspection and maintenance can be daunting tasks. A GIS can help organize the data, provide a means for capturing the condition information from inspection data, and help utilities analyze trends. Having a good picture of the system's condition significantly improves the maintenance program.

Utilities have found that GIS installed on mobile devices is very effective for inspection and maintenance activities since the crews have direct access to the historical information regarding work done on the equipment and the most recent inspections.

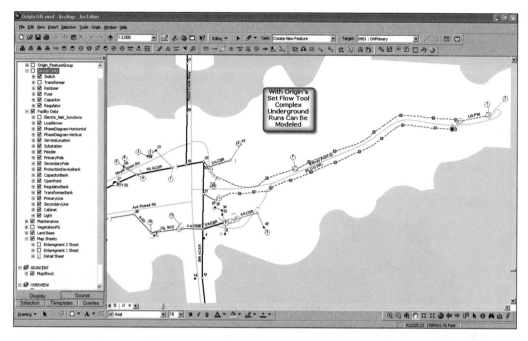

Figure 5.9   Complex underground runs can be modeled using GIS.

Courtesy of Origin GeoSystems

Distribution vegetation management

Many overhead distribution power outages are caused by trees or branches falling on distribution lines and breaking them. Thus, vegetation management for electric distribution mainly involves tree trimming. Utilities clear branches to prevent them from contacting distribution lines. Trimming also provides a degree of separation to protect overhead distribution lines during wind and snow storms. Utilities also may have to remove trees that pose a threat to the distribution lines. GIS users can inventory the trees along the distribution system, analyze tree growth, and choose the trees to trim that pose the greatest threat. Utilities also use GIS to locate dense tree areas to find fast-growing trees.

Utilities typically use contractors for tree-trimming work. GIS users can manage the initial assessment and monitor contractor compliance. Utility tree-trimming contractors often use GIS to manage their own work, whether the utility uses GIS or not. Determining which trees need trimming and sending out contractors with chain saws involves more than meets the eye. Perhaps the biggest challenge utilities face regarding tree trimming has nothing to do with technical reasons to trim. Trimming a tree along a beautiful country road can be an enormous public relations nightmare. Cutting down a historic, but potentially hazardous tree may spark public outcry. GIS can demonstrate the hazards of keeping trees untrimmed. In fact, an arborist will often use GIS in community presentations and point out that trimming can be healthy for trees. Utilities can use GIS to illustrate the significant outages that can occur by not trimming. Following a power outage in a community that opposed tree trimming, the utility can show in a map the correlation between the electrical system damage and trees that were not trimmed or removed. Often, that visualization can be compelling enough to move the tree trimming program forward.

Call Before You Dig

Electric distribution companies in many countries are required to investigate and mark their underground facilities. Whenever someone wants to dig in the public way or on private property, that person is required to file a notice with a clearinghouse organization, often called "Call Before You Dig," which then contacts the local utilities in the area of the proposed dig. The utilities must mark their electric distribution facilities within a prescribed time frame. Without an up-to-date GIS, this process can be tedious and error-prone. Even with GIS, if a large number of changes have not been updated, the utility does not have accurate enough data to confirm that every Call Before You Dig mark-out is correct. This underscores the importance of automatically transferring field data to the corporate GIS as soon as possible.

Figure 5.10   Digging into the ground where various pipes and lines are buried is risky business. GIS can substantially reduce the risk.

Photo by Patrick Dolan

The streetlight business process

Many distribution electric utilities operate the municipal street lighting system, which is relatively simple: Modern streetlights are tapped directly into the low-voltage distribution lines. Photoelectric cells turn on the lights when it gets dark and they shut off when it gets light. While the system may be simple enough, the business process is not. The utility must keep an accurate inventory of the streetlights with the type of lamp, construction (overhead and underground), fixture, and locations of each light. The utility manages the engineering, design, construction, and documentation of new streetlights. It also needs to perform regular inspection and maintenance.

Beyond these issues, the utility must be aware of the role streetlights play in public safety. If someone gets mugged or a car crashes into a pole on a dark street where a lamp burned out, the utility often is blamed. Operators of the streetlight system would be expected to keep accurate records on each fixture but that is seldom the case. In fact, since utilities don't meter streetlights, they may not have a single source of accurate streetlight information. Some utilities report that their engineering records, billing records, and plant accounting records each show a different number of streetlights. Using GIS as the definitive source of streetlight information could solve these problems.

A single entity may not own all the streetlights in a community. In some regions, for example, the local electric utility owns a portion of the streetlights, the city owns some decorative lights and some standard streetlights, and a regional district agency may own the rest. Since the utility owns the majority of the streetlights, citizens call them to report a streetlight outage. If the utility doesn't have an accurate record of which streetlights it owns (and many do not), it will send a worker out to replace the lamp. Only when the worker arrives at the scene can the utility determine ownership of the lamp. Sending workers into the field to check on something they should already know is wasteful.

Since most utilities don't meter streetlights' power usage, they may not keep track of the lights by address. So when someone calls to report a light out, the person receiving the call has to determine which lamp is out by asking for the pole number. Since it is probably dark when the call is made, it's unlikely the caller would search the pole for a tag that may or may not be there. The caller could give the address, but may be driving by and can't make out the address. With GIS, utilities can easily locate the burned-out light based on the caller location. People can also report a burned-out streetlight through a Web site. If the utility doesn't own the streetlight, the Web site can link to the organization responsible for the streetlight, saving the lamp maintenance person a needless trip to the field. Either way, once people report the outages, GIS users can generate work orders that crews can do with routine work, like relamping projects that are already underway.

Some jurisdictions require streetlight system operators to repair streetlights within a specific time frame or face fines. Without a comprehensive streetlight management system, operators would be at a serious disadvantage. GIS should be at the heart of a streetlight management system, integrated with streetlight inventory, billing, outage, supply chain, work order management, and fixed asset accounting.

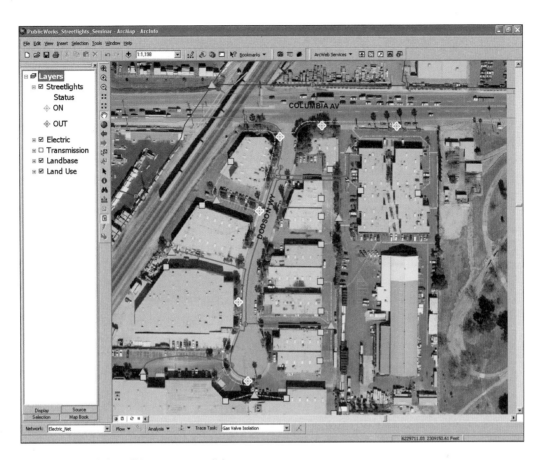

Figure 5.11 GIS helps utilities manage streetlight outages.

Courtesy of City of Riverside

Finally, GIS is the tool of choice for the actual municipal lighting design. Using GIS, streetlight designers can show lighting levels at intersections, heavily treed areas, and areas of high crime. The GIS can show the proper distribution of light and, in fact, use animation to show how lighting levels vary with alternate designs.

Enterprise GIS transforms distribution

Enterprise GIS ties all the pieces of the electric distribution system together. As discussed in chapter 2, GIS can be at the heart of the work order management life cycle. GIS, especially implemented on mobile devices, closes the gap between field and office activities. By having ready access to inspection information, utility asset managers can make accurate assessments of where to repair, maintain, or replace equipment. GIS provides a common view of some of the factors that contribute to poor distribution performance, like where trees cause outages or where squirrels raise havoc or where faulty lightning arrestors are installed. GIS can help utilities assess their streetlighting coverage or pinpoint areas where utilities may be liable. In short, enterprise GIS provides a means to intelligently manage the complex electric distribution system.

6

Electric system operations: Dealing with outages effectively

Snowstorms had hit Mary's town hard during the rough winter and this night was especially bad. Trees had gone untrimmed for several years after complaints that AnyTown Energy was "chopping away at the town's rural image." The overgrown trees made outages more prevalent. Mary's lights went out at 9:23 p.m., right in the middle of her favorite television show. An older, patient woman, Mary figured that the utility company would know she was without electricity. What Mary didn't know was that the electric company relied on someone in the neighborhood calling in to report a power outage. She knew people who worked for the electric company and was confident these good folks would work hard to put her lights back on. Mary went to bed at 10 p.m. in the dark. She awoke at 3:30 a.m. still without electricity and the house was growing colder. She thought she had better call the electric company.

Figure 6.1   Lightning, a common cause of power outages, strikes downtown Seattle on a summer night.

Photo by R. Morley/Photolink/PhotoDisc/Getty Images

AnyTown Energy's customer service representative (CSR) told Mary they were aware of the outage in her neighborhood, but with so many outages, he could not guess when a crew would arrive. Mary pressed for some kind of estimate so the CSR told her to expect power to be restored in about four hours. Actually, the CSR had absolutely no idea how long it would take, since he only knew that there was an outage in Mary's area. The trouble job was in "open" status, meaning that it had not yet been assigned to a crew. Mary wrapped herself in an extra heavy blanket and went back to sleep. When she woke up at 7:30 a.m., the lights were still out and the house was getting dangerously cold. She thought she had better call the electric company again. As she picked up the phone, the lights went on. "Thank goodness," she said to herself. "The crew must have arrived." But then, as quickly as the lights had gone on, they went out again. She thought they must still be working on the problem so she didn't call.

Still no power

By noon, Mary was nervous. Still no electricity. She called the electric company and was shocked to learn that the problem had been fixed that morning at about 7:30 a.m. with all power restored in her neighborhood. The CSR further told her that there were no outstanding trouble jobs in her area. Mary insisted that her power was still out and got annoyed when the CSR suggested she perhaps had turned off all the lights in the house. The CSR said a crew replaced a fuse which restored power to her neighborhood so there must be something wrong in Mary's house. She was equally adamant that the fault was with the electric company.

Mary called back to speak to a supervisor who promised to send out a crew. But the supervisor warned Mary that if the crew determined it was "inside trouble," the electric company would charge Mary $25 for the service call. With a heavy backlog of jobs, it could be many hours, perhaps a couple of days, before a crew arrived, the supervisor told Mary, ending the call. A moment later, the supervisor called back and spoke to Mary in a much different tone of voice. She told Mary that three of Mary's neighbors also reported lights out, and promised that a crew was on the way.

Within an hour, the crew arrived not far from Mary's house, lights flashing, bucket truck rumbling. Mary threw on her old heavy overcoat and rubber boots and rushed to the crew, intent on staying there until her lights were back on and stayed on. The line-worker raised the bucket to the top of a pole and replaced the fuse in a minute. Mary saw that her porch light stayed on. She blew kisses to the crew and dashed home.

Mary's predicament is common. During a storm, a fuse that protects a neighborhood's electrical system blows when a falling tree or tree limb comes in contact with the line. More often than not, the tree limb burns a bit before the fuse blows and falls to the ground. However, after an outage, other tree branches fall onto lines or remain in contact with the lines. Since the power is out, the downstream fuse remains closed. However, when a trouble-shooter replaces the upstream fuse, the new fuse energizes the line. When that happens, the downstream fuse blows.

Cause of the problem found

That's what happened in Mary's neighborhood. The main fuse blew, shutting down the whole neighborhood. Another tree limb came in contact with a line near Mary's house. Because the power was out anyway, the fuse protecting Mary's section of the subdivision didn't blow until the crew replaced the main fuse. That's why Mary's lights came on for a few seconds and then went out again. Because Mary's area was quite a distance from where the crew members were working, they didn't notice that some of the neighborhood was still in the dark. The electrical dispatchers looked at the original calls they had received to determine the most likely cause of the outage. The crew noted the blown fuse, replaced it, and the lights in the neighborhood went back on. The problem was that the workers did not report that they had replaced the fuse until after a number of neighbors had called. The call center assumed that the calls came before the crew repaired the fuse. The utility missed outages because no one in the field reported trouble information in a timely way.

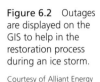

Figure 6.2 Outages are displayed on the GIS to help in the restoration process during an ice storm.

Courtesy of Alliant Energy

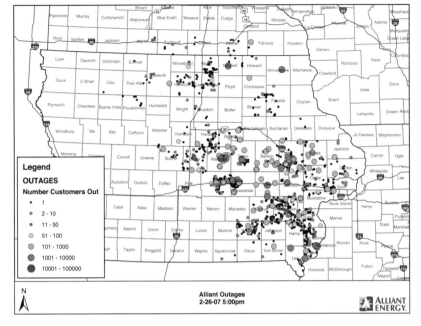

This situation exposes another problem. The original crew did not have data about the downstream fuse in Mary's neighborhood. The department responsible for fuse coordination had not communicated to the electrical dispatchers that this sort of event could happen easily. Somewhere, AnyTown Energy had the data necessary to anticipate this nested outage but there was no enterprise approach, no coordinated source of information, and no workflow to check for this possibility. Had there been a mechanism in place, such as a truly enterprise GIS, things would have been quite different. GIS with a mobile component could view the enterprise data, including the fuse coordination information, to analyze Mary's first call. Crew members with easy access to information about all protective devices downstream of the fuse they were working on would have routinely checked for downstream fuses before leaving the neighborhood. The mobile device driven by GIS data would have immediately uncovered the problem. Mary would have had her power restored four hours earlier and the electric company would have avoided visiting the same neighborhood twice during a time of critical resource constraints, such as a snowstorm.

So what's the big deal about a couple of extra hours of outage? If this were an isolated event, it probably wouldn't be such a big deal. However, the cost of restoration can be significant. For a medium-sized electric utility with widespread outages, the cost can run from $25,000 to perhaps $50,000 an hour. That could exceed half a million to a million dollars per day for labor and logistics. Extending the outage for even a couple of extra hours can be very costly. This cost is in addition to the lost revenue from the power being out and the erosion of public confidence.

Figure 6.3   Ice storms create havoc on an electric distribution system.

Courtesy of Alliant Energy

GIS and distribution system operations

Outage management is part of an overall program managing the everyday operations of the electric distribution system, variously called system operations, distribution dispatching, or distribution operations. The workflow represents the coordination of work based on information received from the field, information available in the office, and the communication of what crews do in the field. The distribution system operations or dispatchers tend to be located in a central control room. They communicate directly to field crews and line supervisors most often by radio. Sometimes the dispatchers are located in remote distribution services centers. In other cases, utilities choose centralized dispatch during the busy times of the day and decentralized dispatch during the slower periods.

Distribution outage management is a process of sorting through information gained from various sources. Among them are real-time operating systems, such as SCADA systems and distribution automation systems; calls directly from customers or as gleaned from interactive voice response (IVR) systems; data from the customer billing/information system, plus data about the electrical network (the GIS representation). Utilities that install automatic meter reading (AMR) are able to poll a customer to determine whether that customer has power or not. All data sources are important, but without the spatial information—the network behavior and connectivity—managing outages is structured guesswork.

Even with good systems in place, including an enterprise GIS, not having the most current information available to all systems weakens the process. Many utilities still allow work order information to pile up without anyone posting the data into the GIS. Of all the processes in electric distribution, restoration is the most sensitive to data currency. That's why some utilities maintain two data systems: one for the general engineering, design, and mapping and the other for operations. Keeping separate records systems can distort reality and always creates more work. All data originates from changes that are generated in the

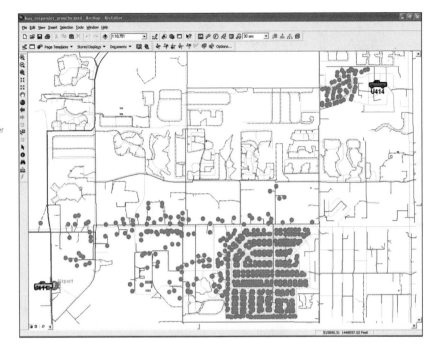

Figure 6.4
This shows a real-time graphic image of an outage in progress.

Courtesy of Telvent Miner & Miner

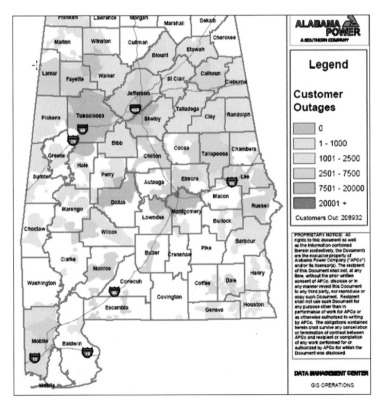

Figure 6.5 Alabama Power mapped Hurricane Dennis on July 11, 2005. This outage density summary operation center map depicts actual and projected wind speeds after landfall.

Courtesy of Southern Company

field as a result of new construction, maintenance, and repair. Maintaining separate records necessitates a complex reconciliation process in addition to a duplication of updates.

The key to successful distribution operations is good data and simple processes. In the example at the beginning of this chapter, the centralized dispatchers may have communicated the restoration order to the crew by simply providing a trouble ticket with the notation: "Area outage reported near intersection of Maple and Pine. Probable cause: tree fallen on wire due to heavy snow. Customer reports seeing a flash. Probable location of disconnecting device: Pole 123/54." The repair crew had to locate the pole, locate the intersection of Maple and Pine, and then perhaps guess that they had the correct fuse size to replace the blown fuse. When the work was finished, the crew noted the repair on the trouble ticket. Perhaps the crew replaced the blown fuse with a slightly different one. If so, they might have noted that on the trouble ticket. In its haste to move on to the next incident, the crew didn't tell the dispatchers until later that it made the repair. The crew had no reason to suspect there was a downstream fuse somewhere else in the neighborhood.

Had workers immediately reported that they had replaced the fuse by entering the data on a mobile field device connected to the GIS integrated with the outage management system, Mary would have had her power back when the first crew visited her neighborhood. Had crew members had access to current information on their GIS mobile device that matched the information available to the dispatchers and CSRs, Mary would have had her power restored at 7:30 a.m. If all the crews had this information, total restoration time for the storm event would have been much shorter and possibly the crew could have restored Mary's power while she was sleeping. If this sort of situation occurs many times over during a major outage event, the wasted time could cost hundreds, perhaps thousands, of dollars per minute.

As utilities install additional monitoring devices in the field, they will require fewer customer calls to determine outage locations. However, with more automation comes an even greater need for current and accurate infrastructure data managed by GIS interfaced with the real-time systems. Textbox 1 lists a distribution system's major processes.

The major processes of distribution system operation

- Switching remotely operated distribution equipment. This is a function of a real-time control system. However, utilities use this technology to integrate the real-time data with the GIS. This allows the wide access of real-time data to be visualized outside the control room. Publishing this data on GIS Web-based services is very effective.
- Directing the switching of manual, nonautomated disconnecting devices to field crews. Nonautomated switching is rarely modeled in real-time control systems. The GIS can manage the operational switching data associated with the disconnecting devices, such as normal tagging information. Examples include time the switch was opened (or closed), who operated the switch, date, time, and other notes.
- Determining the sequence of load transfer under a variety of situations. The GIS maintains all the information and processes to perform these functions.
- Keeping track of the positions of all distribution disconnecting devices. The GIS can be used to visualize the unscheduled positions of switches for the distribution system. This is critical during restoration and operational planning. Sometimes switches remain in the out-of-normal position for months. These out-of-normal situations can adversely impact load transfers if they are not managed well. Circuit loading under normal and emergency situations is determined by distribution system planners. Without an enterprise GIS, those planners will not have visibility into potentially problematic operational conditions.
- Directing the field forces to find faults. Manual trouble tickets rarely give crews and trouble-shooters enough information to find faults. GIS can detail the route to get workers to the pole, manhole, or pad-mount transformer location of the suspected fault. GIS also can identify where the possible disconnecting device is located, along with all the necessary information about that device.
- Assuring the electrical system is safe for workers to make repairs. A properly configured GIS allows dispatchers and field workers to speak the same language. Dispatchers see the big picture and provide accurate instructions to the crews.
- Safety tagging equipment. Tagging data becomes part of the overall network representation. The power of the GIS to perform queries on tagged equipment can assure a higher level of safety assurance for the crews.
- Coordinating the sequence of additions to the electrical distribution network. As construction is proceeding, the GIS can display an added portion of the network as a separate version of the data, thus allowing the dispatchers to commission parts of the network. This eliminates the awkward and costly process of having to maintain two record systems, one for work-order processing and one for operations. Using separate versions from the same core information allows planners and engineers to view the current operations while dispatchers and field workers view new or proposed work that may be within their current work area.
- Formulating restoration plans for major storm outages. This is where the GIS shines. Various scenarios can be developed for crew deployment, looking at potential impassible routes like bridges

Textbox 1

shut down during high winds or rivers subject to flooding. The GIS can help predict outages and equipment damage for certain projected weather conditions, like hurricanes, so that just the right inventory is reserved for delivery to the right location if the storm materializes.

- Keeping track of critical customers. Those with serious medical issues, or pumping stations, wells, and cell towers have always been a high priority for electric distribution companies, even when the restoration process was done manually. The GIS can enhance the way critical customers are treated, beyond being a flag in the customer information system. Crews can be deployed to provide early assessment. The GIS can provide visualization, showing the restoration priorities of these critical customers in the context of the overall restoration process.

- Coordinating the use of customer generation. As more customer and distributed generation sources are added to the system, the GIS can provide the details of their location and their role in the restoration process. Since customer generation can also be a potential safety issue during an outage, the GIS can help flag where crews need to exhibit additional caution.

- Coordinating with the demand side management programs. Utilities often have a separate group within customer care that deals with voluntary load reduction programs for customers with special billing deals. The GIS gives the load dispatchers visibility into these additional resources to optimize the use of load curtailment.

- Performing system analysis. Load flow, short circuit analysis, voltage profile analysis, cold load pickup, protective device coordination, and capacitor application all need the infrastructure data that GIS holds. Often, as in the case with planning, dispatchers maintain separate analysis databases. This results in an error-prone and risky reconciliation process.

Textbox 1

The reality of workflow within a utility is that it takes a finite time to change from one state to another. The enterprise GIS manages the various states so the right information is available at the right time to the right model (textbox 2). This relies on the proper set up of the work and tight integration with corporate supply chain, asset and work management, or ERP systems (textbox 3).

Managing many states of the system

Data within the GIS environment exists in many states:

- As-is data. The state of the system that shows all work orders closed to plant records. This database is not the current state of the power system, since work in progress is constantly changing the configuration of the system.
- Work planned. This state shows those elements of the power system that will be changed, but are not yet in service. The collection of these elements shows the future state of the power system.
- Work under construction. This state shows those elements that are in a state of change in real time.
- Work completed but not energized. This state shows all physical work has been completed, but the electrical system has not been energized. This state would not exist for work done while hot.
- System energized. This state shows those elements that have been changed (built) and now create a change in the electrical network. The complete work associated with this change may or may not be finished.
- Work completed. This state shows the as-built condition of the work as it evolved during the engineering and construction process. This state shows all the work completed after the electrical network has changed. An example of work performed after the network is energized is the removal of damaged cable. While part of the original work order, the removal might be done months later, since it is a low-priority item.

Textbox 2

Outage management using GIS or a standalone system

Outage management consists of some work processes that require spatial and network representations and thus could be developed as a GIS application using GIS tools. Many other outage management system (OMS) processes and functions do not. A number of successful OMS applications are based directly on GIS. There are two advantages to this approach. One, the data model can be used directly without translation. The other is the data itself is as current for OMS as it is for GIS.

However, most outage management systems are built as robust, proprietary, closed, secure, high performance systems. Often, an OMS is operated by dispatchers within the energy management and dispatch centers of utilities along side the SCADA consoles. Since the OMS does require spatial and network data, an interface exists between the GIS and the OMS. The interface does the following:

1. Extracts just the right data for the OMS
2. Validates connectivity and data integrity
3. Optimizes the number of nodes and branches
4. Restructures the data for import into the OMS
5. Reports the status of the imported data

Workflow for managing system operation changes

1. A work order exists and some of that work has already been installed in the field but nothing has been energized.
2. Field changes have been corrected in the work order so the crew must update the GIS immediately using a mobile GIS device, and communicate with the centrally or locally managed GIS in a distributed environment.
3. A switch planner creates a switching order that details the steps needed to bring the work into service (called commissioning).
4. The dispatcher assigns a status to the GIS feature (transformers, cable, wires) denoting that element is to be energized. That status also includes the switching order number and the switching order step.
5. After all the features have been noted for commissioning, the data is reconciled or posted into the as-is state (often called default version). None of the elements is to be energized, nor are any of the existing elements deleted.
6. Dispatchers could then create a study version to perform "what if" switching scenarios before settling on exactly the sequence they wish to follow.
7. When the switching is to take place in the field, the dispatcher simulates the opening or closing of switches or the connecting or disconnecting of cable or conductor. This simulates energizing the added sections and de-energizing other sections. The intent is to reconfigure the network model in the same sequence or order as that occurring in the field.

Textbox 3

The size and complexity of the electrical network will determine which approach is appropriate. There are successful implementations of both configurations.

A hybrid approach uses the standalone OMS for the core outage processes and GIS for visualization, routing, and spatial analysis. Data is populated from the OMS to the GIS on regular intervals. Outage-related GIS applications that are not core OMS functions include outage events maps, the status of switches, spatially orientated restoration status, and the location of trouble crews. That information can be viewed from a Web browser by the general public, media, local government, emergency agencies, and utility executives. The OMS is used for the heavy lifting (managing the bursts of data), leaving the GIS to perform the functions it does best.

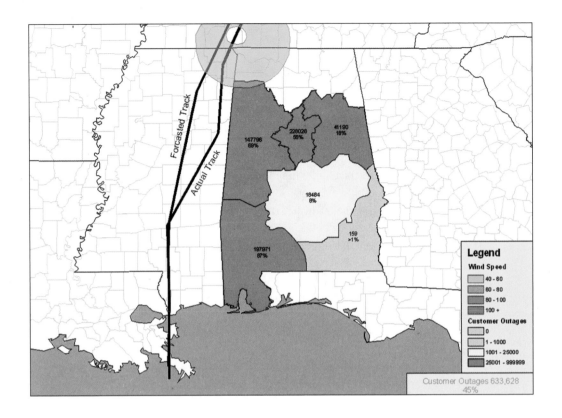

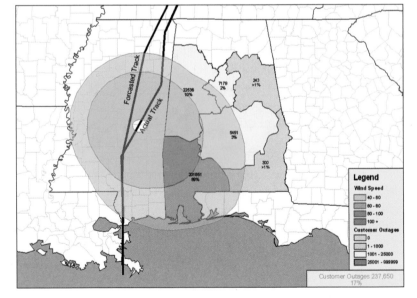

Figure 6.6
Alabama Power tracked
Hurricane Katrina by
forecasted track, actual
track, wind speed, and
customer outages.

Courtesy of Southern
Company

GIS and OMS

Why some utilities have a separate OMS (whether based on GIS or not) from the fully detailed GIS

- OMS deals mainly with geoschematic data; exact geographic representation is not necessary. Network connectivity is critical.
- A vast majority of the structural features like poles and manholes are not needed in the OMS operational model. A standalone or pared down GIS can be optimized for schematics.
- The fully detailed facility GIS contains ten to a hundred times the volume of data needed for outage management.
- OMS must handle rapid bursts of millions of pieces of real-time, telephone, and near real-time data. A pared down GIS or OMS can better handle this workflow.
- The displays, both graphic and nongraphic, must be refreshed with subsecond response.
- OMS requires very high availability and will often require fail-over capability. In this way OMS is more like SCADA. Fail over of a pared down GIS or standalone OMS is simpler to manage.

Textbox 4

Outage management processes

Outage management consists of five iterative processes:

1. Data gathering
2. Analysis and outage minimization
3. Dispatch and crew management
4. Repair
5. Report

Data gathering

As noted above, data for outage management is gathered from real-time systems (SCADA, AMR), telephone customer contact, and calls from police and fire departments, the media, and local government. Intelligent substation automation systems often will be able to accurately determine the distance from the substation to the fault. Early OMS's were referred to as trouble call systems since the only data collected was from telephone calls. As more distribution automation, AMR, and intelligent devices (even smart appliances) are installed, the number of points of monitoring increases dramatically, reducing the reliance on customer call information. The electrical network and its end points are becoming more intelligent.

GIS provides the thread and the context for the intelligent devices and end points. That is, GIS knows how the network is put together and the relationship of the devices to each other and the network.

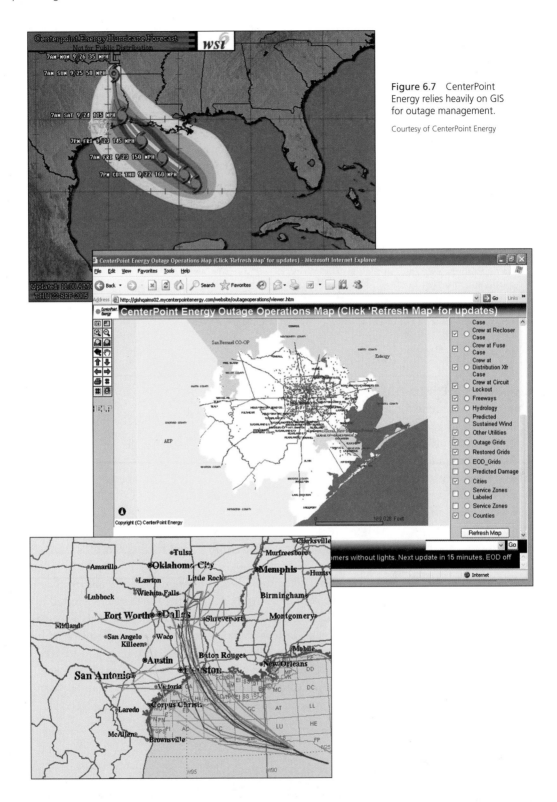

Figure 6.7 CenterPoint Energy relies heavily on GIS for outage management.

Courtesy of CenterPoint Energy

Analysis and outage minimization

Whether collecting real-time data from monitoring devices or from telephone calls, the OMS must

1. determine the events, which involves a logical grouping of data points suggesting either many small events or a few major events;
2. determine the location of the actual failure point (or fault) or points;
3. determine the location of the disconnecting device or devices;
4. determine the customers associated with each of the events;
5. estimate the resources required to repair the problem;
6. determine the sequence of load transfer under a variety of situations; and
7. switch around the problem.

GIS provides both the spatial and the network connectivity data.

Dispatch and crew management

Once the analysis is completed for an event, the work must be assigned to a trouble/repair crew. In many ways, this can be likened to work management, only more immediate. Materials, accounting, time reporting, and scheduling all have to be done. The OMS must aid the field crew to manually switch disconnecting devices safely and effectively.

Spatial and network data managed by the GIS is critical for crew routing, location of emergency resources and materials, and the deployment of additional emergency crews from remote locations and from their homes.

Repair

The OMS must track the progress of the repair work, including percentage completed and revised estimates of the restoration time. This data must be communicated to the customers. The OMS must provide data to assure the electrical system is safe for workers to make repairs and keep track of the positions of all distribution disconnecting devices.

The timing of the assessment and repair is critical for proper analysis. Reporting temporary repairs to the GIS is critical for long-term maintenance and asset tracking and management. Spatially enabled mobile and wireless GIS applications greatly facilitate timely and accurate reporting of repairs.

Report

Reporting during and after the events are critical for media updates, continuous process improvement, accounting, material management, and regulatory compliance. The OMS must be able to capture enough data to calculate the essential reliability measures such as System Average Interruption Duration Index (SAIDI) and Customer Average Interruption Duration Index (CAIDI).

GIS can be used after the fact to assess the relative reliability and effectiveness of work divisions as well to assess the impact on preventative measures such as tree trimming and inspection programs which directly impact an electric distribution system's ability to withstand storms.

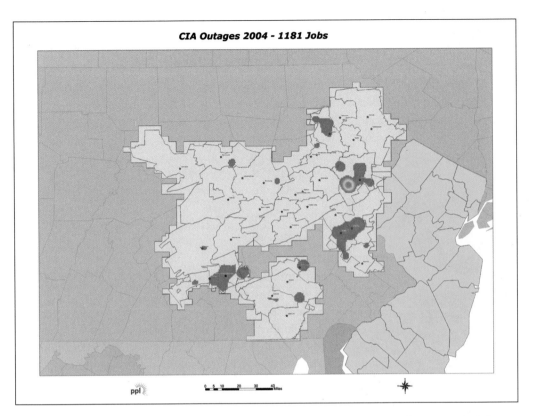

Figure 6.8 This map depicts the location of the 1,181 jobs (call tickets) completed by PPL of Pennsylvania workers in the first quarter of 2004.

Courtesy of PPL of Pennsylvania

SCADA: North Delta Electricity Distribution Company, Egypt

North Delta Electricity Distribution Company (NDEDCO) supplies low- and medium-voltage electrical energy for different purposes among three North Delta Governorates (Dakahlia, Kafr Elsheik, and Damietta), representing approximately one-third of Egypt's population.

NDEDCO turned to ESRI software to manage its electric power facility. ArcSDE is used for quality assurance of geodata entry and management of the utility's geodatabases.

For outage management, NDEDCO implemented a supervisory control and data acquisition (SCADA) system. SCADA monitors and controls the real-time status of equipment in the field such as substation components and certain line equipment. The NDEDCO staff members displayed SCADA information in the GIS so they could immediately see the number of customers affected by equipment failure. GIS also helped engineers prioritize the recovery efforts in a storm or other emergency situation. Integrating SCADA with GIS provided the company with useful information in the spatial analysis of system efficiency.

NDEDCO also used GIS-produced schematics maps. The ArcGIS Schematics extension allowed users to obtain logical views of a utility layout. Users could create easy-to-read multilevel representations (geographic, geoschematic, and schematic) of any linear network and drill down into and manage network information. NDEDCO's GIS produced schematic maps for its medium voltage electricity network and delivered maps online.

From *Energy Currents*, summer 2004

6.9a

6.9b

Figure 6.9a, b, c   ArcGlobe software's whole-earth 3D visualization application enables users to manage and visualize data at a global or local perspective. These are ArcGlobe's zoom-in views of Egypt's Nile River and pyramids.

Courtesy of North Delta Electricity Distribution Company

GIS enables power restoration

GIS is the enabling technology that manages the underlying electrical network configuration and its relationships to land, structures, and other networks. It is designed to handle short and long transactions, manage huge volumes of data, and provide spatial and network information to a variety of applications within the enterprise. OMS, whether a GIS application or a standalone system integrated with GIS, must consume huge volumes of data quickly, analyze the data in seconds, manage the workflow and repair process, and maintain statistics about network performance. GIS integrated with Web services such as weather, traffic, or emergency services provides additional resources outside the utility for effective restoration.

7

Natural gas transmission: Managing assets, minimizing risks

On an August morning in 2000, a dozen people from an extended family were asleep at their campsite along a river under a concrete-decked steel bridge. The bridge in this remote desert area of the southwestern United States supported a natural gas transmission line. SCADA operators noted that the pressure of the line 1100 dropped from about 670 psig (pounds per square inch gauge) to 375 psig. The maximum allowable operating pressure was nearly 850 psig. Operators immediately knew something was very wrong with the pipeline.

The 30-inch diameter transmission line had ruptured, allowing natural gas to escape. The high pressure caused the released gas to generate heat and ignite, severely burning all twelve campers and incinerating their vehicles. No one survived. The fire lasted nearly an hour. The rupture and subsequent explosion left a crater more than 80 feet long, nearly 50 feet wide, and 20 feet deep. Locals could see flames for miles. Investigators found a 20-foot section of pipe nearly 300 feet away. Another section crashed into the bridge, causing serious damage. The fire and explosion destroyed approximately 60 feet of transmission line.

Besides the enormous human tragedy, it cost nearly one million dollars to repair the pipeline, which transported gas west from Texas. California lost much of its gas supply while the pipeline was out of service. The U.S. Department of Transportation (DOT) estimated the cost of that curtailment to California's economy at nearly $18 million dollars a day.

The National Transportation Safety Board, which investigated the explosion, concluded that severe internal corrosion had significantly weakened the pipeline wall, causing the rupture and explosion.

Sadly, this pipeline accident was not an isolated event.

The DOT report on natural gas pipeline safety said that since 1986, there have been nearly 300 fatalities and nearly 2,400 injuries with property damage approaching $300 million.

In the summer of 2004, in an industrial area of the village of Ghislenghien, about 20 miles southeast of Brussels, Belgium, a construction crew pieced a natural gas transmission line that erupted and exploded. Shaken neighbors could see the flames and hear the blast from miles away. Emergency crews from across Belgium and from France, Luxembourg, and Germany rushed to help. A gray haze hung over the rural area as helicopters and about fifty ambulances carried injured to hospitals. Twenty-four people perished in the accident.

Feds step in

Natural gas accidents and environmental disasters caused by pipeline leaks, prompted the U.S. Congress to act. In 2002, lawmakers passed the Pipeline Safety Improvement Act, which President George W. Bush signed into law. The law provides for federal oversight of pipeline design, construction, and ongoing inspection and risk mitigation. The new government regulations required pipeline operators to execute a pipeline integrity management program. Other nations have enacted similar safety standards.

The new regulations require natural gas transmission pipeline operators to meet these mandates:

- Develop and implement a comprehensive integrity management program for pipeline segments where a failure would have the greatest impact on the public or property.
- Identify and characterize applicable threats to pipeline segments that could impact a high consequence area.
- Conduct a baseline assessment and periodic reassessments of these pipeline segments.
- Mitigate significant defects discovered from the assessment.
- Continuously monitor the effectiveness of its integrity program and modify the program as needed to improve its effectiveness.

The DOT, which regulates transmission pipelines, recognized that pipeline safety consists of three essential components:

1. Outstanding, accurate, and coordinated data management.
2. Consistent, methodical discovery and reporting of threats and risks to an oversight agency.
3. Timely mitigation and remediation of risks.

Asset and facilities management: Public Service Company of New Mexico

New Mexico's largest supplier of natural gas services, Public Service Company of New Mexico (PNM), uses its ArcGIS solution to centralize, streamline, and increase efficiency in managing its gas transmission assets, including 1,700 miles of pipeline.

PNM's Gas Transmission Application Management Information System (gTAMIS) replaced a system fairly typical of the industry. Old maps of facility locations and construction drawings remained in various electronic formats, online, and in paper files. Most of the records for the maintenance and inspection of gas transmission facilities were paper based. GIS data was scattered and in various systems and projections. It was difficult and time-consuming to combine data for system-wide analysis and querying.

The gTAMIS application was developed around the company's goal of having one centralized repository for data that allows multiuser access. Designed by POWER Engineers, gTAMIS helps consolidate applications to a standard platform/tool and integrates GIS capabilities with other systems. It allows easy access to information, improves productivity, and supports current and accurate information. It limits redundancy within the utility's internal processes through the centralization of data sources that are accessible online. GIS provides PNM with planning and analytical capabilities through visual mapping of gas transmission system facilities and their selected attribute and operating limits.

PMN uses its GIS for planning, scheduling, and verifying regular maintenance and inspection of gas transmission facilities. In addition, the system provides access, routing, right-of-way, and maps to assist field crews checking facilities. The GIS application uses a multiuser geodatabase and application that allows queries, viewing, modifying, and adding data associated with the transmission system.

GIS enables gTAMIS to create spatial relationships and feature attributes that can be queried and displayed for analysis. Users select specific facilities or data objects to view associated data by querying attributes and historical inspection and maintenance data. Interacting with at least four PNM systems and various other digital documents, gTAMIS is the interface for using existing maps, databases, applications, images, CAD drawings, and multimedia files to display and analyze gas transmission data.

From *GIS for Gas Utilities*

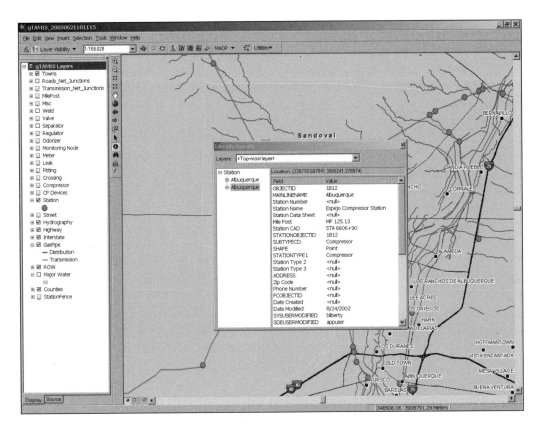

Figure 7.1   The Gas Transmission Application Management Information System (gTAMIS) helps Public Service Company of New Mexico manage its assets. This gTAMIS map shows the table of attributes that appears on-screen after a user selects a feature with the identify key.

Courtesy of Public Service Company of New Mexico

Data management

Natural gas pipeline companies and utilities have been collecting enormous amounts of information about their facilities for years. As noted throughout this book, the information is often fragmented. The critical data—useful for basing decisions such as inspection reports, pigging (pipeline inline inspection) databases, photography, and general facilities reports—has not always been well-coordinated.

This was the situation at our fictional utility, AnyTown Energy, which maintained gas transmission pipeline information in CAD files. Each file contained a representation of information accumulated for a short section of pipe. While in digital form, the information on one CAD file had no relationship to the information on another. In addition, there was no way to query the information on each file. The CAD drawings were created exactly from the gas transmission department's old alignment sheets, manually prepared drawings that display segments of pipe over particular sections.

AnyTown Energy also had a large amount of backlogged work that did not show up on its alignment sheet CAD files. In fact, just to review and update all the alignment sheets, and print and distribute copies to transmission line operators and contractors, took nearly a year. A lot happens in a year that doesn't show up on newly printed alignment sheets. AnyTown Energy maintained a separate digital tracking system for all events and inspections that had occurred along the utility's transmission system. However, none of the events coordinated with the data contained on the CAD-based alignment sheets.

To determine the safety of a natural gas transmission pipeline, the operator must assess the relative risk that the pipeline will rupture and subsequently ignite. Since pipelines stretch for miles crisscrossing nations throughout the world, the task of physically inspecting pipelines inside and out is enormous. Accidents happen when the operators are not aware that a pipeline segment is at high risk. After an accident, investigators often discover there was sufficient data to predict a rupture, but the operator did not have the means to pull the information together to be able to recognize the risk. They may discover that the pipeline segment had a higher risk of rupture than other segments. Operators determine risk by a number of factors. Things like the age and location of a weld or a dent, or when a backhoe hit a section of pipe, are critical risk factors. Perhaps there was an inspection report that indicated a faulty corrosion protection device. If these inspection reports happened to be misfiled, the risk to that section of pipe may be understated.

The data management situation at AnyTown Energy put the utility at risk of missing some critical information that could result in a devastating pipeline explosion. In assessing risk, operators need to know who lives, works, and plays near the pipeline. Should a pipeline erupt and ignite, people must be able to flee quickly. Clearly, a pipeline that runs through remote desert poses a lower overall risk than one near a sensitive structure. Examples of sensitive structures are high-rise office buildings, day care centers, prisons, or hospitals. What makes these structures sensitive is that in the event of a nearby pipeline explosion, the occupants would typically be confined and not easily evacuated.

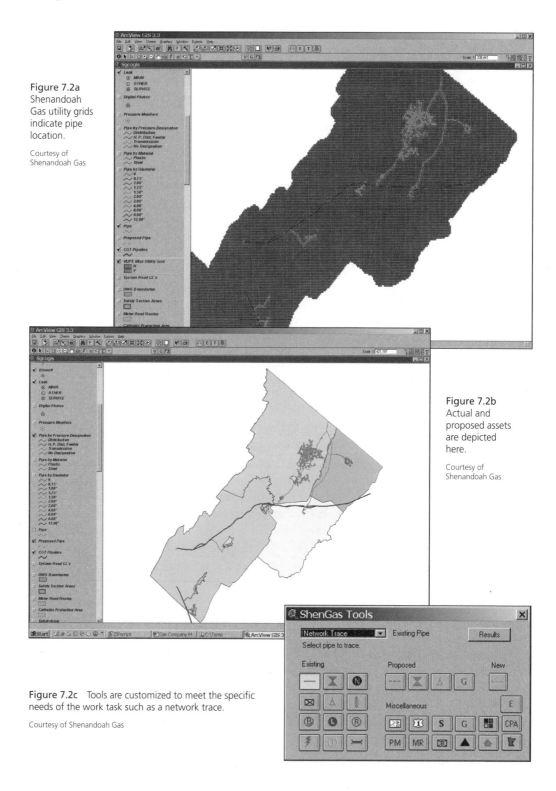

Figure 7.2a
Shenandoah
Gas utility grids
indicate pipe
location.

Courtesy of
Shenandoah Gas

Figure 7.2b
Actual and
proposed assets
are depicted
here.

Courtesy of
Shenandoah Gas

Figure 7.2c   Tools are customized to meet the specific
needs of the work task such as a network trace.

Courtesy of Shenandoah Gas

Data management: Shenandoah Gas

Shenandoah Gas, a division of Washington Gas Light Company, uses ArcView software to maintain its facility data. The service territory includes four counties in the Northern Shenandoah Valley in Virginia and serves 15,000 customers with 359 miles of main pipeline. In this era of deregulation, gas companies strive to do more work with fewer resources. Using ArcView, Shenandoah Gas has greatly improved its facility information management.

The Shenandoah Gas system consists of three custom tools for querying, adding, and maintaining data. The Query Dog querying tool allows users to zoom to a location according to a selected attribute such as a street or intersection. The ShenGas tool is for adding and maintaining facility data. Its button set includes pipe, proposed pipe, appurtenance, and polygon theme and has an individual menu assigned to each button. For example, to edit pipe attributes, the user selects the pipe tool and drills down within that tool to the edit menu. A third tool contains a vast set of application tools such as theme, legend, as-built, and map-to-model tools. All tools were designed to provide user friendliness that requires very little GIS knowledge to operate.

Other applications for Shenandoah Gas' GIS include new facility design analysis, utility grid selection, leak survey area analysis, leak survey walk sheet generation, safety section and critical valve analysis. Also, pipeline integrity high consequence area analysis, mains replacement analysis using mapped leak data, and Advantica's SynerGEE gas pressure and flow analysis.

From GIS for Gas Utilities

The data that pipeline operators need to assess risk includes factors within their control—the ability to maintain accurate and coordinated information about their pipes—as well as information outside their control, such as a trailer park permitted adjacent to their pipeline.

The DOT regulations define special areas that surround natural gas transmission lines. These high consequence areas (HCA) are where people might congregate or live and would have a hard time fleeing from a natural gas pipeline explosion. The pipeline operators need to coordinate all the information in a spatial way along the pipe. They must have access to and coordinate information that surrounds their pipe to properly determine threats and prioritize threat remediation for the highest risk areas.

Shortcomings of alignment sheets

Prior to computer technology, pipeline operators manually captured data on alignment sheets. Users had to match each sheet to the adjacent sheet. Thousands of sheets collectively served as a bible for the engineers and technicians who managed the pipelines. Operators detailed events, accidents, repairs, and inspections along the pipe. Keeping this data current took considerable effort and updating sometimes would fall woefully behind. This backlog of unposted transactions left the operators ill-equipped to make critical decisions. Relocating a pipeline meant recreating the alignment sheets using a cumbersome process to correlate new locations with the original measurement locations. This process was error-prone and time-consuming.

In the 1980s, many pipeline operators converted their existing alignment sheets to CAD systems. While this may have improved the updating process, it did not solve the data problem. CAD did not address the fundamental flaw that the data was uncoordinated and fragmented. CAD is not a suitable information repository, nor can it perform spatial analysis.

Pipeline operators really needed a way to

- capture large, discrete amounts of data spread out geographically;
- coordinate historical documents about events that occurred along the pipeline;
- add new data about events that happened along the pipeline;
- reference linear data geographically, converting linear referenced data to real-life geographic coordinates;
- calculate the high-risk areas of a pipeline;
- coordinate the high consequence areas with the other data;
- adjust the risk profiles based on people moving into HCAs; and
- show all this data in a way that people were used to seeing it, similar to alignment sheets.

Along came GIS

The pipeline industry had been using GIS for asset management. However, the new U.S. government rules and similar rules by other governments made GIS virtually required for pipeline integrity management. That's because GIS is an information system, with a relational database management system at its heart. GIS allows documents to be linked to geographic locations and thus to exact locations along a pipeline.

Extending GIS to integrity and risk calculations was natural for pipeline companies that already used the technology for asset management. In addition to managing the assets, GIS can also manage events that occur along the pipeline. Finding points of corrosion is valuable for asset management as well as for determining the risk profiles for the pipeline segments.

Linear measurement systems

As noted earlier, the pipeline industry has historically used linear referencing, or station series, to record pipeline events. Operators determine fixed points along the pipeline as stations. For example, they will refer to the beginning of a pipeline segment or known point as station 1. They then measure the distance along the pipeline in relation to this station number. So operators refer to 100 feet along the pipeline from station 1 as station 1+100. This value represents a point that determines the location of an event or piece of equipment. So the common language for location is station value rather than coordinate. From an operator's perspective, stationing provides a more reliable form of measurement. Further, construction personnel may not have captured the absolute position of a pipeline accurately at the time of construction. However, they would have carefully documented the relative location along the pipeline. GIS can model the pipeline using its station series. It can also provide a means to transform the station series into real-world coordinates.

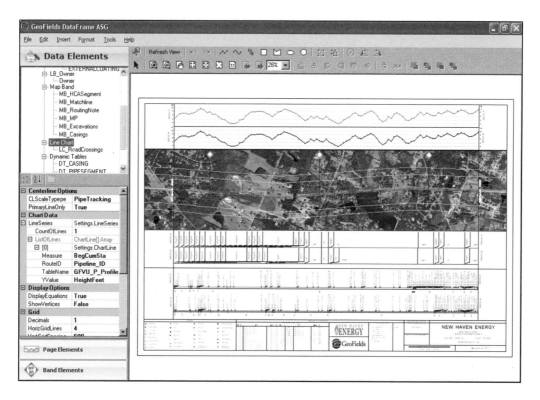

Figure 7.3   GeoFields' RiskFrame HCA and the spatial processing capabilities of ArcGIS combine to identify high consequence areas for gas pipelines.

Courtesy of GeoFields

Facility management: Osaka Gas

Osaka Gas' pipeline operation manages 55,000 kilometers (34,175 miles) of pipeline. The gas pipe facility management system project built on ArcGIS brought many advantages to the company, such as effective data management, workflow efficiency, and interoperability.

ESRI technology has helped Osaka Gas achieve large cost reductions. For example, by using the ESRI gas data model, the company was able to quickly initiate its project. These quick start abilities served to minimize the initial cost and development period for its GIS. Another cost-saving factor is the system's ability to automate CAD drawing importation (location adjustment) which freed up specialists to engage in other facility-related work. GIS-enabled Web applications reduced software costs that had been previously charged on a per-client basis.

The open platform and scalable structure of ArcGIS enabled the company to use its existing hardware and establish a low-cost, flexible system structure for client/server, Web, terminal connections, mobile functions, and so forth. GIS mobile solutions help with field service operations. Construction work orders are transmitted online. ArcPad for PDAs and ArcGIS for Tablet PCs were added to field worker tools to improve services.

Osaka Gas' GIS is primarily designed for pipeline facility management and uses an integrated central control system. The system fulfills the company's added-value goal by providing information to local public sector organizations and supporting Web services for other internal systems.

GIS is integrated with the utility's workflow from facility maintenance to data queries. The online system, built with ArcIMS and ArcSDE, is accessed by 3,000 users at more than 70 internal and external sites.

From *GIS for Gas Utilities*

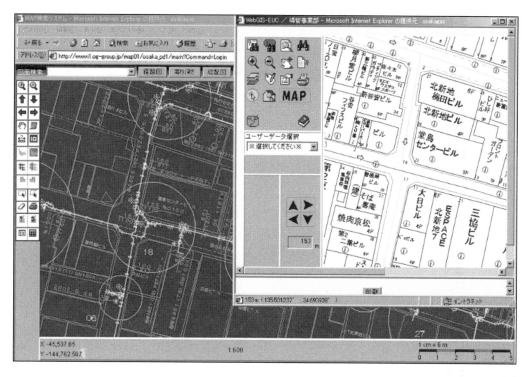

Figure 7.4   Facility maps are available on the Osaka Gas GIS-enabled intranet site. More than 3,000 users access the company's various GIS Web sites.

Courtesy of Osaka Gas

Since GIS is geographically based, no longer is data linked strictly to the linear stationing method. GIS that has linear referencing capability can provide the operator with two views of the data: by pipeline station (critical for historical events data) and by geographic coordinate (critical for modern inspection using GPS).

Pipeline spatial and data analysis

Using spatial analysis, GIS routinely answers the question, "Who lives within 600 feet of my pipeline?" The DOT regulations, many of them data related, define the elements of a comprehensive integrity management program. One of the key elements is creating and documenting HCAs. Operators need geographic and attribute data about the pipeline and for the surrounding region. Further, given that data, operators need a way to perform a dynamic spatial analysis to identify HCAs.

A GIS is not only about points, lines, and polygons. The vast majority of GIS applications involve the integration of raster information, such as satellite imagery. Knowing the surrounding terrain is important for pipeline operators managing assets. Knowing the nature of structures adjacent to a pipeline is essential for pipeline integrity management. Up-to-date imagery integrated with the GIS-based pipeline asset information helps define high consequence areas.

Pipeline operators need to understand the potential risk of every pipeline segment. GIS can manage the complex tabular and graphic representation of the pipeline by weighting the relative risk of each segment. The results can be displayed as a map, highlighting high-risk areas or areas where a potential trailer park, day-care center, or hospital near the pipeline would increase risk.

The GIS provides the flexibility to display all kinds of information about the pipeline in new and enlightening forms. It can also display the pipeline information in forms familiar to operating and maintenance people. However, unlike the past practice of producing alignment sheets using a static CAD system, GIS can provide dynamic, on-the-fly alignment sheets based on the latest data from a common GIS database. This could include any new imagery that surrounds the pipeline segment.

Most pipeline operators have adopted or are in the process of adopting GIS to manage their pipeline data and to provide pipeline integrity management.

With a GIS-enabled natural gas pipeline system in place, data management becomes significantly less burdensome. By creating a GIS model for the pipeline system, operators can manage their pipeline assets (which they must do anyway), have the infrastructure for HCA analysis, and perform a host of other analysis. GIS helps operators easily determine all the elements needed to proactively define a pipeline's risk level. Further, a GIS can provide documentation to prove compliance with the regulations to oversight agencies.

Discovering and reporting threats

Current GIS technology allows operators to manage, coordinate, and identify discovered threats in a standard form and report them to the DOT or other oversight agencies. By capturing and coordinating data in GIS, associating scanned documents (such as historical manual inspection reports), operators will be able to keep pace with ever-demanding regulations in a cost-effective way.

Assume that a pipeline operator has already determined what segments of the pipeline lie within a high consequence area. How would that operator know that someone has permitted a trailer park, a nursing home, a baseball field, or a prison near the pipeline? Instead of spending countless hours researching the files of every planning board or commission, the utility could subscribe to a GIS Web service that would automatically notify the operator of a potential zoning change or new building permits for land close to the pipeline. The GIS could then analyze the project to see if it increases the risk profile for a section of pipe. GIS helps manage threat data, facilitates reporting both internally and to the regulators, and provides visualization of threats on a macro level.

Managing risk mitigation and remediation

GIS provides a platform to help operators prioritize risk. By coordinating and effectively organizing all the relevant data relating to integrity management, operators may find that they can optimize mitigation. For example, if an operator is unsure if a pipe segment is low, medium, or high risk, the operator may take a conservative approach and assume that it is medium or high risk. If that pipe segment cannot be inspected using in-line inspection methods, assessment may have to be direct, requiring expensive and dangerous excavation. Conversely, if the operator assumes that the segment is low risk, based upon inaccurate or uncoordinated data, and it really is medium or high risk, the operator would face severe consequences if an event occurred.

Thus, GIS can help manage mitigation. With solid processes and procedures in place, a GIS platform can give operators the best opportunity to make the proper decisions about mitigation and remediation, being neither too conservative (which may be expensive) nor too optimistic (which may be risky).

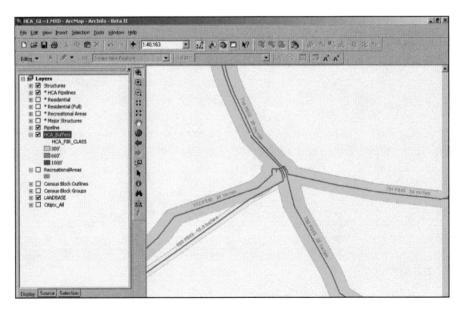

Figure 7.5 High consequence area analysis with GIS generates buffer zones to show at-risk distances from the pipeline and assure safe excavations.

Source: ESRI

Regulatory compliance: Questar Gas Company

Working with ESRI and GE Energy, Questar Gas Company developed its industry-specific pipeline applications. The comprehensive solution was designed for the company's Geospatial Pipeline Maintenance and Integrity Management Support project to meet specific regulatory and compliance requirements.

Questar maintains over 4,000 miles of transmission and high-pressure distribution pipeline across six states and 23,000 miles of immediate high-pressure distribution pipeline serving more than 825,000 customers within 21,000 square miles of service territory.

Questar needed a system with powerful functionality to perform high consequence area analysis, risk analysis, class location determination, maximum allowable operating pressure calculations, and other compliance and engineering functions. The initial focus and vision was to move all transmission pipeline data into the ESRI software environment and to consolidate data into one central repository where it could be accessed companywide by the people who needed it, when they needed it, and from wherever they needed it.

The project helped Questar respond to the U.S. Department of Transportation's Final Rule for Pipeline Integrity Management in High Consequence Areas. The project also helped Questar comply with mandates for natural gas pipeline operators to develop integrity management plans for all transmission facilities that fell under this rule.

ESRI GIS software and applications from GE Energy replaced the legacy transmission pipeline automated mapping/facilities management system and other disparate databases and information systems Questar used to manage its assets. In subsequent implementation phases, the enterprise GIS platform was designed to integrate with existing information systems such as customer information, Advantica's SynerGEE gas network analysis software, PeopleSoft ERP, and FileNet document management software.

The enterprise solution deployed ArcEditor and ArcSDE software. The geodatabase and, specifically, the ArcGIS Pipeline Data Model, provided the basis for the central data repository.

From GIS for Gas Utilities

Asset management

Pipeline operators, just like electric transmission operators, must have a proper inventory of their assets and be able to view them in relationship to the environment. They must understand the condition of their assets, as noted above for regulatory reporting and for safety reasons, but they have to know the condition of the assets so that they can make proper decisions about maintenance and upgrades. As in the case of electric transmission, GIS allows operators to visualize their assets in relation to the world around their pipelines.

GIS helps manage gas transmission

An enterprise GIS can bring the data used by asset and integrity managers directly into the hands of the maintenance and inspection personnel. Data downloaded or transmitted wirelessly to handheld and field devices for remote interaction allows for coordinated activities across many disciplines. Operators can easily view alternatives for expansion based on many factors, such as high-consequence areas and projected growth.

Pipeline inspection involves both visual inspection and electronic surveillance. Intelligent in-line inspection systems draw data from inside of the pipe. Operators can routinely integrate digital in-line inspection data with GIS, giving operators information to assess the internal integrity of the entire pipeline. The GIS can capture inspection data directly, allowing operators to see the complete picture of the pipeline's condition. The GIS can associate any relevant documents with points along the pipeline as well. New systems that use a form of sonar can precisely locate an abnormal sound, such as the banging of a backhoe against the pipe. Having this real-time data in hand, the operator can immediately dispatch a repair crew to the site of a possible dig while the evidence is still fresh.

Once pipeline operators have decided to build a pipeline from point a to point b, GIS helps choose the best route by taking into account economics, ease of construction, possible local opposition, natural disaster factors, security factors, and overall construction risk.

Many pipeline operators will use the GIS to create a master plan for engineering and designing a new pipeline segment. This avoids the extra steps of transcribing the as-is data from the GIS into a design package and, after the construction is complete, posting the as-built data from the design documents back into the GIS.

Vegetation management along a buried natural gas transmission line is not as critical as it is for an electric transmission line, but it is still an important task for a pipeline operator. Vegetation discoloration can be an indication of a gas leak, so a careful assessment of the plants along the right-of-way is important. Overgrown vegetation along a right-of-way can cause community issues. In the event of a rupture and ignition, overgrown brush could exacerbate the spread of the fire. As in the case for electric transmission, GIS is the ideal tool to manage vegetation along a right-of-way.

Gas transmission rights-of-way represent a patchwork quilt of land ownerships. Knowing exactly the nature of each easement, license, and grant along the way will prevent future access problems. GIS is the tool of choice for managing land parcels. Operators monitor the health of the pipeline using sophisticated SCADA systems that tend to be more schematic-based than geographic-based. The GIS can supplement the visualization of the SCADA information presented in a geographic view.

GIS provides the means to consolidate both the facility and imagery data, perform spatial analysis, and provide outstanding visualization so that gas transmission pipeline operators can lower their risk and make better asset management decisions.

8
Natural gas distribution: Sustaining the flow to customers

Early one Sunday morning, AnyTown Energy's emergency customer service representative (CSR) received a trouble call. A frantic customer complained of flickering lights and the smell of burning rubber coming from the basement. The CSR dispatched a troubleshooter to the scene.

By the time the troubleshooter arrived, fire engines blocked the street and debris was scattered everywhere. It looked like a house had been blown off its foundation. Fortunately, no one was hurt. The entire neighborhood was without power. The troubleshooter checked the address of the customer who had reported flickering lights. Sure enough, it was the house that had exploded. The distraught customer, clad in a bathrobe, said that after she had called the electric company, the smell from the basement got really bad. She then ran from the house. Not a minute later, the house exploded with a terrible boom.

After the troubleshooter disconnected the underground secondary circuit feeding the neighborhood, the fire captain gave him permission to disconnect the house service in the basement. On his way to the house, he noticed a strong odor of what he thought was natural gas coming from the catch basin right outside the damaged home. He checked the trouble ticket. "Customer reports a strong burning-rubber smell." The smell he noticed was definitely not burning rubber. In his written report, he failed to mention the natural gas odor.

Later, the troubleshooter determined that an underground arcing fault in an old low-voltage circuit had caused the power failure. This particular section of underground feeder had a history of poor performance and arcing cable faults. Apparently, the fault had been cooking for quite some time but people first noticed the flickering lights that morning. At some point, the arcing fault had created a gas, perhaps from the burning insulation of the cable. The investigation concluded that the arcing fault had melted the rubber insulation of the cables. It was at this point that the customer reported the flickering lights and smell of burning rubber. The liquid insulation then created a gas which filled the basement. Something then ignited the gas. Perhaps it was the basement refrigerator's compressor or the furnace, but no one knew for sure.

The lab tests came back inconclusive. Even the lab wasn't sure that there could be enough gas generated from the burning insulation to cause an explosion.

Long after AnyTown Energy rebuilt the damaged house, the troubleshooter happened to be working near the street where the explosion had occurred. He decided to check to see how well the contractor had rebuilt it. As he walked toward the freshly painted house, he recalled the natural gas smell on that awful day of the explosion. He remembered that the smell came from the catch basin but it never was investigated. Then he saw it: a newly repaved section of street. It was not on the side of the street where the cables run. It was on the other side where the gas lines lie.

The troubleshooter had a friend in the gas operations department check the gas leak management system, a little program he maintained on a personal computer. There it was: across the street from the renovated house was a documented gas leak. Someone reported the leak several months before the house explosion. Per regulation, the gas operations department advised authorities and did everything by the book. The leak had been repaired two months earlier, but well after the house had exploded. All the required reports and field notes were in meticulous order. The troubleshooter thought the best course of action was to forget the whole affair.

Too bad they didn't have a GIS

If AnyTown Energy had an enterprise GIS in place, the explosion described in the above scenario would have been much less likely. All the utility would have had to do was to check the GIS to see if there were any gas leaks in areas where there are old underground cables prone to arcing. Perhaps AnyTown could have prevented the explosion and the expense of the subsequent forensics and legal investigations. No one made the connection until it was way too late.

Just knowing about asset condition isn't enough. GIS uses the common element of location to help utilities understand what assets they own and where they are. They discover risks to their assets: what they do and don't control. The electric department had no access to the gas department's leak inventory. The gas department was unaware of the electric department's cable condition. The cause of the explosion probably was the combination of the arcing fault, the oozing insulation, and the leaking gas that migrated into the basement. No one will ever know.

Every time an electric worker enters a manhole, that worker must test for gas concentrations. It could be natural gas from a leak or sewer gas. Workers don't always do what they are supposed to do. Sometimes they forget to check for gas. Gas that leaks underground will migrate into electric manholes. An added safeguard would be a GIS-based field device with gas leak data in hand for every electric worker who may have to enter a manhole or vault.

As discussed in chapter seven, when a large gas transmission line fails and ignites, the results are catastrophic. Many people are impacted. Loss of the transmission line can devastate whole economies. Natural gas distribution is different. Explosions that result from leaks on the gas distribution systems are local and impact just a few people. However, the impact for those few people can be substantial.

Enterprise GIS allows gas distribution companies to discover connections between assets, customers, and events. It provides new information that may reveal a set of old electric cables subject to arcing. Those same cables could be very close to an old cast-iron gas main. Enterprise GIS illustrates what sections of main are at high risk of corrosion in relation to moist soil areas. It compares the inspection and maintenance productivity of one district to another. Enterprise GIS discovers new things that could avoid small problems or big disasters.

GIS and gas distribution

Utilities that operate gas distribution systems need to a have a solid handle on their assets. Unlike gas and electric transmission systems, the gas distribution system is dense and consists of many short segments of small diameter pipes configured in a tight network. The pipes run up one street and down the next, forming loops. What most distinguishes gas distribution from transmission is that distribution companies supply fuel to retail customers. (Some gas transmission companies supply directly to large customers.) That means that gas utilities must have an understanding of its gas distribution assets in relation to present and future customers.

Gas utilities need to have a complete inventory of their gas distribution assets. They must know the precise location of gas leaks and how the environment surrounding the gas distribution system impacts their assets. They must decide what to fix and what to replace. They also must know that their assets impact other utilities' adjacent assets such as underground electric systems. Since gas distribution lines are underground, they must protect those lines from errant backhoe operators and gardeners digging in their front yards.

As noted in the previous chapter, governments around the world are requiring gas transmission operators to monitor pipeline integrity. Most of the regulations require operators to document and report the findings of their integrity management programs directly to the government. Since pipeline accidents impact many people, government regulators have focused heavily on high-pressure gas transmission integrity management. However, governments are requiring gas distribution system operators to perform integrity management for their systems as well. That's because gas distribution networks continue to pose risk to the public. The consensus of many government officials is that gas distribution systems should have more integrity management than currently exists.

The current regulations in the United States apply to all natural gas transmission pipelines. While the focus of the integrity regulations was on natural gas transmission and the consequences of high-volume, high-pressure system events, the regulations also apply to distribution mains operating at high pressure and in areas of significant human activity. This is because transmission is not defined in the United States by organizational structure, business application, or plant accounting principles. It is defined by variables such as pressure and other engineering principles. This is also true throughout the world. So there are really two kinds of distribution from a regulatory perspective. Regulations define high-pressure distribution mains as transmission lines. Unfortunately for local distribution companies, that means they have to comply with gas transmission line rules, which are fairly onerous in the United States. It may be more difficult to assess the condition of qualifying high-pressure distribution mains than for transmission lines.

GIS can help operators differentiate the low-pressure from the high-pressure distribution lines that qualify as transmission lines from a regulatory standpoint. Distribution operators can apply the GIS applications for transmission to the high-pressure distribution lines.

Asset management: Gujarat Gas Company

Gujarat Gas Company Ltd. (GGCL) is the largest private sector gas distribution company in India. GGCL's pipelines spread over more than 1,800 km (1,118 miles).

GGCL implemented GIS in its engineering, operations, planning, and other functions that require the examination, management, and dissemination of geographic data throughout the company. The basic objective was to create a complete GIS-based asset management system to fulfill the objectives.

GGCL worked with NIIT-GIS Ltd. (ESRI India) to implement a GIS-based asset management solution for its natural gas distribution system. The project involved managing migration of legacy data to the Oracle database with ArcSDE coupled with Telvent Miner & Miner's ArcFM software applications. Using a proven integration approach, the team developed the key interfaces to legacy systems such as GGCL's customer database. To do this, the gas company completed a migration plan that included the following steps:

1. Complete a requirement analysis.
2. Create a software requirement specification list.
3. Perform data modeling and designing.
4. Develop the database.
5. Customize tools and extensions.
6. Execute configuration and deployment.

From *GIS for Gas Utilities*

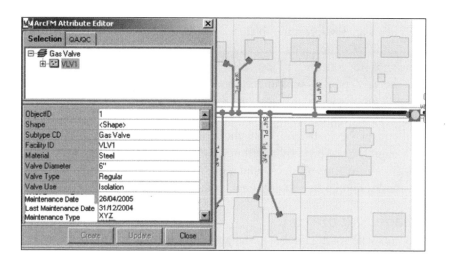

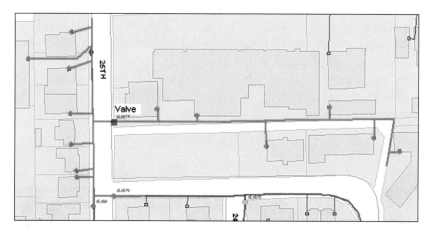

Figure 8.1 Gujarat Gas Company uses ArcFM Attribute Editor to add valve data.

Courtesy of Gujarat Gas Company

Most distribution systems are low-pressure, so they don't rupture like transmission lines. They are almost always in heavily populated areas since they are close to customers. The problem with distribution is not rupture and immediate ignition, but leaks. When a low-pressure gas line leaks, the gas typically seeps underground. The danger is when the gas travels into confined underground areas or basements. Once the gas density reaches a set value, it has the potential to ignite. A common source of ignition is someone turning on a light. Leaking gas could travel a long distance from the actual source, so high consequence areas don't really make sense for low-pressure distribution. Operators can use GIS to associate areas of potential gas leaks to areas of high population density. GIS can help predict the flow of gas from a leak and show the travel and extent of the leak over time.

Third-party damage and one call

Third-party damage occurs when someone other than an employee of the gas utility digs into a gas line. As discussed earlier, most countries have a clearinghouse system in which someone who intends to dig in certain areas must first obtain permission from an agency. These notification agencies go by such names as "One Call," "Call Before You Dig," and "Dig Safe." The agency contacts the local utilities that operate in that area. The utilities are required to mark their underground facilities within a prescribed time frame.

Gas companies rely on accurate, up-to-date plans of their gas distribution facilities in order to comply. If the plans are not current, then the utility must do additional research into what has occurred in the area. Utilities routinely use their GIS to manage the one-call system.

Figure 8.2 Not calling before you dig carries dangerous consequences.

Photo by Doug Menuez/ PhotoDisc/Getty Images

It would seem obvious that gas companies know exactly where each gas line is located underground. Yet dig-ins happen all the time. Why? It's a combination of

- ineffective communication;
- inaccurate or outdated records;
- large backlogs of field changes not posted to corporate mapping systems;
- ineffective processes;
- lack of technology;
- contractors not following proper procedures; and
- human error.

Enterprise GIS and good processes reduce dig-ins.

Condition assessment

Gas distribution utilities need GIS for asset and integrity management, which both require a solid understanding of asset inventory. With integrity management comes additional regulatory oversight and reporting. While asset management largely is an internal process of balancing infrastructure needs with available investment resources, integrity management is about compliance and the consequences of noncompliance within a prescribed time frame. Much of the data and processes that distribution utilities put in place for asset management are the same for integrity management. Like in the gas transmission area, much of the regulatory documentation will be in the form of computer-generated, database-driven maps, and that's what GIS does. This became critical during 2005 along the U.S. Gulf Coast during Hurricane Katrina, along the coastal regions of Asia after the tsunami, and in Pakistan after the devastating earthquake. In the gulf states, gas companies used pre- and post-hurricane imagery coordinated with the gas distribution assets to prioritize gas restoration to impacted areas and to locate their assets in relation to flooded communities.

As noted in chapter 2, GIS provides the foundation for planning and asset management. GIS manages the as-is inventory, location, and condition of the distribution assets. This knowledge may be entirely contained within the GIS or integrated with a work or asset management system.

Mains replacement

A significant challenge for a gas distribution company is to figure out which of its old mains to replace. Gas distribution systems have evolved from wooden tubes, to cast-iron pipes, to steel pipes, and more recently to plastic. Gas companies need a systematic method for replacing mains within the framework of their financial means. GIS maintains the complete inventory of the gas distribution including asset condition, making it a natural platform for managing a main replacement system. The GIS can help visualize which mains have the greatest risk of leaking based on age, soil conditions, and natural disasters, including earthquakes and floods. A GIS or an asset management system can maintain condition information and account for all the parts and pieces. The utility can use the spatial analytical tools of GIS to visualize situations and make better decisions about replacing mains.

Figure 8.3   GIS is used to determine the risk profile of gas distribution mains.

Courtesy of Opvantek

Cathodic protection

The gas distribution system consists of the mains, regulators, valves, meters, and services. But another important component of gas distribution is the corrosion protection system. Corroded, metallic, buried pipe is one of the main causes of gas leaks. While many new gas distribution pipes are plastic, there remains a huge inventory of cast-iron and steel pipes. To battle corrosion, gas distribution and transmission companies install corrosion prevention systems or cathodic protection (CP) systems. The CP system establishes a low-voltage electrical negative potential on the metal pipes (the cathode). This negative potential repels electrons from corrosive materials present in the soil. The CP system consists of positively charged anodes, an electric source, and wire buried with the pipe. Since this important system is like a low-voltage electric system, the GIS needs to model it in relation to the rest of the system. It recognizes isolating and insulating components and test stations.

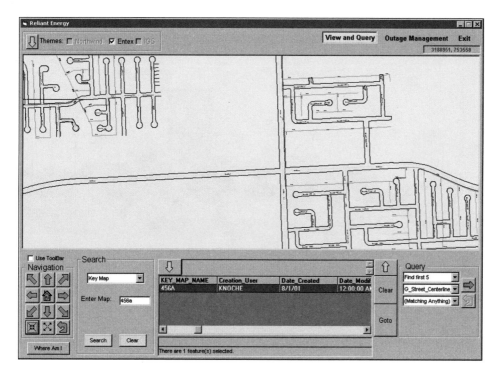

Figure 8.4 Cathodic protection tracking tools integrated with GIS help utilities determine the level of corrosion protection necessary for underground facilities.

Courtesy of CenterPoint Energy

Damage to the CP system increases the likelihood of corrosion on the gas pipes. Even though the CP system is modeled as a separate system, it must be viewed geographically in relation to the gas system itself.

Operations and maintenance

The crews that operate and maintain the system rely on accurate information. If they find a discrepancy between what the operating records display and what is in the field, they must be able to correct the error. A field device that can redline such changes is another tool to improve the overall quality of the data. A large backlog of as-built construction information creates confusion over what is actually installed in the field. In the end, when there is confusion, the utility will often have to visit the field location. If confusion still exists, the utility may be forced to excavate an area to clear up the confusion. An accurate and up-to-date GIS eliminates confusion and saves money.

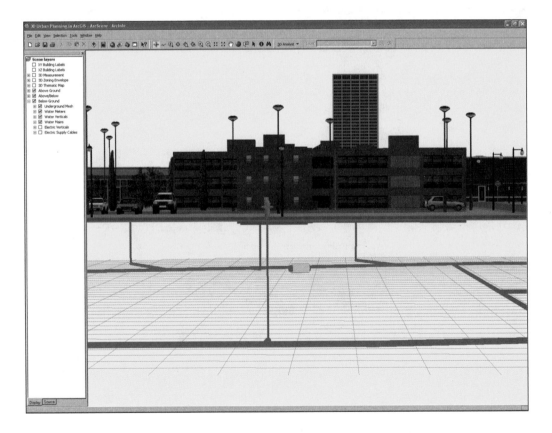

Figure 8.5   A 3D display of gas distribution.

Source: ESRI

Network tracing and customer service

GIS can trace the network to identify customers who are downstream of a main break and determine the best way to supply customers. The GIS can predict where added load may impact the pressure of the area. GIS can model different pressure zones or districts and map the location of regulator stations and pressure control fittings. GIS can simulate the opening and closing of valves. When the utility has to shut down a portion of the gas distribution, whether for a planned repair or replacement, the operator must know how to isolate that section of main to impact the fewest number of customers. Dispatchers can determine where the disconnecting devices are and what customers are involved, and assure that the remaining parts of the network maintain proper pressure. Further, if the utility integrated the customer data with the enterprise GIS, the operator can determine if any customers that provide essential services may be impacted.

Within the GIS, the customer service pipes provide the linkage between gas mains and the customers. In effect, the customers become an integral part of the gas distribution system GIS. An enterprise GIS integrated with the company's customer information system provides a powerful tool for the call center. When a customer calls, the center representatives know everything about the customer's service. They know the pipe size, age, material of the pipe, and exact location of the pipe. They also know if there are gas leaks in the area.

In some instances, gas companies may determine that certain repairs can be done "live"— while the gas is still flowing—by running a pressure analysis. Repairing live can represent a significant cost savings. Again, GIS is a critical component of a total asset management practice.

After a repair or upgrade is completed, the gas company may have to relight customers' gas pilots. By querying which customers were impacted by the gas shutdown and require relighting, the gas distribution operator can use GIS to create an efficient relighting plan that optimizes the route.

Leak surveys and tracking

Gas companies also need to maintain an accurate inventory of leak locations. The leak inventory determines the condition of the gas system. In that sense, knowing the location and severity of leaks gives gas distribution operators the decision-making tools to perform proper and cost-effective maintenance.

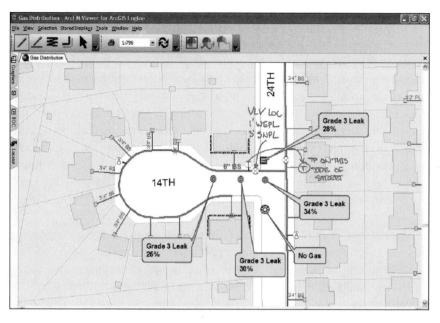

Figure 8.6   Maps locating leaks in a gas distribution system are crucial to a utility's maintenance and safety functions. Redlining is used on a GIS mobile device to indicate gas leaks and becomes part of the enterprise GIS.

Courtesy of Telvent Miner & Miner

Once comprehensive gas leak data is incorporated into the enterprise GIS, operators can
1. map areas of significant concern;
2. co-locate areas of leaks with areas due for replacement, such as replacement of old cast-iron mains;
3. create leak repair reports;
4. immediately update the enterprise GIS upon discovery of new leaks;
5. create a history of leaks should there be litigation or regulatory audit;
6. create leak inspection and survey maps based upon inspection cycles; and
7. create processes whereby gas leak information is communicated to other interested parties (like the electric, public works, and water companies).

New customer demands

Gas distribution companies use GIS to expand their systems to meet the needs of new communities. Knowing the current state and location of available mains in relation to the new communities is critical, and GIS manages this. Companies must be able to provide reliable service to existing customers for their current and projected demands. GIS can be used to design and engineer new gas distribution systems. GIS models the network and routinely interfaces with the most popular network analysis tools. GIS can help gas companies prioritize their main replacement programs in relation to the other activities. GIS shows reported leaks. GIS provides an outstanding framework for distribution integrity management and compliance management. Gas companies model their corrosion protection systems in GIS. They can even include the results of the cathodic protection test results within the GIS. Companies use GIS to capture inspection information from the field. When someone needs to dig underground, companies provide accurate spatial information about the gas lines.

Finally, GIS helps gas companies serve their customers. An enterprise GIS fully integrated into the utilities' financial, asset, and work management systems helps utilities meet customer expectations for new gas products and services.

Figure 8.7   Gas distribution system with network analysis results displayed over accurate imagery.

Courtesy of Advantica

9

Utility customer care: Gaining an edge with GIS

It is uncommon for a city, state, and utility to have technology in place to share information. Without enterprise GIS and good process design, this is how things tend to happen:

A bank needed a new drive-up automatic teller machine (ATM) at the recently opened shopping mall. The bank completed the architectural and engineering work, obtained the rights from the shopping mall owner, and won city approval for the project. The bank planned to open the ATM in six weeks and hired a general contractor who, in turn, hired Jim, a local electrical subcontractor.

Jim contacted AnyTown Energy with the request for the new connection work order on Tuesday of week 1. As noted earlier, AnyTown Energy had a standalone AM/FM mapping system, a standalone work management system, ERP, and a text-based mobile work dispatch system, but lacked an enterprise GIS.

Figure 9.1 Simple construction projects such as a drive-up automatic teller machine installation can become complicated without the integrating features of an enterprise GIS.

Photo by Photolink/PhotoDisc/ Getty Images

Frank, the utility representative, handled Jim's request and entered the data into the work management system. Jim wanted assurances that he would have service in three weeks because he had other projects lined up and could not afford any delay. Frank had no idea how long it would take and suggested Jim check back in a week.

During the week, Frank completed the work order entry form for the ATM, but failed to capture any information on Jim's credit history. In fact, Jim owed AnyTown Energy $340 for a job he did six months earlier. Frank simply reminded Jim to pay the connection fee before the utility would do any work and that the engineering department would determine the fee after it designed the job. But Frank could not estimate how long that would take and Jim was getting worried.

The next day, the customer service planner, Dorrie, found twenty new work orders from Monday alone and the ATM project was number sixteen in her queue. She didn't get to that project until the following Monday when she checked the AM/FM system for the existing electrical system information. But the shopping mall information didn't appear on the system. The work order for the mall was still in the open status, so she knew that no one had posted the as-built electrical drawings and field notes to the AM/FM system. The planner on that job had the mall work order file but was on vacation until the following Wednesday, so Dorrie set the ATM project aside. Jim subsequently learned that his project was "on hold, waiting for more information."

Frustration mounts

On Monday of week 3, Jim talked to another AnyTown Energy employee who said the work order status hadn't changed but he would put a rush on it. The general contractor was pressuring Jim for electrical service so the bank could test the ATM software in a week. On Thursday of week 3, Dorrie obtained the mall work order folder and deciphered the crew's field notes for supply transformer AC-25, the one nearest to the proposed ATM. She then ordered a billing history for the services connected to that transformer so she could calculate the new demand. But the billing department needed at least a week to process Dorrie's request, so she noted in the work management system: "ATM project on hold, waiting for billing data."

By now, the project had fallen far behind schedule. The city wouldn't schedule an inspection until AnyTown Energy connected the service and Jim would have to arrange for the inspection in person between 8:00 and 9:30 a.m. on a Wednesday or Friday since the city accepted no phone appointments.

On the Friday of week 3, Dorrie noted that the ATM work order had a rush on it and that the proposed in-service date had already lapsed. On Tuesday of week 4, billing gave Dorrie information that revealed transformer AC-25 was at its limit and needed an upgrade. She sent an upgrade order for the transformer and a note to accounts receivable to charge Jim $485.83 for the connection fee.

Unbeknownst to Dorrie, when the mall was proposed to the city, the state decided to reroute Highway 44 along the access road to the mall. She also had no idea the ATM was located across a state highway from the transformer that needed to feed it or that the state planned to repave that section. Consequently, Dorrie failed to order a street opening permit from the state.

On Friday of week 4, Jim was shocked to receive an invoice for $485.83. He had quoted a $200 connection fee to the general contractor. Jim decided not to pay it. Now, his project was late, he was losing money, and his next project went to another electrical contractor because Jim was deemed unreliable.

A week later, the state repaved the highway section across from the new, but still not functioning, ATM. On Monday of week 6, an AnyTown Energy crew replaced AC-25 with a new transformer, AC-50. An alert distribution construction supervisor noted that he could not install a service pipe across Highway 44 because he had no street opening permit in the work order file. He called Dorrie, who blamed the mapping department for not updating the plans that would have told her she needed a state street opening permit. On Wednesday of week 9, the state granted the permit and Dorrie noted in the work management system: "Service order design complete—released for construction."

Seven days later, Wednesday of week 10, an AnyTown Energy crew cut a trench into the newly paved highway and the state subsequently directed the utility to repave the entire section. On Friday of week 11, AnyTown Energy powered the ATM. The field crew jotted down notes, indicating in sketch form the change in the service line's location. The work order papers went back to Dorrie for reconciliation. Jim still owed the connection fee and was in arrears for his previous job. AnyTown Energy had to pay a contractor $1,400 to repave the highway.

Long-term consequences

Three months later, a fault in the primary cable feeding AC-50 blacked out a portion of the mall. The bank called AnyTown Energy to complain that the ATM was out of service but the utility had no record of the ATM existing, except for a reference in Dorrie's work-order folder. Since the electrical dispatchers were unclear as to which transformer fed the ATM, they requested a field crew to find out. That delayed restoration by more than two hours, adding about $400 to the cost of the restoration and forcing five stores in the mall to close early.

The following year, one of AnyTown Energy's drafting technicians added the as-built electrical construction details for the mall to the AM/FM system by comparing the design sketches with handwritten field notes. She sent the work-order details to plant accounting, including paper plots that showed where the crew added the new equipment. However, they showed the original transformer, AC-25, not the upgraded transformer, AC-50. Plant accounting manually added the plant data to the ERP system. Two months after that, the technician posted the upgrade work order for transformer AC-50 to the mapping system. Plant accounting got the revised work order, and the new service to the ATM finally appeared in the system several weeks later. More than a year after the project started, the bank finally got a bill for the electricity usage of the new ATM. Plant accounting completed the asset information.

Jim got out of the electrical contracting business, still owing the utility almost $900.

Best-case scenario

The above example was a worst-case scenario and not all the work orders will go this poorly. But ineffective processes often lead to bad results. With integrated processes—the hallmark of an enterprise GIS—the ATM project would unfold something like this:

Jim applied for an electrical permit from the city's inspectional services department. The city issued the permit, noting that the contractor must contact the local electric utility to install the service and connect it to the grid. The city's Web service automatically advised the electric utility of the newly issued permit.

Jim called the utility's 1-800-CONNECT toll-free number. The utility call center representative asked for the permit number, which the permitting system validated, initiating the electric service work order. The automated work order system captured data from the city's Web service about the general contractor, the electrical contractor, and the bank. The utility representative discovered that Jim hadn't paid his last installment of a $340 negotiated settlement from a prior project. Jim paid his outstanding balance by credit card over the phone and the representative released the new work order. Jim supplied some basic electrical demand data and location information and said he needed the service in three weeks. That would give him time to complete all of the electrical work within the general contractor's six-week total construction deadline.

GIS shortcuts

The utility representative pulled up the data on his online GIS and did a quick load analysis. Since the GIS was integrated with the customer billing and customer relationship management module of the company's ERP, the data was current up to the last billing cycle. The GIS design module calculated the total demand on the supply transformer. The analysis showed that the demand for the ATM would exceed the transformer's capacity so the utility would have to install a larger supply transformer. The representative verified that the utility could complete the service in three weeks as requested. Jim paid the $484.50 connection fee again by credit card and he got the work-order confirmation number. The utility published the work-order confirmation number on the Web. The city set the electrical inspection at 9:00 a.m. on the day after the utility completed the service. Jim learned he could do all this work online as long as he had a valid city electrical permit.

The GIS showed the closest service point was across the state highway. The utility representative submitted on the Web a street opening permit request to the state highway department. The state issued the utility a permit electronically. The state's system immediately posted the permit details to its GIS. Trenching detail from the automated design in the utility's GIS was accessible on the state highway's engineering GIS. The state's highway GIS is the primary source of data for the highway department's maintenance system, including all repaving projects. Since the highway department planned to repave that section of the roadway as part of an infrastructure upgrade surrounding the new mall, it allowed the utility to use inexpensive cold patch for pavement repair after the trenching.

The utility's automated work management system ordered all material for the new transformer and service. It generated a one-call digging markup request using data from the GIS. It scheduled a job site delivery the day the electrical connection work was to begin. It created a meter billing cycle. The system assigned the crew based on the human resources module of the ERP accounting for vacations, vehicle maintenance schedules, and scheduled work.

Three weeks later, the crew received the GIS-based construction work order on a mobile device. The crew supervisor noted that the one-call contractor marked the street, showing the location of the underground utilities. The crew trenched the street, installed the transformer, and performed the service. The crew also installed a new handle on the pad-mount cabinet and moved the service three feet south. This information appeared on the GIS mobile device as a redline to the work order design. Later that day, the data from the mobile device populated the GIS and the maintenance management system. All as-built data for this project became part of the GIS during an upload from the mobile device at the end of the shift. The crews installed the meter.

The city completed its inspection. The ATM went into service.

The integrated accounting system added the work's financial value to the utility's asset base. The GIS showed the new service and upgraded transformer. Plant accounting closed the work order. The customer billing system reflected the new load. The state repaved the road on schedule.

The technology in place included an enterprise GIS with mobile devices integrated with the work management, billing, CRM, financial, and supply chain systems (an ERP). It had Web access to the city's inspectional system and the state's engineering GIS. The city and state also had complementary Web services with an automated inspection and permit processing system. The GIS had design capability integrated with electrical system analysis algorithms and standardized design templates.

Table 9.1   Comparing Impacts

Here is a comparison of the costs and customer service impacts of the workflows in the two scenarios:

Metrics	Optimal time frames	Cost	Typical time frames	Cost
Elapsed time	3 weeks		70 weeks	
In-service date	3 weeks		11 weeks	
Time to work order close out and documentation completed	3 weeks		70 weeks	
Call center costs: work-order group	10 minutes	$ 5	40 minutes	$ 20
Engineering	30 minutes (review)	20	12 hours	480
Billing department			2 hours (research)	40
Mapping department	10 minutes	5	2 hours	40
Plant accounting processing			2 hours	40
Billing call center to resolve summary billing issue			20 minutes	10
Lost revenue from ATM			8 weeks ($5 per week)	40
Jim's lost payment			$485.50 plus $340 ($340 from prior bill)	825.50
Extra cost of paving				1400
Total costs		**$ 30**		**$2895.50**
Customer service impact	**Smooth**		**Painful**	

While $2,895.50 (table 9.1) doesn't seem like a lot of money for a large electric utility with millions of dollars in annual revenue, this example illustrates how a process can benefit from good workflow design. The impact can be dramatic when viewed in the context of the annual workload. If the utility processes 10,000 work orders of this type in one year, the annual cost would be nearly $3 million dollars compared to $30,000. A typical electrical utility with a million customers is apt to process from 5,000 to 15,000 service orders per year, depending upon the region's growth. The integrated enterprise GIS plays a key role in this process.

Serving utility customers

Customer care is a major business process within electric and gas companies. As emphasized above, the key to outstanding customer care is integrated information. Since so much of what matters to customers relates to location, integrated spatial information is critical. A utility's information technology budget is largely devoted to customer systems. The customer records represent a major asset of a utility company. Payment and usage history, location, rate category, metering type, and criticality of supply are vital pieces of information. A spatial context for the data, however, is often lacking.

Sometimes utilities maintain equipment links within the customer system showing, for example, a link between the customer and the supplying transformer or even the supplying circuit. Utilities used these links for early outage management systems and transformer load management (TLM) systems. These links tend to be updated on a catch-as-catch-can basis and lack current information. In our above example of how things can go wrong, updating the customer record to the facility record probably would have occurred after the work order was closed, months after the ATM was energized. Utilities keep track of critical customers that provide essential services, such as well stations or cell towers. They also keep track of customers with serious health issues. These critical customer lists are often buried in the customer billing systems. Without the integration with the GIS and a good process in place to keep the data current, utilities might fail to pay attention to critical customers during major outages.

A better way is to locate each customer within the GIS, then build the proper relationships between the customer and the gas or electric equipment. This arrangement more properly models the real-world relationship of customer to distribution equipment. In the above example, the GIS provides the link from the customer, the ATM located at the mall, to the electrical system, transformer AC-50. Lacking that link or having the data about that link as a standalone process or system can inhibit field crews. They would be unable to quickly locate the supply transformer, for instance, because they cannot access information critical to their jobs.

The effective interaction with customers is essential to the utility's success. Certainly keeping the lights on or the gas flowing is key to customer satisfaction. However, there are a number of other processes involved in a utility's customer care.

Upgrading management and service: City of Lexington

The City of Lexington, North Carolina, worked with ESRI business partner Geographic Technologies Group (GTG) to design a GIS plan for its public utilities, starting with the electric department. The GIS included an ArcGIS Engine field editing tool, ArcIMS, for organization-wide dissemination, and ArcGIS for data maintenance.

Field crews collected data about each asset and took a digital photograph of every pole. An ArcIMS software-based data browser solution to view the collected data was a key to the project's success. The electric department needed to view its assets and the region's infrastructure and also needed to link to the city's customer information database. GTG created a seamless integration between ArcIMS and the customer data.

Another critical aspect of this project was ArcGIS software's ability to maintain data. One function of GIS allows field staff to perform disconnected editing of the database. These edits are returned from the field and the data is checked back into the database. City officials found that digitizing information was time consuming but worth the effort. Once they had facility data in the inventory, they could solve all kinds of problems such as instantly knowing which assets needed servicing.

GIS improved customer service, eliminating expensive, labor intensive tasks associated with adding new customers. Before GIS, a new utility connection required city employees to drive to the site to do the research, mark the lines, and develop a plan. GIS enabled them to do much of the work in the office.

GIS also improved asset management, providing accurate data to do circuit and capacity studies on various wire sizes and determine if the wire in place was too small for the loads. GIS provided Lexington Public Utilities with plant accounting values that would be critical if the utility should move into a regulated environment subject to rate approval by the North Carolina Utilities Commission.

Above all, the technology developed by GTG was easy to learn and use with workflows that were simple and intuitive.

From *Energy Currents,* spring 2006

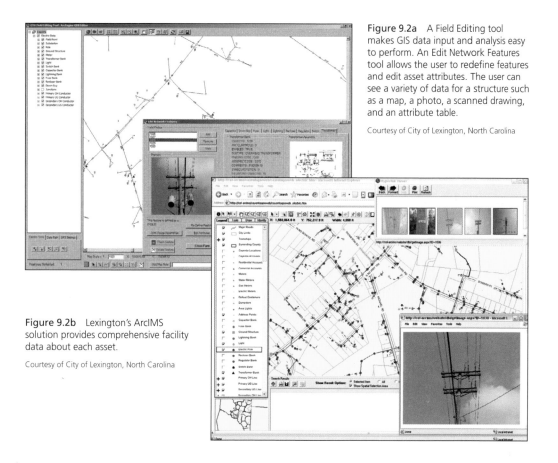

Figure 9.2a A Field Editing tool makes GIS data input and analysis easy to perform. An Edit Network Features tool allows the user to redefine features and edit asset attributes. The user can see a variety of data for a structure such as a map, a photo, a scanned drawing, and an attribute table.

Courtesy of City of Lexington, North Carolina

Figure 9.2b Lexington's ArcIMS solution provides comprehensive facility data about each asset.

Courtesy of City of Lexington, North Carolina

Metering and billing

It may seem like a simple thing: read the meter, send the reading to the billing system, calculate the bill, send it out, and collect the money. However, customers have different rate schedules, move around, and sometimes don't pay on time. Occasionally, the meter is unreadable. All of these factors complicate the billing process. When the utility cannot read the meter or when utilities serve customers in places with no meters, they have to estimate bills, a process that often triggers disputes.

While utilities handle the vast majority of bills without a problem, some billing issues can create an enormous workload for call centers and billing employees. For example, a modest-sized gas utility with half a million customers sends out a bill to every customer once a month. That represents six million bills sent out annually. Assume the utility has problems with only 5 percent of the bills. Assume that the utility spends fifteen minutes on average dealing with the customer's billing issue. That translates into 75,000 worker hours per year devoted to billing issues. That would keep thirty six people busy full time. So anything that a utility can do to reduce the number of billing issues would pay off handsomely.

GIS can help manage the meter reading process. Billing systems tend to be extremely accurate so the bills are usually correct, assuming the meter has been read properly. Billing accuracy problems are almost always due to an estimated meter read or some special meter read. Meter readers who cannot access the meter or get to the meter during the scheduled route will estimate usage. Special meter reads occur when customers move or when utilities replace a meter or have found one to be faulty. Utilities use GIS to manage meter-reading routes, such as dynamically readjusting the routes for changing situations, like new construction in an existing neighborhood. GIS can be used to analyze where billing issues most commonly occur. If access is an issue, GIS can determine where to surgically insert automated systems in certain problem areas. GIS can help determine patterns for meter readers.

Many utilities are moving toward automated meter reading. GIS can play a strong role in the planning and rollout of the systems. GIS can help to dynamically manage routing during the difficult transition from manual to automated systems. Once the automated system is in place, GIS can serve as an ideal monitoring tool.

While reliability of supply is probably the most important customer issue, billing is often not far behind. Utilities that strive for high customer satisfaction work just as hard to improve the billing process as they do to keep the gas flowing or the lights on.

Managing customer orders

Customers' orders often trigger other processes. Examples of orders include a new service, a private property streetlight, a meter test, a lighting rebate, or an energy survey. A utility installs new pipes, lines, and transformers while also managing many other customer-related tasks. Since these activities almost always involve a customer or a customer's agent, making accurate appointments, optimizing travel between appointments, and scheduling tasks can be daunting. GIS helps in visualizing the work, finding patterns to create efficient routes for technicians, sales people, and inspectors.

Call center

The utility call center is the heart of the customer care operation. Here, customer representatives receive billing inquires, gas smell reports, conservation questions, electric trouble calls, turn-on and shut-off requests, streetlight outage notices, and complaints about meter malfunctions, high bills, and even loud line trucks working the area. To the vast majority of customers, the call center is the utility.

Outage management: Kootenai Electric Cooperative

Kootenai Electric Cooperative serves approximately 17,000 members and encompasses more than 1,216 miles of power lines in northern Idaho and eastern Washington. Kootenai's digital story began in 1994 with an effort to improve the accuracy of system maps.

GPS, a new technology at the time, was used to key in features of the system such as poles and transformers. The company's linemen performed 95 percent of the data collection using GPS. With its database growing and GIS emerging on the utility industry scene, Kootenai acquired ArcView and began making truck maps for its field personnel.

At first, there were printouts but then GIS users progressed to laptops in trucks that were loaded with system data, which they downloaded at the office to take into the field. GIS analysts perform database editing and helped collect data in the field. Kootenai also uses an automated meter reader (AMR) system integrated with GIS and other utility systems.

GIS integrated with engineering design software makes it easy to automatically query the database and obtain facility data such as a pole's type, height, size of attached transformers, and cross arm type. This data is extracted into the design software for building the asset. In addition, every meter on the system has a key identification number that ties the meter into Kootenai's AMR and outage management system.

Kootenai uses an outside power line carrier system that allows employees to query a meter over the power line, either from GIS or from an external program. During a power outage, an employee queries the database for meter data and status. Power line data is accessed to determine if the outage is at the meter. If it is, then a dispatcher determines if the neighbor's power also is out by looking at the GIS map. The dispatcher then draws a polygon around a target set of meters and the integrated AMR/GIS shows meters in that section that are on or out. With this information, crews can be sent to the problem site.

The outage system is also tied into a communications service that can manage 1,400 member calls per minute, logging where the power is out and when the call came in. GIS automatically creates an outage map that refreshes every five minutes.

From *Energy Currents,* fall 2005

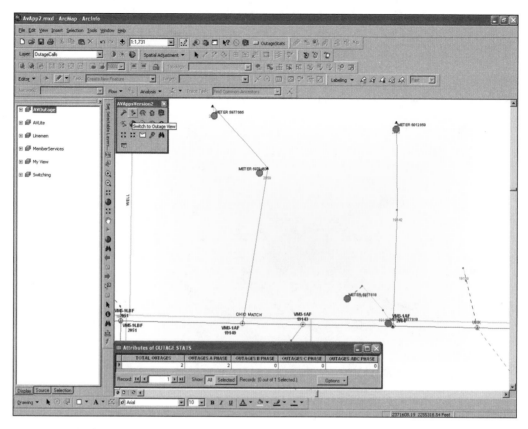

Figure 9.3   ArcView and AMR integration shows outage status.

Courtesy of Kootenai Electric Corporation

Some utilities have installed GIS to help the call center better communicate with customers. They populate the GIS with information to locate trouble and emergency locations and to track crews. Real-time monitoring of where technicians are fixing broken meters and similar information keeps each customer service representative aware of what's going on within the territory. When a customer calls about smelling gas, the call center representative can quickly view the known locations of gas leaks and the locations of gas company field crews working the area, quickly and accurately informing the customer.

Customers certainly want their meters fixed, their streetlights turned on, and their power restored. They also want to know the current status of their issue. This level of communication using GIS goes a long way in really caring for the customer.

Credit and collections

Nearly every utility sets aside a certain portion of its annual operating budget for bad debt, its uncollectible customer bills. Utilities simply write off the debt and sell the receivables to a collection agency, usually for pennies on the dollar. In the United States, utilities have reported between 0.2 to 0.7 percent of their revenues as bad debt. So for a medium-sized utility that generates a billion dollars in annual sales, that amount could be as high as $7 million dollars each year. If the average bad debt is $1,000, the average utility writes off 7,000 customers' debt each year. The reasons people don't pay their utility bill usually fall into one of four categories: they forget to pay, they cannot afford to pay due to unemployment or medical setbacks, they are chronic delinquents, or they deliberately attempt to defraud the utility.

GIS is a wonderful tool for evaluating demographics. By using simple demographics, utilities can decide the most effective way to collect on bad debt. Harassing phone calls to the elderly or the poor are ineffective. However, personal visits by trained collection personnel in affluent neighborhoods may be very effective. GIS can help track chronic delinquents. GIS can help collection agents optimize their time by selecting the right neighborhoods to visit or to call.

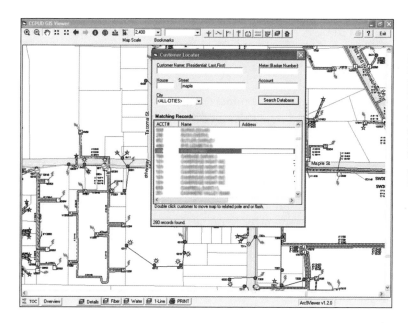

Figure 9.4   The Customer Locator tool provides the user with a form for searching the customer information table. The user can select one piece of information or multiple fields to filter a search.

Courtesy of Chelan Public Utility District

The only real leverage a utility has to force payment is to shut off service. However, a shut-off almost always involves dispatching a technician to the property. At any given time, the utility has thousands of people so far in arrears that the utility is contemplating writing off their debt. The cost associated with shutting them all off is enormous. GIS can help with the logistics to determine which customer to shut off and provide optimal routing for the technicians to follow.

Demographic information combined with customer nonpayment information properly segments the customers. Collection personnel then can establish effective programs to collect from nonpayers before they become bad debts. If utility officials knew, for example, that a cluster of nonpayers included a large elderly population, they could send gentle reminders with perhaps offers to do energy audits that would lower their electric and gas bills. The utility could study areas where delinquents do not occupy buildings they own, looking for patterns of nonpayment or excessive late payments. These people may in fact live in affluent neighborhoods.

While utilities in the United States face a bad-debt problem of less than 1 percent of revenues, utilities in less-developed lands tend to have much more serious nonpayment problems. GIS can help isolate and identify these chronic nonpayer regions and provide the data needed to attack this serious problem.

Bad debt is a growing problem with utilities. As energy costs increase, the number of people not paying their utility bill will increase. GIS can help utilities optimize their limited resources to make the best effort to reduce bad debt write-off and increase revenues.

Revenue protection

Some customers steal energy. Like collections, this problem can be extreme in some parts of the world where widespread theft of energy is common. GIS can help visualize significant mismatches between known usage and actual consumption using the GIS technology's advanced network modeling. Utilities can use GIS to visualize areas plagued by energy theft.

Marketing

Marketers increasingly rely on GIS to create business maps to organize, analyze, and visualize customer behavior. For a gas utility, customer behavior starts with what kind of fuel they use. Marketers also analyze customer demographics to understand future uses. For example, the demographics for a proposed new subdivision may indicate that people with small children are the most likely potential buyers. However, in ten years that subdivision may be populated with large energy consumers, such as families with teenagers. So marketers use GIS to target neighborhoods for particular products and services. While electric companies have a captive market, gas companies compete with other sources of fuel. Thus, gas companies perform market analysis, trending, and target marketing. Electric companies will often target market segments of the community to conserve or participate in conservation-related programs.

Theft reduction: Electricité Du Liban

Ravaged by seventeen years of civil war, Electricité Du Liban (EDL), the state-run energy company utility in Beirut, Lebanon, initiated an ambitious plan to rebuild its utilities. A new geographic information system to model and manage its electric infrastructure was a key element in the reconstruction plan. The GIS application provided for an energy correlation (EC) analysis that targeted illegal power tapping. Electricity theft represented a significant revenue loss for EDL, about 10 percent of the total energy delivered to municipal Beirut.

The EC compared actual consumption based on billing to measured usage on feeders and distribution transformers. The EC analysis between primary feeders and distribution transformers highlighted the distribution transformers that required inspection. The analysis between the distribution transformers and the end customers carefully compared the billed kilowatt-hour (kWh) usage to actual usage to detect the nontechnical losses (theft) on the distribution network.

After locating the network areas with abnormal nontechnical losses, violation removal teams were dispatched to eliminate illegal network connections and take appropriate actions against violators. Continued monitoring of transformers through EC analysis is vital to reduce recurring network violations. The EC program led to a tremendous decrease in nontechnical losses.

From "A Fundamental Utility Restoration and Evolution Using GIS" by Bernard Pertot and Bilal Abou-El-Hassan presented at the 2004 ESRI User Conference, August 9–11, 2004, in San Diego, California

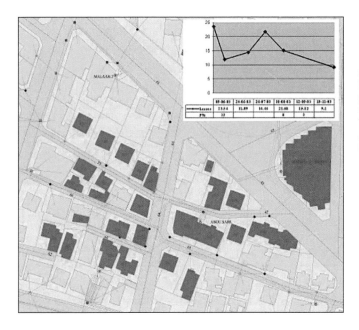

Figure 9.5   The electric utility in Beirut, Lebanon, uses GIS to reduce power thefts and improve customer collections. This map tracks losses for a single distribution transformer.

Courtesy of Electricité Du Liban, Khatib & Alami

Utilities can use GIS to target locations for advertising. If the gas utility wants to encourage new customers to use gas or switch to gas, they could target key billboard locations. They can also target direct-marketing campaigns to areas the utility wants to reach.

Economic development: Nebraska Public Power District

The Nebraska Public Power District (NPPD) uses an innovative ArcIMS application for economic development. The Web-based GIS tool enables users to conduct detailed searches for available economic development sites using both spatial and tabular queries.

Results are provided in both map and text form. GIS Workshop, a leading GIS and spatial integration consultant, developed the groundbreaking Internet project. NPPD completed an application that helps the district serve its constituents, surrounding counties, and others interested in accessing economic development data.

The user-friendly GIS environment helps people perform queries based on their specific needs. Site selectors can search for an exact type of property or building in a given community. They can also perform advanced spatial queries to narrow their search to sites that meet their specific infrastructure needs, providing a unique growth opportunity to agencies in the economic development market.

ArcIMS was customized to integrate various datasets from multiple sources, resulting in up-to-date site selection information. The customized interface provides a user-friendly means of extracting information quickly and easily. The wide range of search criteria includes site and building type and size; city, community, and region; and interstate, railway, and commercial airport drive times.

Once users have a map and a list of sites, they can access even more detailed information about a selected site including pricing, description, construction type, square footage, and photos. A spatial data layer control option allows users to view any combination of parcel, street, and aerial imagery for a specific property. Demographic, consumer spending, and other business data is available with just a few mouse clicks.

As the sponsor of the economic development portal for every city and county in Nebraska, NPPD provides a streamlined user interface for people to upload and download data about their communities. Moreover, the application simplifies how communities add, edit, and delete industrial real estate information.

From *Energy Currents*, summer 2005

Figure 9.6a Nebraska Public Power District Web site visitors can analyze the economic development of a target area such as this demographic report showing income levels, population by race, and age distribution. The site also links to economic trends, market access, education, and other relevant studies for site assessment.

Courtesy of Nebraska Public Power District

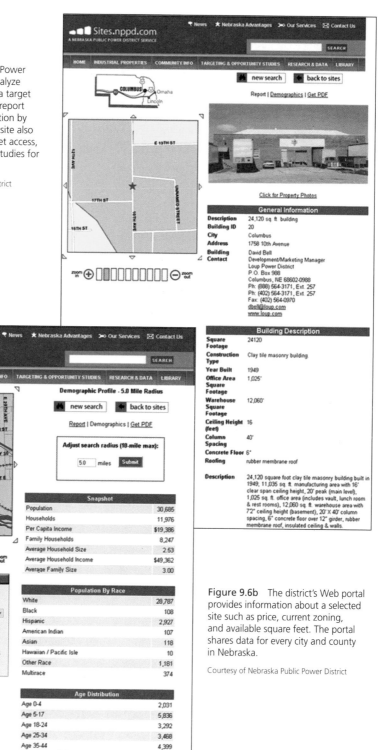

Figure 9.6b The district's Web portal provides information about a selected site such as price, current zoning, and available square feet. The portal shares data for every city and county in Nebraska.

Courtesy of Nebraska Public Power District

Demand side management

Demand side management (DSM) is one way to offset new distribution system expansion. DSM services reduce the demand on the system by improving energy utilization. Utilities are often required to offer services like relamping with energy efficient lighting fixtures, replacing old appliances, or offering rebates for energy efficient climate control systems. A related activity is offering peak shaving or interruptible services. These discount offers allow utilities to shut off a portion of their load during energy shortages. They can use GIS to visualize those areas where supply or distribution capacity may be tight. They then can target those areas for conservation programs.

Customer care

Utilities are using GIS as a common tool to care for their customers. Integration with customer billing and relationship management systems are becoming common. That's because customer location is so key to managing connections, collections, meter reading, meter repair, private property street lighting, trouble location, and many other customer interactions. More and more utilities want to understand customer behavior. They are looking for tools to draw connections between the service they provide and the impact that service has on its customers. In responding to customer needs, utilities need to organize their work in the most efficient way to meet increasing customer demands. They need to make and meet customer appointments. Utilities also need to understand how best to leverage their assets in relationship to their growing customer supply demands.

GIS is not just about making maps. It's about empowering the utility to fully care for its customers in the most cost effective and intelligent way, using GIS integrated with the critical customer care IT systems.

10

Supply chain logistics: Making the most of movement

Supply chain logistics is the effective movement of material and people for the purpose of performing a utility's work. With enterprise GIS, the movement is fluid and cost-effective. Otherwise, the supply chain can be hindered by weak links inherent with an AM/FM system, as this chapter illustrates.

AnyTown Energy's business case justifying its AM/FM system focused on improving worker productivity. One targeted area was cutting the high cost of field investigations for design work. Old operating maps and records were so inadequate that designers in distribution planning had to visit the field for every work order they created. AnyTown Energy's AM/FM advocates reasoned that with good records, designers would not need to verify equipment in the field. With thousands of work orders each year and each field visit averaging at least an hour, AnyTown Energy expected substantial labor savings. What the company failed to grasp, however, was the root cause of poor quality records, manual or otherwise, and that the AM/FM system would not improve the situation.

When AnyTown Energy built the AM/FM system, the project team simply converted the existing records into a new CAD-like format. The format nicely replicated the old maps, but did not capture network connectivity. During data conversion, the contractor discovered inconsistencies, such as old documents showing the same transformer on different poles depending on the map they were converting. Without a complete field audit, there was no way to know for sure which operating map was correct. So, the project team came up with arbitrary rules for the data conversion contractor to use when populating the data in the system. The data conversion contractor never recorded where the inconsistencies had occurred. The information about those inconsistencies in the old records system was lost.

Erroneous assumptions

AnyTown Energy's project team assumed it would take less time to update the data in the new system than to update the old paper maps, and that the mapping technicians would have plenty of time to correct the data. The team believed that the data would improve over time. The AM/FM system was essentially a mapmaking machine and the old system had no built-in quality checks on the input. Before converting the data to the new AM/FM system, AnyTown Energy had accumulated a significant backlog of work orders that had to be posted to the old manual maps. Since the drafting technicians were checking the new AM/FM system against the old manual maps during the data conversion process, they fell further behind posting work orders. The net effect was that when the new system came online, all of the old mapping system problems resurfaced. Plus, the backlog of unposted work orders had increased considerably.

Expecting significant labor savings, AnyTown Energy had reduced the drafting and designer workforces. While it took less time to update the work orders with the AM/FM system than with the old manual methods, AnyTown Energy had fewer people to do the job and the backlog remained.

The following scenario details the breakdown of a system tied to AM/FM processes:

AnyTown Energy's distribution planning designer needed to detail design a work order created by the new distribution automation group. The job required that a crew replace a manually operated line switch with a new remote control switch. Since the new switches were larger than the old ones and had additional control boxes, the designer had to make sure that the switch would be mounted on a pole at least 40 feet high. She did a quick scan of the AM/FM system and found that the old switch was mounted on a 35-foot pole. So, as part of the project, she would specify that the crew install a larger pole.

To design the work order, she zoomed into the area of the old switch on the AM/FM system, created a screen dump of that area, pasted the screen dump into a word processing document, and added the various construction notes. She manually counted the material needed for the job from a hard copy of the work order sketch. She then manually entered the data into the work management system. She printed out the data from the work management system and assembled the work-order package in a file folder.

GIS in the field: Burbank Water and Power

The electric division of Burbank Water and Power (BWP) in Burbank, California, is improving the way geospatial information is deployed to and from field personnel by using cutting edge technology for its mobile GIS applications.

The municipality was already using ArcGIS software and Telvent Miner & Miner's ArcFM for its enterprise GIS. But it was wrestling with the processes of decoding field notes, entering valid information into the geodatabase, and redistributing new paper maps. BWP found a solution. By taking the Microsoft Windows XP Tablet PC edition operating system into the field and combining it with GIS and wireless geodatabase connectivity, BWP has placed the power of an enterprise GIS on a device that fits in the palm of one hand.

Using Tablet PCs equipped with ArcEditor, field workers create redline notes directly on the map with a digital pen. With ArcEditor, digital ink can be stored inside the map document file (.mxd) or within the corporate geodatabase. Examples of GIS functionality include the ability to make notes about a specific geospatial location, highlight features on a map, sketch shapes that indicate GIS editing tasks are required, create thematic redline layers, and mark the site of a damaged asset or dangerous condition.

By using Tadpole Technology gesturing tools, the user quickly and easily navigates and annotates a GIS map without relying on an awkward keyboard. Once uploaded to the company's database, the information can be viewed across the enterprise on both Tablet PCs and desktops. To accommodate shared data, Tadpole Technology's GO! Sync is used to move the electronic annotations directly into the geodatabase. GO! Sync provides secure data reception and transmission across the network, requiring minimal interaction with the mobile users. Burbank's solution takes advantage of 802.11 wireless network features built into the Tablet PC, ensuring that mobile work teams are provided with accurate, up-to-date geospatial information in the field.

Engineers receive a redline map layer from the file, make edits, and enter them into the geodatabase. The engineer erases the red layer and returns the clean digital map to the field worker. This dramatically reduces paper printouts, improves data entry, and decreases data update turnaround time. Engineers no longer have to maintain the personal geodatabase on disconnected field units. Instead, GIS maintains it automatically.

From *GIS for Municipalities and Cooperatives*

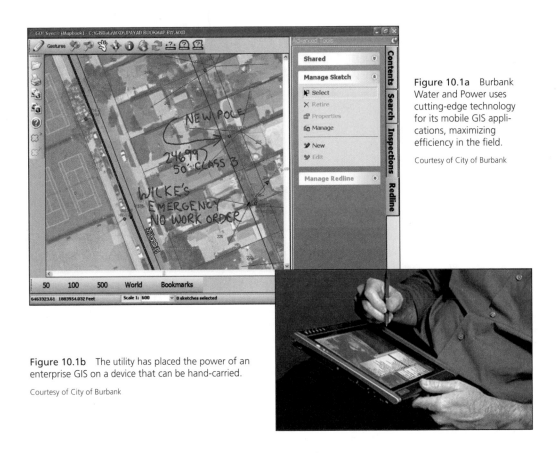

Figure 10.1a Burbank Water and Power uses cutting-edge technology for its mobile GIS applications, maximizing efficiency in the field.

Courtesy of City of Burbank

Figure 10.1b The utility has placed the power of an enterprise GIS on a device that can be hand-carried.

Courtesy of City of Burbank

An office clerk copied the contents of the folder and faxed the work-order package to the field construction supervisor.

Three weeks later, the construction supervisor arrived in the field office early, as usual, to set up her daily crew schedules. She was bogged down by the constant paperwork created by the new work management system. The supervisor managed three overhead line crews in the southeast region. Each crew consisted of a crew chief and one or two line workers. The work management system assigned ten jobs to her region that had to be completed that day, but none was particularly tough. The problem was four jobs from the previous day were unfinished, so the supervisor would have to juggle the schedule to get all the work done. If she didn't catch up, she would have to authorize overtime. She certainly would like to avoid overtime since AnyTown Energy's management was on a rampage to reduce it.

She scheduled five jobs each for crews one and two, and four jobs for crew three. One of crew one's jobs was No. 6385, the work order created by the distribution planning designer.

After briefing the crews on the day's jobs, the construction supervisor returned to the office to process the previous day's work orders. Much of the paperwork involved trying to make sense of the crews' field notes submitted at the end of the day. She hoped to get out to one or two of the job sites sometime later in the morning.

GIS in the field: CoServ Electric

CoServ Electric, a not-for-profit utility serving approximately 110,000 customers in northern Texas, has extended the functionality of its GIS solution to include mobile services for workers in the field. CoServ purchased viewing and editing technology from Telvent Miner & Miner.

Before implementing ArcFM Viewer and the Redliner extension, CoServ Electric printed paper maps, detailing everything from switchgear locations to underground cables, for its operations team to use in the field. ArcFM Viewer enabled CoServ Electric's line workers and service technicians to quickly view, query, or analyze current GIS facility data.

The utility places a lot of physical equipment in open fields and over time, the landscape is altered by development, making it difficult to find them. With GIS in their trucks, workers can access digital maps to find the equipment. The system also makes mapping and switch status information available on mobile units so workers can view the same data as dispatch to make collaborative decisions. This feature is particularly beneficial during storms when workers' safety must be ensured as they respond to emergency calls.

The new application improved communication between dispatch and field crews and facilitated better record keeping for editors. Line workers in the field could quickly view mapping inaccuracies and contact editors to make changes. With the Redliner extension, crews can mark digital maps using a stylus and send notes back to editors for integration into the enterprise.

From *Energy Currents*, fall 2006

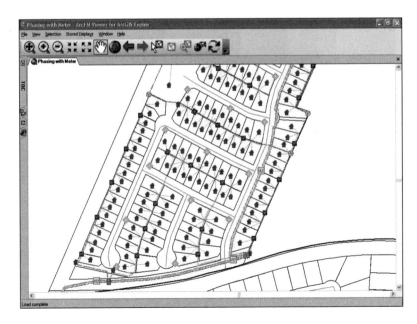

Figure 10.2 Phasing with meter is shown in ArcFM Viewer for ArcGIS Engine.

Courtesy of CoServ Electric

Crew one's chief and line worker drove their line truck to the stockroom for the material they need for the day's five jobs. They waited in line to get their material, which included the new automated line switch for work order No. 6385. Later, they headed for the pole yard, located a mile or so from the service center, to pick up the new 40-foot pole. After stopping for coffee, they arrived at the first job at 10:00 a.m. and completed a simple overhead service installation in 40 minutes. The second job, work order No. 6385, was 15 miles north. The crew chief noted that the project required a digger crew to dig the hole for a new pole. He figured that by the time they got to the job, it would be close to 11:30 a.m. and they would barely get started before it was lunchtime. He decided to start the job in the afternoon and arranged to meet the digger crew at the work site at 1:30 p.m., but failed to notify his supervisor.

At 11:15 a.m., the supervisor completed her paperwork and decided to check on the switch replacement project in person. The crew chief, meanwhile, noticed that the third job was nine miles to the south, estimated he could get there by 11:15 a.m. and complete the job by noon. On the way to that job, he saw crew two replacing a lightning arrester and stopped to chat with the crew chief. They got to the site at 11:30 a.m. and decided to have lunch before tackling the job.

The supervisor arrived at the site of work order No. 6385 at 11:40 a.m. but found no crew. She radioed the crew's truck but since the chief and line worker were eating lunch in a sandwich shop, no one answered. The supervisor decided to track down another crew after making a mental note to give the crew one chief a warning later in the day.

Crew one had lunch, completed the simple repair of a bent switch handle, and returned to the site of the automated line switch job at 1:15 p.m. While waiting for the digger crew, the chief and line worker secured the bucket truck, unloaded the material, and began to lay out the job. The line worker began to remove the supports holding the new pole to the pole trailer, when the chief noticed that there was a new nonautomated switch mounted on a brand new 40-foot pole. The digger crew arrived and was sent away.

Crew one packed up the gear and left the job site at 2:30 p.m. While driving back to the pole yard, the crew chief noted on the work orders what he saw in the field and radioed the supervisor with the bad news. She had bad news of her own for the crew chief.

Crew one left the pole yard at 3:15 p.m. and completed the fourth job on the work schedule without incident, arriving back at the service center at 4 p.m. The crew completed three of the five jobs scheduled for the day. The supervisor authorized overtime for the three crews to complete all the projects on the day's schedule.

A series of breakdowns

So what's the cost to AnyTown Energy? Wasted time, wasted effort, and wasted money. This simple process had a number of breakdowns. First, the designer in distribution planning did not have enough information to properly do her job. Someone in the company had to know that a pole scheduled to be replaced had already been replaced. Someone should have known about an active project to replace the manual switch with an automated one. No one checked the accuracy of data that the company converted from the paper maps nor had anyone graded the individual elements of data for accuracy. Since AnyTown Energy stopped

Figure 10.3 GIS is an invaluable tool for managing field crews efficiently and minimizing wasted effort.

Photo by PhotoDisc/Getty Images

field checking every work order, the designer could not have known that the data from the AM/FM was incorrect. There was no direct connection between information from the field and the AM/FM system, nor was there any relationship between the designs and the system until long after the work was done. It's no wonder there was wasted effort in the field.

The material management group did not prestage the material so crews had to wait in line at the warehouse. Without accurate designs, prestaging the material at the job site would be a waste of time. The crew chief went to another job site unaware of how to optimize work processes. He actually increased total travel time for the day when he thought he was being efficient.

The supervisor had no idea where the crews were located at any given time, so she traveled to a job site only to find no one working there. She also had no concept of how to schedule jobs to minimize travel time for her crews. In fact, in one case the crew one chief passed another crew on his way to a job.

In the end, all the jobs were completed but at a significant increase in cost. Crew one drove to a job site but did no work and drove back to the pole yard to return the pole. The digger crew drove to the job site and left without accomplishing anything. The supervisor wasted time driving to the job site. Calculating wasted fuel, labor costs driving around, and the overtime required to complete the projects probably doubled the cost of each job.

In this scenario, the workers were supposed to move the new automated line switch from inventory to operation. They were supposed to move a 40-foot pole from inventory to the street. Instead, someone moved another switch from inventory to the field. Then crew one moved the automated switch, all the associated parts, and the pole back to inventory. These missteps adversely impacted the supply chain process.

- Inventory levels were higher than they should have been.
- People needed to maintain additional warehouse space.
- Supply chain workers had to perform additional handling.
- The purchasing department had to account for parts that were supposed to be installed in the field.

Enterprise solution: Orlando Utilities Commission

The Orlando Utilities Commission (OUC) is the second largest municipal utility in Florida, serving the electric and water needs of a rapidly growing resort area that attracts more than 35 million visitors each year.

OUC relies on good equipment, preventative maintenance, and dedicated employees to serve more than 190,000 customers in the cities of Orlando and St. Cloud and adjoining portions of Orange and Osceola counties in central Florida.

Facilities and outage management play key roles in the utility's daily operations. OUC set out to create a business case for a GIS solution to maintain and distribute important geospatial data to water and electric field crews and engineers.

OUC needed to streamline its business and data management processes to support utility operations and reduce duplicate operating costs. The enterprise GIS would need to accurately represent the water and electric distribution systems and provide a geodatabase that could be efficiently updated and managed. OUC officials further needed a GIS that would be a useful and reliable tool for operations, engineering, and other internal groups as well as for customers.

OUC turned to ESRI technology to help the company:

- develop a seamless graphic/database source to produce better, more up-to-date maps
- establish a centralized geodatabase to eliminate duplicate datasets
- shorten the time to search for information
- reduce the work involved in preparing for operational analysis
- provide better maintenance and facilities management
- provide wider accessibility to maps/reports
- centralize facilities database management
- create more effective communication
- improve access to city/county planning data
- improve data sharing capabilities
- increase response to changing business needs
- create cost savings through a centralized business and data management system

OUC partnered with ESRI Professional Services to implement this foundation GIS solution. Two ESRI business partners, Telvent Miner & Miner for technical consulting and M. J. Harden (now part of General Electric) for data migration services, joined the team as subcontractors. Implementing the foundation GIS and data conversion at OUC was completed in two years. ESRI's long-term partnership agreement to support OUC and help with future phases was extended for three years. Besides simplifying data maintenance, the geodatabase improved communication and geospatial information sharing within OUC and between OUC and several local and state agencies.

From *ArcNews*, summer 2003

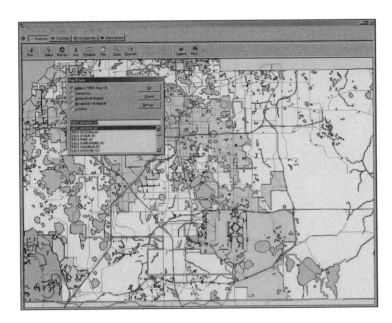

Figure 10.4 The Orlando Utilities Commission uses GeoLocation tools for navigating its service territory.

Courtesy of Orlando Utilities Commission

The GIS solution

How could a fully integrated enterprise GIS have helped? AnyTown Energy would have to make a commitment to clean up its backlog of field data. The utility perhaps would rank the quality level of its data in the GIS. Then the designer would know whether data she relied on could be trusted without a field visit. While utility technicians are in the process of cleaning up the data, she could use a mobile design system based on the GIS data itself. So when she suspected the data was incorrect, she could perform the design in the field but have the proposed design be part of the GIS.

AnyTown would have to change procedures to dynamically update the GIS from other processes. For example, someone ordered the old 35-foot pole replaced after an automobile struck and broke it. But the ordering and recording of the new pole never made it into the GIS. Since the designer had to requisition the new pole out of inventory, a link or trigger from the materials system could easily have alerted the GIS. Someone likely created a maintenance work order, and had it been referenced into the GIS, the designer would have known not to specify the new pole. Had she placed her work order directly into a GIS connected to the enterprise, the person writing the maintenance work order would have seen that a new automated switch was being planned for that pole location. That person could have altered the maintenance plan to replace the old switch with the new automated one. Had AnyTown Energy installed vehicle tracking into the trucks, integrated with the GIS, the supervisor could have located her crews instead of driving to a job site where no one was working.

GIS in the field: Northeastern Rural Electric Membership Corporation

Northeastern Rural Electric Membership Corporation (NREMC), a major electric utility cooperative in northeastern Indiana, implemented an advanced field GIS. ESRI business partner Tadpole Technology provided its mobile GIS solutions, GO! Sync (Mapbook) and GO! Sync (Redline), which use ArcGIS Engine technology.

NREMC had used viewing and syncing software but most of it was a patchwork of applications that required much human interaction to work. The mobile GIS solution leveraged existing GIS investments for greater efficiency and productivity. GO! Sync (Mapbook) and GO! Sync (Redline) seamlessly integrated with NREMC's ArcGIS platform. It made spatial data and functionality available to field crews and other utility staff working remotely. They could view, search, trace, route, link with GPS, and more.

Staff members could view asset network data; create or change digital as-built design; capture remote data such as downed, repaired, or new infrastructure; and provide descriptive report data. The newly captured and updated data could then be uploaded to the enterprise GIS.

The solution provided the ability to distribute data changes quickly across the organization. After initial setup, GO! Sync could distribute map changes with little or no human interaction. The application is customizable, allowing NREMC to tailor symbology and searches as needed. In addition, the electric network tracing tools, combined with the redlining functionality, allowed field crews to make better, more informed decisions for the complex facility plant.

The GPS interface and routing provided NREMC with more accurate direction-finding capabilities. Customer service representatives, linemen, dispatchers, staking engineers, tree crews, locators, and marketing and accounting personnel all benefited from the GIS solution.

From *Energy Currents*, fall 2006

The GIS would provide a communications framework involving multiple departments. Without that framework, the logistics of a simple switch replacement became overly complicated with AnyTown Energy's personnel working in a vacuum instead of collaborating. GIS could have helped properly schedule all the crews in the southeast region, minimizing travel time.

Despite all of AnyTown Energy's automated systems—the digital AM/FM system, the automated work management system, and the automated materials system—the utility's personnel ended up doing a lot of manual work that could have been done automatically with the help of GIS.

Logistics and GIS

A significant portion of a utility's annual expenses is devoted to the process of moving material and people from one place to another; dealing with vehicles, warehouses, garages, service centers, property, office buildings, and security. Supply chain logistics processes keep the core businesses going.

Materials management

Gas and electric utilities need to maintain large inventories of materials. Since crews need ready access to material, such as valves, pipes, brackets, poles, connections, and flanges, material managers need the material and equipment close by. Automated supply chain and material management systems keep track of where material is delivered, including major warehouses and local service centers. Material management systems can work effectively with GIS to identify locations where nonwarehoused material may be located. This becomes critical when crews need a piece of equipment during an emergency. A spatially enabled materials management system allows utilities to quickly locate materials and promptly dispatch them to the crews.

Material managers can use the GIS to identify where odd pieces of equipment are installed. It doesn't make good sense to stock spare parts for rarely needed items. It is wiser to replace the odd equipment with more standard equipment and lower the carrying costs of the spare parts. Just like many families have a junk drawer full of chargers for cell phones they don't own anymore, utilities keep spare parts for outdated equipment. If they must keep spare parts, they should be located as close to the equipment as possible.

Material managers refer to the three S's of lean supply chain logistics: simplify, standardize, and substitute. In choosing material, the simple one often has the lowest life-cycle cost. For a utility, it's probably best to standardize a few common sizes than to finely engineer every situation to a unique application of a material. For example, a utility may normally carry 15kVA (kilovolt-amperes), 25kVA, 50kVA, 75kVA, and 100kVA single-phase transformers. It may find that standardizing with two or three sizes saves money in the long run. The utility does this even though it may install a transformer that is larger than required. It's best to replace a nonstandard item with a standard substitute. GIS can help material managers assess and perhaps tag the GIS equipment that has become nonstandard. A designer working on an upgrade project would quickly notice a piece of equipment within her work-order area that is nonstandard. She then could make the substitution as part of the work order.

The process of simplifying, standardizing, and substituting provides purchasing managers greater leverage to negotiate better prices for material. The cost of a thousand 25kVA transformers is probably lower than the cost of five hundred 25kVA transformers and five hundred 15kVA transformers.

Inventory

Inventory costs for a utility can run high. The effectiveness of a materials process can be measured by inventory turns, which is counting how many times a piece of material leaves inventory. A high number of turns means the company is using the material effectively. A low number means that a piece of material languishes in inventory for a long time. GIS can help uncover material in inventory that the utility no longer needs. This keeps the inventory moving and increases the inventory turns. For example, suppose there are twenty 15kVA transformers located throughout the various service centers and warehouses. Suppose further that the utility no longer specifies 15kVA transformers for new work so it's no longer a supported standard. GIS could identify where 15kVA transformers may be needed for spares and correlate the locations with the transformers in stock. The utility could then unload the surplus, thus reducing the inventory levels. Lowering inventory reduces carrying costs, storage space requirements, and the labor to manage the storage space.

Warehousing

While some utilities are moving toward procuring material just when they need it (so-called just-in-time procurement) rather than stocking the warehouse, utilities still need to manage hundreds of thousands of parts to run the complex infrastructure. Utilities hold this material in warehouses or service centers. Determining the location, size, capacity, staffing, and maintenance of warehouses can be complex. Utilities can use GIS to assess their warehouse utilization, whether centralized or distributed. Warehouse managers can use GIS to map deliveries from the warehouses to the service centers or crew locations. This routing exercise may show that the utility spends excessive time moving material from one place to another. Material dispatchers can use the GIS to model alternative scenarios: What would the material flow look like with an additional warehouse in a newly growing area? What would happen if the utility closed down its central warehouse? The cost of running a warehouse can be significant and doesn't always get the attention of senior management.

Fleet management

Vehicles used by utilities require constant maintenance. Garage personnel need to carefully maintain electric bucket trucks to assure proper insulation qualities. They need to certify booms and test buckets. Vehicles must be reliable to respond quickly to gas leaks. Like warehousing and inventory, the fleet management process is rarely noticed by senior management until budget time. It's at that time that senior management asks the question, "Do we have too many vehicles?" or "Why do we have so many vehicles?"

Most utilities use some form of fleet management software. This software focuses on improving maintenance cycles for the vehicles. The idea is to take vehicles out of service in the least disruptive ways to perform the maintenance based on the vehicles' overall use, not just mileage. The systems often integrate with the vehicles' computers.

Automated vehicle location (AVL) is another common fleet management system. AVL systems include some form of GPS tracking installed in the utility's vehicle plus software located in the fleet dispatcher's control room. Fleet dispatchers can then track the current location of each vehicle and they can also retrieve the history of each vehicle's movement. The system can track stopping times and measure the speed history of a vehicle. These systems, like fleet management systems, are often standalone.

Utilities that integrate fleet management and AVL systems with GIS greatly enhance the value of both systems. AVL measures where the vehicles are or have been. Fleet management software measures the behavior of the vehicles and the people who operate them. Utilities that integrate AVL with their GIS can show everyone in the enterprise the location of vehicles in relation to the utility's assets and jobs. Not only is a utility truck located on Elm Street, it is located three blocks from a blown fuse or a reported gas leak. If the designer knew in advance that the digger derrick truck was scheduled for an overhaul at the same time that she has scheduled a pole replacement, the utility would have time to bring in a replacement truck instead of finding out later that the digger was unavailable.

A utility fleet is expensive. Utilities use GIS throughout the enterprise, not just for operations. Customer care, energy supply, maintenance, buildings care, station operations, IT, legal, and environmental organizations all use vehicles for their work. GIS can save utilities lots of money, especially in conjunction with work management, fleet management, and AVL systems. GIS can effectively answer the senior manager's question about why they have so many vehicles. Utilities that use GIS to manage their fleet can be sure that they have driven excess travel, and thus unnecessary cost, out of the business.

Material testing

Utilities need to test equipment and material regularly. This testing may involve an intricate process of material removal from the field, delivery to a testing facility, disposal of hazardous waste and faulty material, and sometimes repair or rebuilding of material.

GIS can help with optimizing the many steps of the supply chain logistics process. GIS can help material testing professionals locate the right material to test, based on use patterns and exposure to weather. Examples include electric relays, valves, remote terminal units, oil filled transformers, and switches. As governments issue new environmental regulations, utilities need to know where objectionable material is located. When handlers find hazardous material, they must make sure they transport it in the safest and most environmentally sound way. Material handlers can take advantage of the intelligent routing capabilities of GIS and its ability to do spatial analysis of the surrounding environment.

Facilities management

Utilities operate a vast array of facilities from office buildings to city gate buildings to substations to power plants. In addition to the electric and gas equipment that needs to be maintained and inspected (by the transmission or distribution crews), there are a number of facility tasks that need to be addressed. Examples include cleaning services, snow plowing, painting, roof repairs, landscaping, cafeteria services, furniture moving, personnel relocation, office supplies distribution, and printing services.

GIS can be an effective tool for facility managers to locate where equipment is stored, such as lawn mowers, plows, rakes, hedge trimmers, and portable sump pumps. Facility managers can use GIS as a gateway into their facility maintenance plans. They can use GIS to analyze weather patterns on their buildings, predicting when best to reinforce roofs to dispatch crews during snowstorms. They can use GIS to identify high crime areas or areas of significant vandalism.

Facility managers can use GIS to keep track of where people are located. As employees and their equipment move around, GIS helps to optimize space utilization. Service centers and shops, like warehouses, are expensive to operate. GIS can help facility managers determine the best location for facility maintenance staff, answering questions like, "Do we really need four service centers? Will three do? If so, where should they be located?"

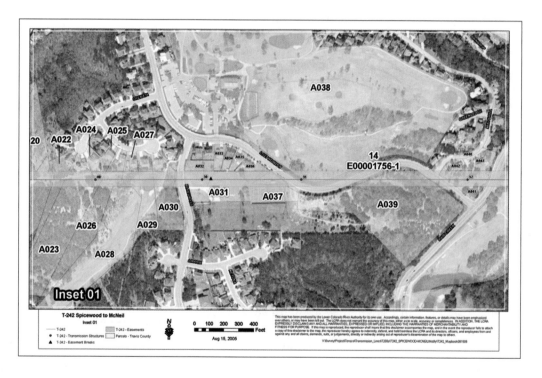

Figure 10.5   Online map book supports transmission line easement maintenance for the Lower Colorado River Authority.

Courtesy of Lower Colorado River Authority

Easement management: Lower Colorado River Authority

The Lower Colorado River Authority (LCRA) Transmission Services Corporation implemented various GIS applications to support its easement management processes. LCRA is a quasi-state agency founded in the late 1930s with central Texas as its predominate service area. LCRA maintains more than 3,200 miles of line and uses GIS to manage data and support processes for more than 8,000 transmission line easements.

The GIS applications increased LCRA's landowner notifications from six to more than eighty lines per year. Researching and notifying property owners along transmission lines have historically been the purview of the company's real estate group while the maintenance group dealt with landowners.

Often the real estate and maintenance groups filed landowner information in their individual departments, resulting in redundancy and incomplete processes, negatively affecting public relations.

Using ArcGIS software, LCRA reduced confusion by smoothing interdepartmental workflows, performing research, accessing and delivering data, creating reports, and integrating with other systems.

GIS helped LCRA collaborate its landowner notification program. The company's GIS group compiled all the GIS data into an ArcIMS site and developed map books that allowed groups housed in different buildings to access a common map or dataset while communicating with each other.

Understanding data needs and distinctions helped the GIS group construct a simple data model useful for connecting GIS data with other documentation. During the initial planning phase, data was categorized by one group that performed easement reviews and another group that provided customer service. Based on these two groups' functions, databases were created to serve as the foundation for building the application.

People with legal, engineering, and real estate backgrounds in the easement review group agreed on a common vocabulary and compiled a list of constraints. An engineering constraint, for example, is the width of the easement and a maintenance constraint is ingress and egress to and from the easement with specific authorizations.

Service personnel must sometimes traverse private properties and Texans tend to know their landowner rights. To maintain good relations and reduce legal confrontation, LCRA's administrative board mandates that landowners be notified of activities on the transmission line. A notification detail report is a useful checking device that guarantees all processes are completed before maintenance and building activities start.

Decades old easement documentation in the form of hand-drawn maps and other hard-copy data was converted into a digital format so it could be served through ArcIMS and ArcSDE to create map books. Data layers enable system users to create reports such as the special conditions reports used by the maintenance group to determine if the field worker is allowed to service the site or needs to call before accessing the site.

From *Energy Currents*, spring 2006

Rights and permits

Utilities are constantly requesting rights and permits to work on public and private properties. AnyTown Energy discovered that forgetting to get a street opening permit from the state resulted in a long project delay. Many communities require substantial documentation before they will grant a right, permit, or easement. This documentation often involves a plan of the existing environment that indicates the site of the easement, right of location, or permit. A common example of this documentation is a plan that shows the location of a new pole. A utility cannot simply install a pole wherever it wants. It normally has to get an official permit from the municipality. If a utility does its proposed designs within the GIS, then producing the plan for the pole permit would be a simple presentation of the information already contained in the enterprise GIS.

Often the department or group that seeks rights and permits is different from the department or group that performs the designs. GIS can help align these groups since they are using the same information but for different purposes. Utilities often maintain a record of various rights, permits, and easements in a database. Normally, each easement has a legal description. The legal descriptions that are contained within a document management system combined with the easements documented in the GIS provide a powerful tool for anyone in the utility that needs that information for a piece of property the utility is interested in.

GIS finds the way

Logistics involves much more than finding the shortest path from one place to another. It is a critical business process within utilities. That is evident by how much money utilities spend to move people and material around. The cost of maintaining a large fleet, a number of warehouses, service centers, and buildings is substantial. GIS helps utilities assess their current logistic processes as well as helps logistics managers find better ways to move people and equipment quickly and effectively to support their operations. GIS can implement the three rules of supply chain logistics—simplify, standardize, and substitute—to significantly cut costs and improve operational efficiency. Many industries have saved lots of money by improving the supply chain, and since utility supply chain processes are spatial, GIS can be a key tool in supply chain logistics processes.

11

Shared services: Saving money, avoiding legal snags

In her campaign speech for mayor of Roseville, Marsha Thomas pledged to ferret out waste by restructuring the administration. It won her the election. She looked at every way to increase revenue while reducing costs. In her prior career as legal counsel for Roseville, she knew that by improving record keeping and organizing finances, she could save the city a lot of money.

When Mayor Thomas reviewed the city's many tax revenue sources, AnyTown Energy stuck out. She dug a little deeper and noticed three substantial city expenses: charges for streetlights, connection fees for the fire alarm system on AnyTown Energy's poles, and a large fee for access to AnyTown Energy's conduits for the city's private fiber-optic network.

Mayor Thomas wondered if AnyTown Energy was as bad at record keeping as the city. If so, the city probably was being overcharged for the connection fees and streetlights. She further assumed that the city was under-collecting property taxes from AnyTown Energy. So, she issued a challenge to the utility to document the number of poles, pad-mounted equipment, switches, streetlights, and fire alarm connections and the length of wire. She questioned AnyTown Energy's distance calculation for city-owned fiber-optic cables occupying the utility's underground conduits.

Joe, AnyTown Energy's plant accounting department manager, fielded the request. He promptly replied to the city with the number and age of the properties that the taxes were based on, the number of connections and streetlights, and the mileage of underground conduit. However, Joe knew the city didn't just want a reiteration of what AnyTown Energy charged. The city wanted verification and that was going to be a problem.

Mayor Thomas was furious and sent Joe a fiery letter demanding that AnyTown Energy prove the numbers were correct. She asked for street-by-street counts. In the meantime, she directed the public works department to count the poles, pad-mounted equipment, streetlights, and fire alarm connections in a new part of Roseville. She reasoned that if the utility kept bad records, it would likely be behind in the newer parts of the city due to the rash of construction.

Figure 11.1 The City of Painesville, Ohio uses GIS to inventory poles.

Courtesy of City of Painesville

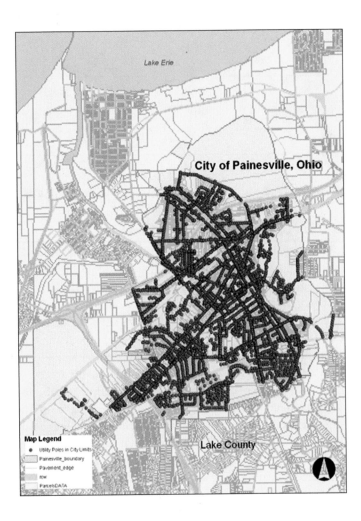

Regulatory compliance: City of Painesville

Municipally owned electric systems must comply with government reporting guidelines, including one that requires detailed financial statements about the full cost of providing services. Utilities must meet the reporting and depreciation requirements of the Government Accounting Standards Board's (GASB) Guideline 34 by producing acceptable methodologies and practices for infrastructure maintenance and an infrastructure inventory for the past twenty years.

The City of Painesville, Ohio, operates utility services including water, electric, storm water, and sewer, and its government regulation compliance system relies on GIS. Painesville's GIS also supports asset management for electric operators, system maintenance, and capital improvement planning.

The city contracted with Metcalf & Eddy (M&E) to implement a utility management system built on ArcGIS. The success of the initial GIS project for sewer services led to applications for electric and water services. M&E set up the GIS database structure using ArcSDE. A utilities data collection service, TransMap Corporation, performed citywide infrastructure data inventory including manholes, utility poles, roadway systems, traffic signals and signage, and fire hydrants.

An inventory of poles inside and outside the city limits was collected on handheld computers loaded with ArcPad and GPS. The pole inventory list included pole tag information, pole type, attachment types, number of primary and secondary wires, and line voltage.

To meet the GASB cost-out requirement, Painesville used a publicly available materials cost index history. The cost is input to the GIS model along with other tables containing infrastructure information. Tables are related to each other using common identification features. GIS connects the tables to a basemap to produce infrastructure map data layers.

The city gains many benefits as byproducts of regulatory compliance. GIS enables the city to manage and audit joint pole use, increasing revenues. The infrastructure inventory can be used to create an accurate GIS circuit map. GIS is also proving useful for Painesville's capital improvement planning, such as estimating a projected road replacement cost.

From *GIS for Municipalities and Cooperatives*

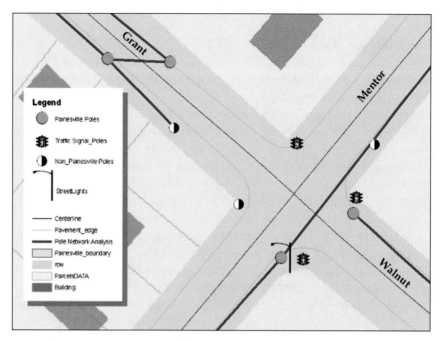

Figure 11.2a   Painesville's pole inventory map.

Courtesy of City of Painesville

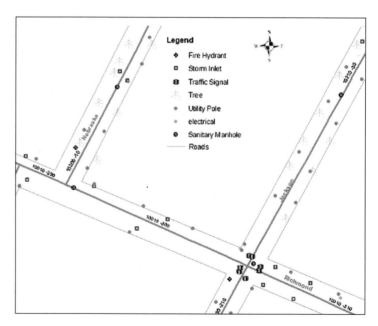

Figure 11.2b   A citywide infrastructure map shows many city service departments with detailed asset information.

Courtesy of City of Painesville

Joe forwarded the mayor's request to AnyTown Energy's mapping department. The AM/FM system could not count the electrical equipment by street. So, the mapping people had to manually count everything, which took three days. Unfortunately for Joe, the numbers the mapping department came up with didn't match the numbers in the accounting system. The poles and pad mounted equipment shown on the maps exceeded the number in the accounting system. The number of streetlights and connections and the mileage on the maps were different from the accounting system.

Joe notified the city that AnyTown Energy had some record-keeping discrepancies but was confident the numbers were now correct.

Mayor Thomas' suspicion was confirmed: AnyTown Energy's records were as bad as the city's. She checked the purportedly correct listing for equipment from AnyTown Energy against what her public works employees counted, and she saw discrepancies. The equipment that formed the property tax base was undercounted so she anticipated a tax-revenue windfall. Plus, the utility had over-counted streetlights and connections, which would mean lower costs to the city. She fired back her response to AnyTown Energy. Based on her field audit, she demanded increased tax revenues and an immediate reduction in the city's connection fees. She threatened to sue the utility if it did not agree to her demands.

With three different sets of numbers from the accounting system, the mapping system, and a field audit, AnyTown Energy was in no position to argue. The utility promptly agreed to the city's demands.

GIS would have helped

AnyTown Energy didn't have an enterprise GIS integrated with the accounting system. It had no process to assure that as equipment was added and removed, those changes would be documented within the plant accounting system. Neither the accounting system nor the mapping system reflected any of the information contained in the large pile of backlogged as-built work orders. The long process of getting corrected data from the field contributed to AnyTown Energy's inability to come up with consistent accounting of its property.

AnyTown Energy had an automated work management system, an automated plant accounting system, and an automated mapping system. Yet, the utility spent considerable manual effort to maintain these systems.

Keeping the balance sheet healthy

Whether private or public, utilities account for the financial value of their assets on their balance sheets. They must calculate the depreciation of their assets. To do this, the utilities must record the value of various assets when they are installed. Utilities install, replace, and repair wires, pipes, valves, and transformers every day, and keeping these records straight is a daunting accounting task. So it's easy for utilities to lose track of their assets' value.

In 2002, the U.S. Congress passed the Sarbanes-Oxley (SOX) Act to protect investors from accounting abuses that occurred during the Enron and WorldCom collapses. The SOX regulations set higher standards of accounting for all publicly traded companies. SOX also created additional oversight of accounting practices. In the United States at least, investor-owned utilities need accurate financial reporting. In the above example of fictional Roseville clashing with AnyTown Energy, the value of the utility's assets reported in the financial system did not accurately reflect its real asset base. An audit would show the discrepancy. So, AnyTown Energy's balance sheet was in error, which could cause significant legal liability. It could also diminish public confidence in the company and negatively impact the company's stock price. Finally, a poor audit generally forces the company to spend money it hadn't planned on spending.

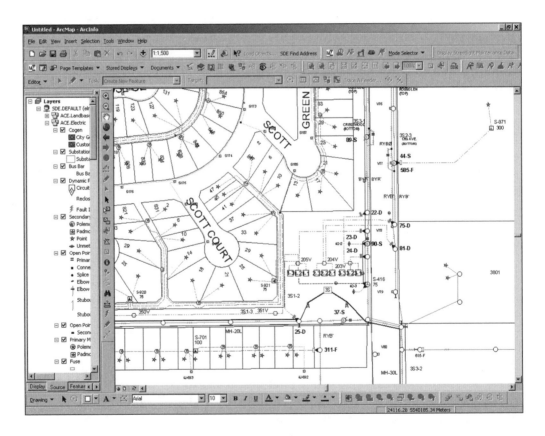

Figure 11.3 Typical underground primary lines originating at circuit breakers in a substation and converting to overhead distribution lines.

Source: City of Medicine Hat

GIS across the board: City of Medicine Hat

Medicine Hat, a city in Alberta, Canada, generates, transmits, and distributes electricity to 26,500 customers within its 195-square-kilometer (75-square-mile) service area. ESRI Canada provided an enterprise GIS solution for the city. The city's Internet site iMap uses ArcIMS to provide the public with tools for viewing and interacting with data about the city. An intranet version makes data available to more than six hundred employees.

The city's utility departments use the Telvent Miner & Miner ArcFM suite of software for facility and network management. The enterprise GIS database contains all of the utility's asset information such as transformers, lights, poles, and distribution lines. ArcFM enables users to quickly define and recall map sheet collections for map production.

Map production tools in ArcFM allow users to select the page templates, stored displays, documents, and map sets that precisely define layers, scale, and map elements necessary for the general management of the utility. GIS has improved operations by automatically updating maps that used to be manually changed. It also assists with billing for joint use of poles by cable, phone, and other companies. An attribute is defined for each company that has items on poles. Billing personnel can run a query that returns all the items for a particular company using poles. By tracking all of a company's items in the geodatabase, the accuracy of billings is improved with additional revenue generated.

The city provides e-services on its iMap Web site that allow the public to report on different municipal areas and utilize map-based functionality. A local resident, for example, can use the Web site to report a malfunctioning streetlight. The utility department then creates a work order and a technician is assigned to investigate and repair the light.

Medicine Hat's electric utility maintains more than 9,000 streetlights and provides street lighting to outside organizations, such as Alberta Transportation. GIS helps with the billing to those organizations.

Citizens can call the Alberta One Call system to coordinate with the utility to locate any underground facilities prior to excavation work. Staff can estimate the work involved by looking at the infrastructure on a map. Field crews then can stake the locale and use laptops loaded with facilities data in a personal geodatabase.

Medicine Hat is responsible for paying taxes on its transmission and distribution lines based on the length of line. Codes are assigned to different types of lines. GIS generates a report and calculates the total span of line for each code. These totals are then submitted to Alberta Assessment as required.

Staff uses ArcFM Designer to prepare work sketches for electric line construction in a subdivision. GIS ensures that engineers are working with the latest design changes during construction.

From *Energy Currents*, fall 2005

Fully integrating GIS with financial systems gives companies a single source of the inventory for their assets. The plant accounting system can then follow the GIS. If utilities use GIS for design and integrate it with work management, they have an accurate means to keep the plant inventory (and age and cost) accurate. If utilities eliminate the backlog of unposted work orders, the value of assets in the field would match the value of assets on the books. By adopting mobile design and as-built reporting, the utility can prevent work order backlogs.

Reporting assets

Besides keeping accurate records of their assets, utilities need to report on the assets in different ways for different purposes. Location often forms the basis for that reporting. For example, many utilities serve multiple districts, municipalities, and counties. It is important to be able to report the value of assets according to those political subdivisions. GIS can answer the question, "How many miles of low-pressure gas mains are in the town of Roseville and what is the current depreciated value of those assets?" In the case of AnyTown Energy, there was no easy way to do basic geographical counts. GIS simplifies this task and can answer temporal questions such as, "How many poles were installed and how many were removed in fiscal year 2007 in Harlow County?" GIS can answer questions about age and depreciated assets such as, "How many electric regulators are fully depreciated within the downtown section of Rosewood?"

Had AnyTown Energy immediately answered the mayor's question with a GIS map showing the location and value of its assets, the mayor surely would not have entertained thoughts about challenging AnyTown Energy. Providing detailed accurate information instills confidence and generally results in better and fewer audits.

Taxation

Many jurisdictions charge sales tax for their electric and gas use. They ask the utilities to collect the taxes on their behalf. Sometimes, the sales tax depends on overlaying jurisdictions. For example, a unified school district may span several municipalities and there may be a sales tax specific to the district. However, each municipality may have differing sales tax rates, so the problem for utilities is to accurately compute the consumption sales tax based on multiple jurisdictions. GIS can routinely handle polygon overlays for taxation purposes. When a new customer signs up for gas or electric service, the utility must determine the exact sales tax for that specific customer. Since the customer might be calling from a new subdivision, relying strictly on lists of multiple jurisdictions is error-prone and time-consuming. With GIS, utilities can precisely place the new customer, determine the exact taxation jurisdictions, and correctly calculate the sales tax.

Since municipal boundaries change, utilities that link these boundaries to their customer information systems and use GIS to capture the correct tax jurisdictions can routinely and automatically determine exact sales tax rates. Those that rely on manual methods may find that some customers are paying the wrong amounts for sales tax, causing complications.

Electric and gas utilities are often among the largest local property taxpayers. As noted in the above example with AnyTown Energy, it's critical to know exactly how much a utility's property is worth in a specific tax jurisdiction. If a utility undercounts its facilities, it may unexpectedly incur a tax liability. If a utility is over-reporting property value, then it is simply paying too much tax. It's unlikely that a municipality will reimburse a utility for years of over-reporting property values.

GIS linked to the plant accounting system assures the utility pays exactly what it owes in property tax. In addition to avoiding embarrassing audits or negotiations with sharp lawyers turned mayors, utilities can automate the process of property tax reporting.

Third-party attachments

Around the world, electric utilities continue to hang their equipment on wooden poles despite a growing trend to bury wires underground. These poles are convenient structures for other entities to use. Third-party attachments are equipment that cable, telephone, municipal fire, and fiber-optic companies hang on the utility poles for a fee. Keeping track of these connections can be difficult, since cable and telecommunication companies, like electric utilities, are doing work on these poles every day. So, third-party attachments involve many transactions. A utility that doesn't know how many poles it owns at any given time is unlikely to have a solid handle on the number of third-party attachments.

GIS helps utilities keep current on third-party attachments. Field crews with mobile devices can verify the accuracy of attachments. Aside from the obvious revenue benefits of knowing what devices and cables are attached to their poles, utilities need to know who to contact should a pole be damaged and have to be replaced.

Some third parties that fail to contact the electric utility when they attach their equipment face fines for unauthorized attachments. Having the attachment information in the GIS helps utilities keep up with the ever-changing third-party situation. The GIS can be used to provide analysis, such as answering the query: "Find the route of a third-party attachment and locate any pole in the route where no attachment is found." This may uncover a number of poles where attachment authorization is missing and fees are unpaid.

Many utilities have an extensive system of underground conduits. Any unused conduit is a prime candidate for revenue production from cable, telecommunication companies, and fiber-optic providers. Utilities can use GIS to find a complete underground path for their cables. Once the telephone companies install the cable, the GIS can help manage the location of the third-party cable. The GIS also can help with accounting input to assure revenue flow.

Streetlights

Early electric system entrepreneurs formed companies specifically to light community streets. Today, a combination of electric utilities and municipalities provides street lighting to communities, sometimes both in the same area. Since utilities typically don't meter streetlights, they charge municipalities based on the number and type of streetlight. So, utilities base revenue from street lighting on their own count of fixtures within a given community. Due to the uniqueness of streetlight billing, some utilities have standalone systems that manage this billing.

Land management: American Electric Power

GIS helps American Electric Power (AEP) manage 300.000 acres of land used for various purposes in the generation, transmission, and distribution of electricity. The investor-owned, Ohio-based utility founded a century ago has a generating capacity of more than 42,000 megawatts and serves almost five million customers. Its long history of innovation includes building the first long-distance transmission line and the first super power plant in 1917.

AEP manages land in fourteen states and property plays a key role in its operations. GIS ensures staff members have accurate maps for various land-related issues, including sales, leases, development of generating capacity, easements, and land rights. AEP's real estate agents use GIS maps to fulfill land information requests by potential buyers. The utility's legal department uses GIS maps for documenting property boundaries and land attributes, such as acreage, soil type, elevation, and mineral content.

Before GIS, AEP's Land Management Department had to make do with hand-drawn maps, boundaries sketched on U.S. Geological Survey topographic maps, or drawings provided by a surveyor. These maps had to be checked for accuracy and updated, and often had to be redrawn or copied. In many cases, one paper map would contain information pertaining to multiple deeds, complicating the research process.

But GIS dramatically improved the process. AEP's GIS specialist, Mike Williams, now maps the utility's ownership parcels from a legal description on a project-by-project basis initiated by real estate transactions or a grant of land or land rights. UCLID's IcoMap for ArcGIS technology converts survey measurements from scanned documents into digital formats, saving time and assuring accuracy. By using IcoMap, workers can key in calls 50 to 75 percent faster than by manually keying in mete and bounds. Time-saving quality assurance features allow users to edit individual lines and quickly correct mistakes.

Particularly impressive to Williams is the ability of ArcMap to integrate spatial data with tabular information from property descriptions, which are transferred into an Oracle database. AEP's GIS is an important communication tool that helps staff more accurately visualize the utility's property boundaries but also perform queries that were not possible with paper records.

In a potential sale of timberland, a field crew uses ESRI's ArcPad on a Trimble GeoExplorer GPS unit to help locate property corners or markers. The crew is able to collect information on access roads and forest inventory to update the GIS data back in the office. AEP's real estate agents use the same equipment to earmark acreage for a hunting or agricultural lease.

Williams has found that GIS makes AEP more efficient, productive, and competitive. The utility is trying to centralize records while serving a staff that is spread over numerous states and reliant on those records. GIS makes it much easier to manage that information. AEP is working toward having all land management records online and then using ArcIMS to make the GIS accessible to staff via the company's intranet. Other departments would then have access to accurate information about the company's land.

From *GIS Solutions for Power Generation and Transmission Services* with contributions from Paige Medlin of USLID Software

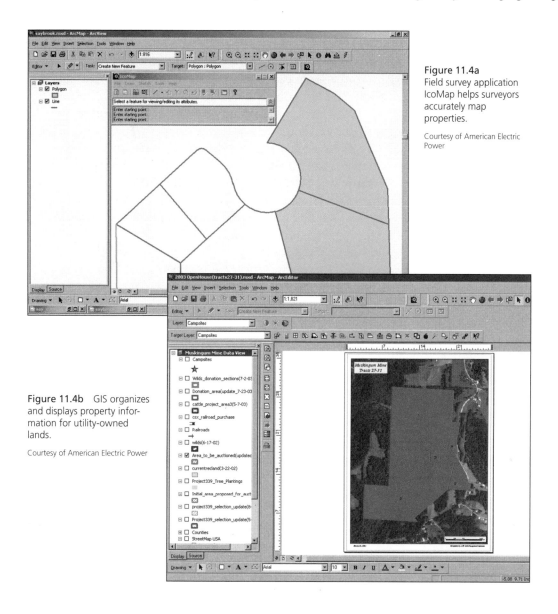

Figure 11.4a
Field survey application
IcoMap helps surveyors
accurately map
properties.

Courtesy of American Electric
Power

Figure 11.4b   GIS organizes
and displays property information for utility-owned
lands.

Courtesy of American Electric Power

Integrating streetlight management with GIS is natural. Using GIS, utilities can easily count streetlights. They can integrate new streetlight maintenance work orders into the
accounting system, thus making sure that the utility has an accurate count of streetlights
and type. When a utility gets a call that a streetlight is out, it can accurately identify which
streetlight is involved by querying the person who called.

Lighting engineers can use GIS to model streetlight patterns and create effective designs.
Safety officials can use these models to determine the adequacy of the lighting in areas
where security is an issue. If a crime or accident occurs in a location where a streetlight was
out, the utility could face liability and public relations issues.

Real estate

A utility clearly owns the land that a substation or generating station sits on. However, utilities may have purchased land years ago anticipating expansion of their facilities or simply on speculation. Having all of the land ownership captured in the GIS and available to the enterprise benefits the company. While many utilities use GIS to manage their land, it is not common that land ownership is visible to everyone in the company. Suppose the planning department anticipates it will need a new transmission substation in two years to supply a new area of town. Suppose further that at the same time, the manager of the real estate department closes a lucrative deal to sell land the utility has owned for years in that same area. Later, the planning department asks the real estate department to find a suitable site in that area. The real estate department just sold the perfect parcel. Far-fetched? Perhaps, but not integrating the real estate data with the planning department data certainly increases the probability of missed opportunities.

Utilities also may own land they lease to third parties. It is important to have a common understanding of the landholdings and all the legal aspects of the land in relation to the utilities' facilities. As noted earlier, utilities spend a lot on simple logistics, moving people and material from one place to another. Knowing that a utility owns a vacant piece of land usable for permanent or temporary staging could be important. The key idea is that by showing all land ownership in the same data structure (the GIS) allows the utility to better coordinate its overall operations.

The utility can use the GIS to plan for future land acquisitions. The utility may decide that having staging areas during emergencies could improve overall operations. It may be looking to optimize the siting of service centers.

While GIS is a popular and common tool for managing real estate, it can be a powerful coordination tool when the real estate data is part of the overall utility enterprise GIS.

Perhaps the most difficult real estate issue is managing various rights-of-way for gas and electric transmission. As noted in chapters 4 and 7, rights-of-way are patchwork quilts of various easements, licenses, and land leases. Keeping the parcel data along with the legal descriptions of the land can help utilities better manage their activities along the rights-of-way.

Environmental impacts

Due to its ubiquitous presence in the community, utility equipment has many opportunities to impact the environment. GIS is critical in assessing the environmental risk of such equipment. For example, some heavy electric equipment contains insulating oil. Should a rupture occur or the equipment be struck by an errant automobile resulting in oil leaks, the utility needs to know exactly where the oil will migrate. If there is a nearby stream, the impact on water resources could be serious and the utility would be liable for any harm. Gas utilities use a variety of chemicals in their operations, which, if leaked, would cause damage to the environment. Knowing where these chemicals are stored in relation to sensitive areas can save the utility a lot of grief and costs in the event of a spill.

Utilities that maintain and repair their own vehicles have a host of chemicals and fluids to manage. A GIS that shows environmentally sensitive areas in proximity to fleet garages helps mitigate damage and, should a spill occur, helps the cleanup process.

With an enterprise GIS, utilities can see vegetated wetlands in relation to oil-filled equipment, underground tanks, and chemical and fuel storage facilities. That information can help utilities decide to either replace the equipment or build barriers to protect the sensitive areas from harmful spills. When a spill does occur, utilities have relevant information for a timely response.

Figure 11.5   GIS shows the effects of a planned reservoir.

Courtesy of Companhia Paranaense de Energia

Utilities don't necessarily have to store and maintain environmentally sensitive information directly in the GIS. They could subscribe to a Web service that provides up-to-date information about floodplains, wetlands, sensitive habitat nesting grounds, or any area where a spill could cause a serious environmental problem and also cost the utility in public image and fines.

Some utilities have to manage contamination on their own property. GIS helps them monitor the progress of the cleanup.

Sometimes, driving a bucket truck over an environmentally sensitive area can be a violation of an environmental regulation. GIS can communicate information to the field forces to avoid such an intrusion and the stiff fine that results.

GIS helps utilities visualize the environmental impact of power plant emissions. Should an emission system failure occur, the utility can model the path of the pollution and take appropriate action to notify those communities and agencies impacted.

GIS helps utilities make good decisions, such as how close to place facilities near environmentally sensitive areas or what could be done to prevent a potential chemical or oil spill from spreading to a river stream. GIS helps utilities communicate. By identifying environmentally sensitive areas within the GIS, crews know where they can and cannot work. GIS helps utilities collaborate. Utilities can work with local conservation commissions and environmental agencies to plan their facilities in the most environmentally friendly way.

Finally, utilities can use GIS for total environmental risk assessment. They can ask the GIS the question, "Show me where a failure of our equipment could cause the most environmental damage."

Security

Critical infrastructure protection has taken on a new meaning with the increase in terrorism around the world. Electric and gas utility systems top the list of critical infrastructures. Utilities spend increasing sums to assure their systems are secure from terrorism, vandalism, and theft. GIS can help utilities visualize the various security devices installed throughout the service territories. Gas and electric utilities have video cameras, door alarms, motion detectors, and a host of other security devices. Linking these devices to a geographic location can help utilities respond to violators. However, just displaying the location of an alarm on a map isn't enough. Having the alarms displayed in relation to the infrastructure gives the utility a better handle on the degree of the threat. If the utility is using GIS for fleet management and automated vehicle location, it can discover where the closest crew is and direct that crew (along with the police if necessary) to the location where the violation has occurred.

GIS can help utilities discover inherent weakness in their system. For example, GIS could discover single points of failure, including where transmission lines cross waterways, potentially cutting off large communities, or where high-pressure gas transmission lines cross critical electric transmission lines. Other, less obvious examples include losing critical rail transport to a coal-fired plant or cooling water supply to a nuclear plant. GIS can help utilities develop scenarios of various incidents to better prepare them for attacks on their critical infrastructure.

One other important way GIS can support the utility's security initiatives is through data sharing. GIS can provide a common language for different agencies to share critical infrastructure information among themselves. Electric and gas utilities can share information with pipeline companies, water agencies, and the government. Of course, the data sharing must be secure.

GIS can be critical to plan for and respond to security threats. Utilities have used GIS for security applications in standalone applications. Integrating security into the enterprise GIS allows utilities to continuously analyze their systems for all types of threats.

Information technology

IT asset management

Utilities depend heavily on information technology (IT) for nearly all aspects of their business (including GIS, of course). Utilities can use GIS to help them manage the locations of their IT equipment. Routers, computers, phones, printers, servers, remote terminal units, sensors, microwave equipment, private radio transmitters and receivers, networks, hubs, and much more equipment are scattered throughout the gas and electric systems' buildings and facilities. Managing these assets is a challenge. Knowing the location and condition of the equipment can ease this burden.

Telecommunications in utilities

Utilities provide some degree of telecommunication services in competition or collaboration with local telecommunication companies. Some utilities have firmly entered the communication market. Since utilities own underground conduits and poles, they can certainly leverage that investment for a telecommunications business. Utilities were early adopters of fiber-optic communication systems for their internal relay protection systems. They can use the spare fibers for other commercial applications.

Like electric and gas utilities, telecommunication companies use GIS extensively. As utilities provide more telecommunication services, GIS for this purpose will increase. If they integrate the telecommunications system within their utility GIS, they will be able to easily coordinate telecommunications asset management with the utility asset management rather than having a standalone system just for telecommunications.

Electric utilities can leverage wires for voice, video, and Internet service using broadband over power lines (BPL) systems. While still in its infancy, this technology may grow. Like other communication systems, BPL requires devices to be located throughout the service territory, which involves significant asset management. Utilities can use GIS to document the BPL equipment. Utilities can use GIS to determine where radio interference causes problems with other nearby communication systems, like amateur ham radio operators.

Human resources

Can GIS help manage people? Sometimes. Since enterprise GIS is a platform integrated into the utility's IT infrastructure, there is no reason why the GIS cannot access employee home locations from the payroll/human resources system. Utilities can find significant productivity improvements by staging materials directly at job sites rather than having crews pick up their equipment at depots or service centers. Likewise, for some utilities it may make sense to restructure some of the work so that employees can report directly to the job site. Knowing where an employee lives in relation to a proposed project could affect how the jobs are scheduled and dispatched. This could be even more important during the response to an emergency.

Health and safety

Utilities strive to assure their employees work safely. Most utilities carefully measure their safety record because it's important and subject to regulatory oversight.

A good record of what's in the field makes the workplace safer. Confusion, missing information, and inconsistent information breed accidents. So utilities that install enterprise GIS and improve processes to eliminate backlogged information will see fewer switching errors, less confusion, and fewer accidents. By using GIS to optimize travel time, employees will travel fewer miles to accomplish the same tasks. Fewer miles statistically correlate to fewer vehicle accidents.

Utility health and safety departments track lost time caused by motor vehicle accidents. GIS can help discover patterns of accidents related to location. For example, if there are more accidents in one particular area, are there environmental, weather, or traffic factors that make one region more prone to accidents than another? If not, perhaps one region is not as aggressive on safety or training as another region. Utilities may discover that a section of roadway is narrow, heavily treed, and has a history of accidents. They could alert crews to avoid that roadway, if at all possible. Subscribing to a public safety Web service could highlight areas with high accident rates. Those areas can be displayed in the enterprise GIS.

Utilities monitor employee health. Using GIS, they may discover that certain employees experience some unexplained health issue in the same location. They can check for patterns. Utilities can monitor areas of high crime and provide additional coverage or police details. Using GIS, utilities can see crime or suspected health problem areas in relationship to their facilities and the planned work.

GIS can help manage employees in sometimes unique and surprising ways. The result is better communication and productivity and improved safety records.

Public relations

Utilities are very concerned about their public image. Why? As a corporate citizen, maintaining a positive image is the right thing to do. It also is a very good business strategy. Utilities with unreasonably high rates, extended outages, and poor customer response find themselves in the headlines of local newspapers. Investors will shy away. Bad public relations could result in higher costs or make it more difficult or expensive to raise capital. Bad PR usually results in expensive investigations, audits, and additional work.

Most utilities regularly perform customer satisfaction surveys. Those surveys tend to measure factors such as satisfaction in billing, reliability, community service, communication, and aesthetics of their facilities. While these factors are good measures of the company as a whole, they don't tell a complete picture. Suppose a utility's billing rating needs improvement. The utility has to ask itself, is the dissatisfaction with billing uniform over all its territories or good in some areas and bad in others? By viewing the ratings geographically, utilities may discover pockets of people that suffer from poor billing. That probably means the issue isn't so much with the bill per se, but with the accuracy of the meter reading in their area. Or, it might be that a large percentage of people in an area have estimated bills. Looking at the geography of estimated bills compared to satisfaction ratings may give the utility the concrete evidence they need to improve meter reading, not the billing system.

GIS is a wonderful communication tool. Many utilities publish outage information over the Internet so the media, politicians, and the public can understand the extent of outages and can make appropriate plans. Most people understand that power outages are often unavoidable. What people find most frustrating about power failures is the lack of communication. Gas companies have to deal with serious customer concerns during a gas outage, especially during cold weather. Customers with good information can take early steps to find shelters if they know the outage will be prolonged.

Utilities can use GIS to inform the public about ongoing projects. Often gas companies have to dig up streets, which impacts merchants and traffic. An informative Web site that gives detour information or projected completion dates along with helpful dynamic maps for their customers can be priceless.

Rate making

Governments regulate most utility rates. Utilities have to prove their rates are fair. Regulators require utilities to research the rate patterns of all classes of customers. This is done using special interval meters strategically placed at representative customer sites. The collected data samples form the basis for rate analysis. GIS can help display the various rate classes to help utilities place the correct research meters at their proper location.

To create fair rates based on sample meters, utilities have to calculate the cost to supply each rate class. For example, a utility has to allocate the costs of the generation, transmission, and distribution systems to a particular class of rate payer, like certain residential, commercial, or industrial customers. This can be a tedious manual process because it requires an accurate model of the distribution system and a definitive understanding of how the various rate classes are geographically distributed.

GIS is a natural mechanism to help utilities calculate the cost of supplying a particular rate class. Using tracing and demographics, utilities can create automated systems to perform cost of service studies and track the cost of service for any class of customer. This helps utilities fine tune their rates structures as they go along so they don't have to develop a long and arduous cost-of-service study every couple of years prior to a rate filing. GIS can help utilities simplify rate making and provide an easy way to report to the regulators the methodology of their rate cases in a graphic, easy-to-understand way.

Corporate

The CEO, general manager, minister of electricity, or simply the boss of any complex electric and gas company wants to know how well the utility is operating. In other words, he or she needs so to see a common operating picture (COP) of the utility. Enterprise GIS can be an integral part of the COP, since electric and gas utilities are so geographically distributed. Generally, the COP displays the company's key performance indicators. Since metrics about customer service, safety, environmental performance, and a host of other factors vary widely over the various districts and divisions in the utility, the COP can illustrate where things are and are not going well.

The corporate office is concerned about business continuity. Utilities can use GIS to build a number of emergency scenarios, such as what would happen during a major flood, earthquake, or terrorist attack. The GIS can illustrate the impact on primary, backup, and support systems, and it can also show the location of critical data centers and the consequences of something happening to them. GIS can be one component of a comprehensive business continuity planning study.

GIS serves the needs of shared services

Location plays a critical role in most of a utility's shared services functions, so it's not surprising to find GIS users in many different departments. What is less common are shared services groups using an enterprise GIS. These groups can share applications and data with all the other organizations within the utility. Utilities can visualize the spatial data to discover patterns and to show hidden relationships. Using enterprise GIS in shared services is yet another way to create a unified picture of the utility.

Figure 11.6   Determining joint usage on power poles can be challenging as this photo taken in Tyumen, Russia, illustrates. GIS can help.

Photo by Patrick Dolan

12

GIS: Making the enterprise business case

For years, AnyTown Energy was content to be a middle-of-the-pack utility in the region, neither outstanding nor poorly rated. The company earned investors a stable return and its stock price kept pace with the industry average. However, as energy prices and customer demands for service increased, a flurry of skilled workers retired, the infrastructure deteriorated, and AnyTown Energy's ratings slipped. Several embarrassing safety audits, an increase in motor vehicle accidents, and lower reliability had attracted unwelcome media attention.

AnyTown Energy found itself below average in nearly every category of a utility's benchmarks. Company officials realized they had retained tried and true processes that had served them in the past but were too cumbersome for today's challenging environment. The CEO was worried and the board of directors demanded improvements. A top management consultant assessed operations and recommended an enterprise GIS.

AnyTown Energy successfully implemented the GIS along with many of the consultant's other recommendations. In two years, AnyTown Energy's benchmark ratings once again were positive and trending toward its best-ever performance metrics. AnyTown Energy had built a strong business case for the enterprise GIS, confident that the technology would improve the company's most important functions.

Starting with the strategic plan

The strategic plan identifies a utility's top priorities. Utilities face various natural challenges, including hurricanes, snowstorms, earthquakes, and wildfires. Each region has its own regulatory and political environment. Some countries have a single state-owned utility. Others have a combination of investor, state, and consumer-owned utilities. Some utilities serve wealthy, demanding customers, while others serve abjectly poor communities. Some utilities have a single strong union. Others have many weaker unions or none at all. Despite these differences, electric and gas utilities generally have the same four critical stakeholders: customers, shareholders, communities, and employees.

Utilities typically craft their performance metrics as a scorecard that records the demands of the four stakeholders. The scorecard measures areas that utilities believe are critical to their mission. Boards of directors rate executives on how well the company meets these metrics. We can visualize the scorecard as four quadrants, each quadrant representing one of the stakeholders. A successful utility strives for balance in all four areas. If money were no object, that would be easy. Since one of the quadrants of the scorecard is shareholder, it is critical that a utility not spend more than it can afford. Cost-cutting measures, such as staff reductions, elimination of overtime, and reduced funding for emergency responses often reduce customer service. Such measures also diminish employee morale and can lead to negative political and community impacts.

The ideal situation is to show improvement for all of the stakeholders at the same time. How is this possible?

AnyTown Energy had fallen behind in filling requests for new service. It had to cancel customer meetings with contractors and constantly reschedule crews. Employees were hassled by irate developers and customers while complaints from the public utilities commission piled up. Managers kept busy writing excuse reports. Overtime expenses soared just to keep up with the workload. Each stakeholder was unhappy.

Enterprise model: CenterPoint Energy

Headquartered in Houston, Texas, CenterPoint Energy is the nation's third largest combined electricity and natural gas delivery company, serving more than five million metered customers, and is Houston's third largest employer in the energy industry.

CenterPoint Energy provides electric transmission and distribution service for the Houston metropolitan area and natural gas distribution service in Arkansas, Louisiana, Minnesota, Mississippi, Oklahoma, and Texas. CenterPoint Energy also owns and operates two interstate pipelines, gathers natural gas, provides maintenance and technical services to third-party clients, and installs its remote wellhead monitoring and measuring product, ServiceStar.

CenterPoint Energy uses GIS throughout all of its operation. The company's enterprise implementation has created a central organization that manages the relationship with ESRI as well as all the applications, data models, and workflow processes associated with maintaining data in the GIS. Implementing base asset information is the platform from which additional applications and business values are derived. Increasing integration adds value for decision making.

CenterPoint Energy's Land & Right of Way Division acts as property manager for acreage within the Houston metro area. Critical to effective property management is the ability to view from the desktop as much information as possible and reduce costly field visits. GIS makes such data as how the asset was purchased, current uses of the asset (leases, grants, easements, etc.), the asset's physical boundaries, and acreage within the asset, all readily available to the agents. GIS assists the division in managing approximately $5 million of annual revenues related to property usage and has saved the division more than $80,000 per year in labor costs.

The custom addressing application facilitates the company's responsibility for assigning 50,000 to 60,000 new Houston-area addresses annually, relating them to the specific transformer that feeds the premise. Once created in GIS, this information is automatically transferred to the customer information system. The transferred information contains the results of polygon processing and coordinates used for map-based dispatching. This automated data feed process has saved CenterPoint Energy $50,000 annually in addressing alone; but it also facilitates a much more significant cost avoidance in crew dispatching.

CenterPoint Energy uses the GIS database to track and manage the number of communications attachments in many ways. Reports of attachments by area, owner, type, and other categories are easily generated in text or map format. Legal text and map images are merged to produce a contract document that shows the specific poles leased to a communication company within the area on the map. The GIS data is also used to produce pole counts and generate lease attachment billings. The pole attachment application with GIS data assists CenterPoint Energy in managing $6 million in annual revenue.

CenterPoint Energy saw a rapid increase in requests to locate underground facilities and also needed to locate more facilities for a gas company it had acquired. The company's Line Locating Division responded by creating a system that integrated GIS, new technologies, and process

Continued on next page

Continued from previous page

reengineering to save CenterPoint $1 million in its first year. MapObjects supported by data from a very large ArcSDE geodatabase produced digital maps and processes that resulted in fewer field locate queries and increased efficiencies in the locates that were performed.

CenterPoint Energy uses a custom application to facilitate customer requests for streetlight conversions. Users create a selection set of streetlights from ArcMap via the Interactive Select tool or by spatial constraint. The lights are automatically assigned a default light type to be converted, which can be modified as required. After the new light types have been confirmed, the information is automatically sent to a streetlight work management system database and a work sketch is automatically generated for maintenance crews to perform the work. Changed attribute information is automatically updated in the GIS, eliminating manual digitizing. This GIS-assisted streetlight conversion process has saved the company $40,000 a year.

ArcLogistics Route is a commercial off-the-shelf application that provides CenterPoint Energy with an efficient means of handling meter rereads. Inconsistent meter readings are kicked out of two separate billing systems (gas and electric) daily. In the past, the gas and electric rereads were handled separately, but ArcLogistics Route could process both lists of rereads for efficient routing. This processing merger has saved CenterPoint Energy $40,000 in reduced overtime and fleet costs.

From *CenterPoint Energy GIS: Technology for Your Enterprise,* reprinted with permission

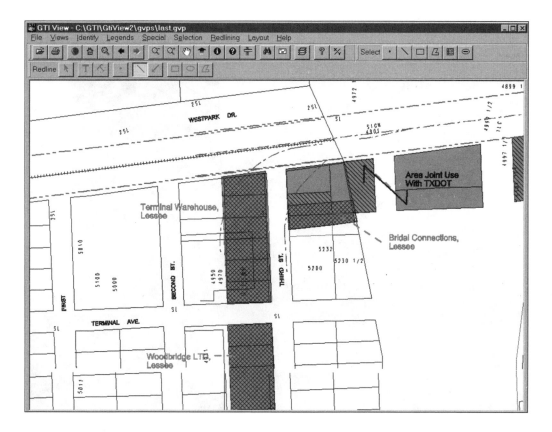

Figure 12.1   GIS helps CenterPoint Energy's Land & Right of Way Division manage more than 70,000 acres of land, providing desktop views of crucial property data.

Courtesy of CenterPoint Energy

Adding more people and working people longer were not viable solutions. If it were to improve, AnyTown Energy could not continue awkward processes that negatively impacted all four stakeholders. We have seen in previous chapters that uncoordinated systems increased employee frustration. The utility unnecessarily delayed a customer's request for new service. Inaccurate records affected employee safety. In most cases, AnyTown Energy overspent on operations because of poor processes and a lack of enterprise GIS.

For the business case to be compelling, the GIS must have a positive impact on the key strategic metrics of the company.

Figure 12.2   Delivering energy from source to user involves numerous spatial issues that an enterprise GIS is designed to handle efficiently.

Photos by (a) Comstock Images—Power and Energy/Jupiterimages; (b) Scott T. Baxter/PhotoDisc/Getty Images; (c) Comstock Images—Industrial Strength/Jupiterimages; (d) Russell Illig/PhotoDisc/Getty Images

AnyTown Energy's situation

AnyTown Energy built its standalone AM/FM system in the late 1990s by converting its old hand-drawn operating maps. As a result, it lacked a standard map coordinate system so it couldn't use GPS to locate points accurately. When AnyTown Energy converted its maps, the map products included detailed electric and gas distribution plats, or grid sheets, each scaled at 1 inch equaling 50 feet. AnyTown Energy also had a number of overview maps at varying scales. When the company converted the detailed plats, it never coordinated the overview maps, so these maps were separately maintained even though some of the information overlapped. In addition, the electrical engineering group maintained one-line switching drawings and the gas operations separately maintained pipe schematics. Again, both sets of drawings contained duplicate information.

The gas transmission group maintained all alignment sheets in a separate CAD-based system. The electric transmission group maintained hand-drawn strip plans and transmission system plan and profile drawings with associated rights-of-way. As noted in earlier chapters, technicians performed gas and electric designs by plotting the existing facility information and hand drawing the revised facilities on the plotted maps from the AM/FM system. Other than editing the as-built information onto the digital maps, AnyTown Energy had no spatial applications.

The utility distributed the AM/FM system maps in much the same way that it distributed the hand-drawn maps. When a significant number of changes occurred on a particular detailed plat, one-line switching drawing, gas schematic, transmission strip plan, or gas transmission alignment sheet, the mapping group plotted out the drawing, made copies, then mailed the copies to interested parties throughout the organization. However, a shortage of clerical staff in some of the regions prevented regular filing. In some areas, the operating groups kept a record set of prints that they redlined or marked up with corrections and changes. This posed a problem. Before someone replaced the new print with the old one, he or she had to transfer the redline to the new replacement print.

Goals of utility's GIS project

AnyTown Energy's GIS project team established these goals for the enterprise GIS:
1. Create a single source for all spatial data. This includes all land, gas, and electrical transmission and distribution facilities, generation, storage, and support facilities.
2. Spatial information is referenced to a standard coordinate system for GPS to locate all facilities.
3. The GIS accepts commercially available raster imagery.
4. Throughout the enterprise spatial data is distributed over the Web.
5. Mobile devices update spatial information from the field and synchronize quickly with the data maintained in the office.
6. Designs are created and maintained within the GIS environment.
7. The GIS is integrated with or replaces corporate systems such as the customer, supply chain, SCADA, work, leak, integrity management, and outage systems.
8. All output products, detailed maps, overview maps, schematics, transmission strip plans, and gas transmission alignment sheets are derived from the enterprise GIS.
9. The local municipalities are leveraged for land-base maintenance.

Enterprise model: Southern Company

Southern Company's enterprise approach to GIS enables its four operating companies serving millions of customers—Alabama Power, Mississippi Power, Georgia Power, and Gulf Power—to improve customer service, cost containment, and profitability.

Each of the four utilities operated an independent GIS with limited sharing of infrastructure and support. This resulted in duplication of efforts in maintaining, administering, and supporting GIS across the various business units including distribution, transmission, land, economic development, and marketing.

Recognizing the need to leverage common business requirements, centralize information technology architecture, and optimize GIS investments to meet the needs of the whole organization, Southern Company established an enterprise GIS (E-GIS) in 2003. The project aimed to streamline technology, save money, provide value to each operating company, and enhance opportunities for business support and growth.

A GIS core strategy team included management representatives from all four operating companies that were reporting directly to Southern Company's IT steering committee. The team developed a collaborative strategic E-GIS vision across companies and business units and finalized an enterprise site license for ESRI software.

Enspiria Solutions Inc., a Denver, Colorado-based consulting and systems integration firm experienced with utility GIS projects, came on board to help develop an E-GIS plan for architecture. The plan included hardware, software, and network requirements along with an implementation road map showing cost and savings estimates. The plan was a framework for management and control of the enterprise-wide system used by the four operating companies.

The E-GIS solution consisted of an ArcGIS platform based on ArcSDE with ArcObjects and Telvent Miner & Miner's ArcFM toolset. E-GIS was set up to be the central database for distribution, transmission, and land records across the enterprise. It also provided consistent, high-quality data to other systems such as feeding data to the outage management systems at the operating companies to ensure optimum response to hurricanes and other disasters.

The ArcGIS platform serves as an enabling technology for addressing future Southern Company business needs. The E-GIS project positioned Southern Company to optimize business processes and decisions.

From *Energy Currents,* spring 2006

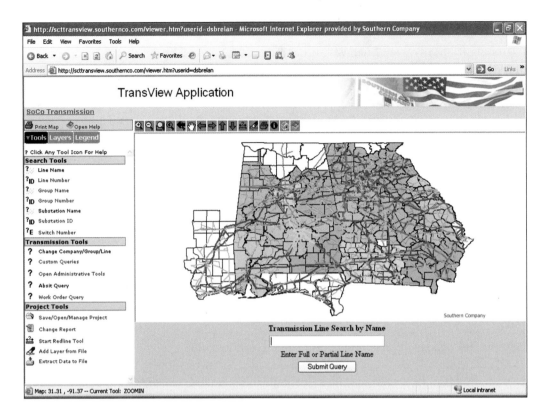

Figure 12.3   Southern Company's TransView Application leverages ArcGIS to provide system-wide query and work design for all four operating companies. This is a full view of Southern's service territory.

Courtesy of Southern Company

The AnyTown Energy GIS project team had to develop the business case to obtain funding for the enterprise proposal. The business case needed to show a strong positive investment value, but it also had to address AnyTown Energy's nagging operating problems. That meant that the business case had to be as financially prudent as any investment. It had to show that implementing a GIS would help close the gaps in the strategic metrics that meant the most to AnyTown Energy.

The methodology first calculated the costs of building the GIS, and then calculated the financial benefits. The business case identified how much the GIS would contribute to closing the gaps in the operating plan, such as improvements in reliability or customer satisfaction. Intangible benefits like "better looking maps" or "making my job easier" were not included. Factors such as labor, material, fleet, overtime, contractor, inventory carrying costs, cycle time, and customer satisfaction needed to be evaluated as they were before and after GIS to completely develop the business case.

Cost factors

Digressing from AnyTown Energy's specific project for the time being, this section describes in general the financial implications of an enterprise GIS. Building and integrating an enterprise GIS within corporate information systems involves major external and internal costs. The components of an enterprise system are:

- core GIS software for the desktop, servers, and mobile devices
- application software for system planning, right-of-way management, fleet management, utility work flow management, and gas and electric design
- integration software with interfaces to legacy systems, middleware, and adapters
- utility-specific data models
- a database management system
- hardware and networks

Enterprise GIS requirements

At the heart of enterprise GIS is the core software with essential modeling tools to build and edit utility facilities and customer and land features. Text, sound, photos, CAD files, and scanned documents are among the attributes that could be linked to features. The software places intelligent and non-intelligent text, deals effectively with raster files and imagery, and imposes business rules, domains, and relationships.

An enterprise GIS must have application design tools and be able to customize the work flow and build configuration scenarios. It should allow users to create process models and have scripting capability. The development tools must allow an interface to the various tools so that engineers can perform electric and gas network load analyses.

One of the most important functions of an enterprise GIS is managing spatial data. Whereas CAD systems manage drawing files, a GIS manages spatial and non-spatial data and must be able to edit, input, and manipulate data. Since data exists in so many forms, a GIS must have the capacity to import, export, and bulk load data from various formats including CAD files, spreadsheets, legacy databases, and even old AM/FM systems. A GIS has to process different land projections. As noted throughout this book, a GIS needs to create many versions of the data, must allow for multiuser access and editing, and have quality assurance tools for data integrity specifically for utility data.

To accomplish the concepts in this book, an enterprise GIS must perform spatial and raster analysis. It must maintain the connectivity of facilities, like wires, pipes, roadways, and rights of way. To take advantage of the connectivity, a GIS must trace the electrical net-work to upstream fuses or downstream customers and create the shortest path for a gas technician to a report a leak. It must have intelligent routing, so the utility can use the GIS for meter reading or to route and schedule technicians and crews.

Visualization brings the power of GIS to life. A GIS needs tools to control the display and create thematic displays, such as where tree trimming crews should be sent. A GIS must be able to render the displays in 3D and allow for animation. Predicting the path of a potential oil leak from a power transformer can help the engineers design a better con-tainment system. A GIS must allow for surface visualization for things like transmission clearance assessment. From executives to the people in the field, utility people need to visu-alize data in nonspatial ways, like in schematic and isometric forms.

Of course, a GIS must produce high-quality maps so advanced cartography is required. It must publish maps in a variety of ways, from map books to view-only files, and be able to publish all kinds of utility maps on the Web. It must have an advanced report-writing function.

An enterprise GIS requires new servers, network equipment, and desktop and mobile clients. The extent of the hardware and network infrastructure is dependent on the existing IT system and capability to handle the additional load of an enterprise GIS.

Implementation

Implementation steps include:

- data modeling
- software implementation, configuration, custom application (if required), and integration
- data migration/conversion
- training
- post implementation costs

Data modeling

A data model is critical when creating an enterprise GIS. A data model contains all the features, relationships, and dependencies of the GIS components. Attributes, naming con-ventions, and domain rules (the valid values that an attribute can have) are all part of the data model. The end result of the data modeling exercise is a database schema.

Workflow technology: Kissimmee Utility Authority

Kissimmee Utility Authority (KUA), Florida's sixth largest utility serving 61,000 customers, wanted the most advanced technology available to upgrade its mapping and engineering geographic applications. KUA needed a system that could be accessible to many of its 260 employees rather than confined to the isolated desktops of a few workers.

In 2003, the utility selected ESRI and Telvent Miner & Miner software for its GIS because of these companies' open standards-based architecture, reputation for success, and expertise in the electric and gas industry. The complete suite of products running on top of a single, seamless geodatabase created an easy-to-use, one-stop shop solution for the company's facilities management, outage, and business needs.

All ArcGIS and ArcFM software products use a single, comprehensive geodatabase that provided KUA with a complete workflow that streamlines and integrates business processes. The new GIS cut down on data conversion and import/export by nearly 75 percent from previous methods involving independent and isolated applications.

ArcEditor and ArcFM were used for data creation, editing, and maintenance. ArcIMS was used for Web data distribution within KUA, and ArcSDE integrated GIS within the company's relational database management system. ArcFM Designer provided utility design capabilities. ArcFM Viewer gave field personnel remote viewing capabilities. ArcFM Responder was used for outage management. Conduit Manager allowed users to track underground conduit systems and Network Adapter provided an interface to popular interactive network analysis tools.

The GIS project met all aspects of KUA's business and operations needs, including automated mapping and facilities management, outage management, design, customer service, finance, systems operations, and field operations.

From *Energy Currents*, summer 2004

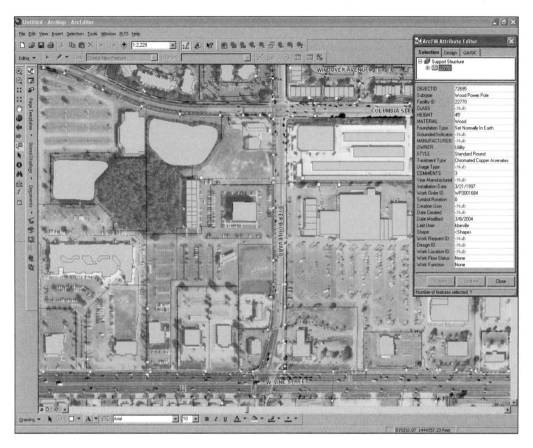

Figure 12.4   The ArcFM extension Attribute Editor helps users perform validations by using a QA/QC tool. This tool uses basic database validation principles, such as relationship connectivity rules, to validate attribute values.

Courtesy of Kissimmee Utility Authority

Software implementation, configuration, custom application, and integration

This step involves setting up the software, tuning the database, building any custom application tools, and building the integration with other applications. It may involve creating adapters to legacy systems to work with enterprise application interface tools. Integration of document, financial, work, and outage management, and SCADA systems occurs during this step. This step can be a substantial effort if the utility does not adopt more standardized processes. Estimating the cost of custom applications can be a challenge. Regardless of the complexity, utilities must methodically manage custom applications and interfaces, even simple ones.

Data migration and conversion

Obtaining or creating good data often represents the largest cost of a comprehensive enterprise GIS project. Usually data migration and conversion fall into these categories and many projects will use a combination of all three:

- Direct conversion from paper sources. While most utilities converted much of their facility data into some digital format, there still is data in raw, hand-drawn form. This would include digitally scanned drawings and maps.
- Building the data from field inventory. Some utilities have determined that their paper (or digital) data sources are too out of date, incomplete, or inaccurate to convert. So they rely on a process of direct field data collection. Today, that usually involves collecting the GPS location of critical network devices.
- Digital data migration. This involves converting CAD, AM/FM, or legacy GIS data to a more modern platform and may require considerable manual data correction.

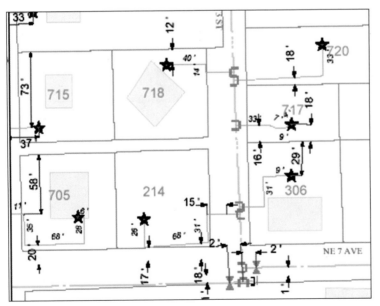

Figure 12.5 To convert gas paper maps to GIS, raster maps are scanned and rectified to coincide with the county land base. Gas features are then traced on-screen and include attributes and dimensions.

Courtesy of Gainesville Regional Utilities

While utilities often have data in electronic form, they need to create internal processes to improve data quality. Utilities that have used CAD or even GIS for mapping alone may not have sufficient data quality for enterprise applications. As discussed throughout this book, utility maps need only to look good. GIS applications, however, rely on the proper database design including data connectivity. Utilities that have used CAD systems have found that creating a gas network model, for example, requires weeks of work, even if the data is in electronic form. A properly designed GIS data model with a good data maintenance tool saves time. Gas utilities can utilize the GIS gas connectivity model for network analysis. However, there will be a cost associated with fixing the network connectivity data from the legacy CAD, AM/FM, or an older GIS dataset.

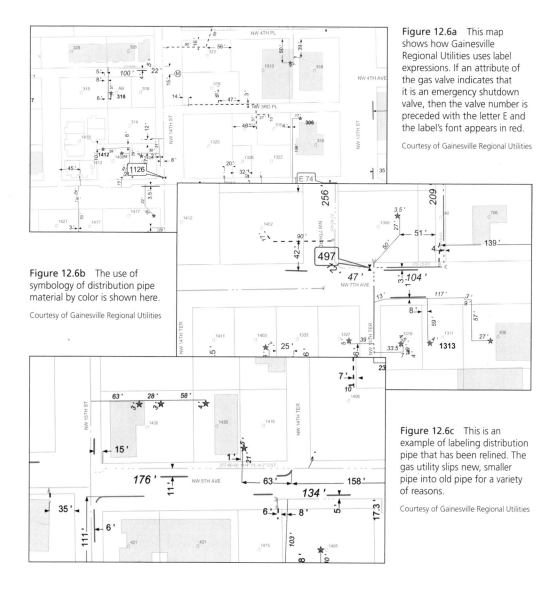

Figure 12.6a   This map shows how Gainesville Regional Utilities uses label expressions. If an attribute of the gas valve indicates that it is an emergency shutdown valve, then the valve number is preceded with the letter E and the label's font appears in red.

Courtesy of Gainesville Regional Utilities

Figure 12.6b   The use of symbology of distribution pipe material by color is shown here.

Courtesy of Gainesville Regional Utilities

Figure 12.6c   This is an example of labeling distribution pipe that has been relined. The gas utility slips new, smaller pipe into old pipe for a variety of reasons.

Courtesy of Gainesville Regional Utilities

As described earlier, many utilities have used GIS data for their outage management algorithms with disappointing results. Inconsistent phase data, tiny discontinuities in the connectivity data, and inconsistent links between the network and customer data have plagued utilities. They have wrongly assumed that their mapping of electronic data is good enough for outage management. Utilities must address these inconsistencies and data-quality issues before they can use the data for advanced applications. Like the gas model, electrical connectivity has to be outstanding for engineers to use it to predict outages. In fact, no connectivity is probably better than bad connectivity for outage management. Lax enforcement of connectivity rules during the creation of CAD drawings can result in a nightmare for a utility.

Many utilities, like AnyTown Energy, created their own mapping coordinate systems. For convenience, they created mapping grids. These grid designations often ended up in the databases of related systems, such as unit of property accounting systems, customer systems, and trouble call systems. Internally, these grid systems work well, creating graphic references. For example, some utilities number their poles or gas valves according to the company's grid numbering system, so that a pole within a certain grid would have a pole number starting with the grid number. A whole host of business processes embed the grid numbering system. Over time these nonstandard mapping systems become inaccurate and incompatible with governments' state plane coordinate systems or standard land projection systems. As a result, external data sources or GPS are of little value because the facilities are not properly oriented with the external data sources. Rectifying the grid or projection system could involve considerable effort.

Some additional data costs to be considered include:

1. Data cleanup. This is often a manual process and can be labor intensive. Again, connectivity needs to exactly model the physical network. There are some complex electric distribution networks that require very careful modeling. Examples include secondary networks and underground residential development networks that require single-phase modeling.

2. Backlog reduction. Utilities often have a large backlog of as-built data left on the shelf or in filing cabinets. Lacking current data can significantly diminish the benefits of an enterprise GIS because engineers and designers have to verify the condition of the system with a costly field visit.

3. Field verification. Even if direct field inventory is not used, it is often necessary to check equipment in the field. With underground systems such as a gas or electric distribution system, this may be impossible. However, the field inventory can verify valve or switch locations, missing addresses, and other hardware to indicate field accuracy. Sampling data in the field can help gauge the accuracy of the paper or digital sources.

4. Organization of associated documents. A significant benefit to a utility is the organization of associated engineering and technical drawings, images, and reports. The ability to link company records to sections of a gas or electrical facility can save considerable time and effort, especially in cases of accidents or regulatory queries.

5. Land-base reconciliation. As we've seen, many utilities based their old manual mapping systems on an arbitrary grid coordinate system. Utilities should seriously

consider adopting the standard land base system used throughout the region by governmental agencies that conform to GPS standards. If they do, there will be an additional cost to adjust the electric and gas facilities to this standard. There will also be the cost of changing other corporate systems that buried these grids within their systems.

6. Training. Training costs are often underestimated. Even if the project is a migration from an old GIS to a new one, people will be required to change their old familiar habits. The cost of training includes the core costs of training programs, training materials, internal labor costs for the participants, and on-going internal and consultant costs during the roll out phases of the project.

7. Ongoing support costs. An enterprise GIS platform is heavily dependent on the commercial database management system. The speed and performance of the graphic editing, attribute editing, tracing, and spatial analysis all rely on the condition of the database. The GIS creates a large number of transactions to the database. Consequently, database administrators must continuously monitor for performance, which includes reallocation of data, tuning, adjusting database parameters, and reindexing.

Other annual ongoing costs include:

- hardware and software maintenance costs
- support for custom software
- refresher training
- internal help desk support
- system administrator support for the enterprise GIS

Table 12.1   Costs of AnyTown Energy's GIS project

Cost Category	Capital	Operation/ Maintenance	Cost
Data migration		X	$ 3,000,000
Hardware	X		750,000
Software	X		500,000
Implementation	X		750,000
Training and support		X	250,000
Total costs	$ 2,000,000	$ 3,250,000	$ 5,250,000

Annual ongoing costs are $500,000.

Table 12.1 shows AnyTown Energy's costs for its enterprise GIS project based on the requirements described above.

Utilities categorize costs as expense or capital depending on the particular regulatory jurisdiction. Expenses are costs that do not contribute to the asset value of the system, like the labor associated with lubricating a valve and the cost of the grease. Capital costs add value to the plant, like the labor associated with installing a pole and the cost of the pole. From an accounting perspective, utilities book expenses in the year they are incurred. Utilities amortize capital costs over the life of the asset. They often book raw data migration as a capital cost because the digital data itself is an asset. However, utilities usually consider migration of data they previously converted (and presumably capitalized previously) as an expense.

AnyTown Energy's mission statement

AnyTown Energy's business case started with an understanding of what the company is and what its core strategic issues are. The following is an excerpt from the mission statement in the company's annual report;

> We are AnyTown Energy, a full-service electric and gas transmission, distribution, and generation company with long traditions of quality and commitment. We have been providing reliable electric and gas service to our customers since 1892. We fully expect our commitment to service excellence to continue for many years to come. Our mission is to be the top utility in the region. We are committed to our key stakeholders. We are determined that our shareholders receive a fair return on their investment. We strive to meet our customers' demands for service and that we continuously keep the lights on and the gas flowing. We strive to be a good neighbor, respecting the environment and the community we serve. Finally, we are committed to our employees to provide a safe and secure workplace.

This mission statement articulates the commitment to the four stakeholders. Based on these commitments, AnyTown Energy created a handful of strategic measures. These measures capture what the company cares most about. Each has a target. The gap between the target and the actual performance determines the level of funding for an improvement initiative. The business case for GIS begins with this corporate strategy. It involves linking the identified gaps from the corporate strategy and working collaboratively with people responsible for filling the gaps by showing how GIS can help close those gaps. Table 12.2 illustrates the metrics, measures, and gaps.

Before we develop the business case for our fictitious utility, let's expand on its profile. AnyTown Energy is a combined electric and gas utility serving a mixed urban, suburban and rural territory. It serves 500,000 electric and gas customers over a 10,000 square-mile service territory. It has an extensive electric and gas transmission system. Table 12.3 shows AnyTown Energy's financial and operational details. An actual financial profile would be

Table 12.2   AnyTown Energy's metrics, measures, and gaps

Goal	Actual	Target	Gap
SHAREHOLDER			
Earnings per share	$1.18	$1.30	$0.12
Average percent overtime per employee	15%	10%	5%
Operations and maintenance spending	$330,312,500	$300,000,000	$30,312,500
Total annual capital spending	$108,437,500	$100,000,000	$8,437,500
CUSTOMER			
Average days to complete new electric customer connection	20	10	10
Average days to complete new gas customer connection	60	30	30
Reliability—System Average Interruption Duration Index (SAIDI)	120	90	30
Response time to gas leaks in minutes	20	15	5
Customer satisfaction (scale of 1 to 5)	2.5	4	−2
COMMUNITY			
Hazardous liquid spills into environmentally sensitive areas	10	5	5
Complaints to the local public utility commission	200	125	75
Time to prepare integrity management filings to the DOT in months	12	6	6
EMPLOYEE			
Reportable injuries and motor vehicle accidents	50	40	10
Switching errors	4	0	4
Gas explosions	5	0	5

Table 12.3   AnyTown Energy's profile

SHAREHOLDER		EMPLOYEE COSTS	
Revenue	$2,000,000,000	Number of employees	2,000
EXPENSES		Fully loaded unit cost per employee*	$75,000
Energy	$1,350,000,000	Average hourly rate	$36
Operations and maintenance (O&M)	$330,312,500	Total straight time fully loaded employee cost	$150,000,000
Depreciation	$50,000,000	Percent employee overtime hours	15%
Non income taxes	$25,000,000		
Current year capital carrying costs	$16,265,625	Total number of overtime hours/year	624,000
Debt service	$50,000,000	Cost of overtime	$33,750,000
Income subject to tax	$178,421,875	Percent of expense	75%
Income tax	$60,663,438	Employee expense (straight time)	$112,500,000
Net income	$117,758,438		
Number of shares	100,000,000	Employee capital (straight time)	$37,500,000
Earnings per share	$1.18	Employee expense (overtime)	$25,312,500
		Employee capital (overtime)	$8,437,500

*Fully loaded costs include adders for benefits such as health care, vacations, and holidays.

Table 12.3   AnyTown Energy's profile *(continued)*

OPERATIONS AND MAINTENANCE		ANNUAL CAPITAL SPENDING PLAN	
Employee costs—straight time	$112,500,000	Capitalized straight time employee cost	$37,500,000
Overtime	$25,312,500	Overtime	$8,437,500
Contractor costs	$20,000,000	Capitalized contractor	$10,000,000
Fleet expense	$22,500,000	Capitalized material	$40,000,000
Non employee IT	$30,000,000	Capitalized fleet	$7,500,000
Materials	$75,000,000	Other	$5,000,000
Vegetation management	$20,000,000	**Total annual capital cost**	**$108,437,500**
Bad debt	$10,000,000		
Inventory carrying cost	$10,000,000	Capital related to delivery system	75%
Other	$5,000,000	Delivery related straight time labor	$28,125,000
Total operations and maintenance	**$330,312,500**	Delivery related overtime labor	$6,328,125
		Delivery related contractor costs	$7,500,000
Percent maintenance	40%		
Total maintenance cost	$132,125,000	Delivery related fleet costs	$5,625,000
Total straight time labor costs of maintenance	$45,000,000	Total delivery system capital costs	$81,328,125
Total overtime labor costs for maintenance	$10,125,000		
Cost of contactors doing maintenance	$8,000,000		
Total fleet costs for maintenance	$9,000,000		

Note that delivery costs are broken out, since the business case deals primarily with the delivery aspect of the business.

far more complicated, but the intent here is to capture the major items that significantly impact the company.

The company's income statement is the heart of the financial aspect of the business case. If the impact of the GIS is significant, it ought to reflect on the bottom line, namely the earnings per share, which is one indication of profit.

Employee labor is one of the largest cost components of a utility. As noted earlier, employee costs are either expense or capital. Overtime is the standard time and one half of employee straight time. All labor costs and savings are based on the average labor costs for the company. In a real business case, specific labor rates would be used for the specific employees involved.

Operations and maintenance costs are all expense, since the work does not support increasing the value of the plant. These costs have a direct impact on the net income and the company's earnings.

Electric and gas utilities are capital intensive. Due to increasing customer demand, replacement of depreciated and obsolete assets and expanding services, utilities spend more capital dollars each year than most industries.

Benefits assessment

The business case examines a number of processes, first without, then with the enterprise GIS. It estimates the impact of the GIS on the particular process and links that impact to one or more of the key metrics of the company.

The examples in table 12.4 (a to s) describe some of the business case processes. This list could be expanded to include such items as the impact on inventory carrying costs, the costs of siting a generation facility, automating one-line diagrams and pipe isometrics directly from the GIS, meter reading, and billing improvements. The values indicated for improvement, such as the percentage reduction in labor to complete a work order or design, are estimates based on discussions and interviews with utility managers who have implemented GIS. The improvements are not due entirely to the GIS, but also require the utility to adjust workflows. Finally, the savings are a result of an integrated approach to GIS, not multiple instances of a standalone GIS.

Table 12.4a   Business case processes: *Load forecasting*

AREA OF SAVINGS	
Use of the GIS for load forecasting	

DESCRIPTION OF PROCESS IMPROVEMENT	
AnyTown Energy performs load forecasting manually but the enterprise GIS and widely available demographic data would allow the company to automate the process and more accurately assess substation and gas main requirements	

CURRENT LEVEL OF PERFORMANCE	
Labor hours to complete	120
Spending on substation upgrades due to load growth	$5,000,000
Spending on gas main upgrades	$4,000,000
Substation breakers overload due to an underestimated loads for a rapidly growing region resulting in an outage. Number of times per year	2
—Average outage time in hours	2
—Customers out	5,000
Total customer hours out	20,000

PROPOSED LEVEL OF PERFORMANCE	
Labor hours to complete	8
Spending on substation upgrades due to more accurate projection of loads	
—Electric savings	1%
—Gas main upgrade savings	2%
Hours of elimination outages caused by lack of accurate load forecasting	20,000

BENEFIT	
Labor savings in hours	112
Straight time capital labor savings dollars	$4,038
Capital material spending electric	$50,000
Capital material spending gas	$80,000
Reduction in System Average Interruption Duration Index in minutes	0.00033

CORPORATE METRICS IMPACTED	
Earnings per share, operations and maintenance spending, total annual capital spending reliability	

Table 12.4b   Business case processes: *Distribution planning*

AREA OF SAVINGS	
Use of the GIS for distribution planning	
DESCRIPTION OF PROCESS IMPROVEMENT	
AnyTown Energy performs planning manually but the enterprise GIS would enable the company to automate the process and have consistent planning models	
CURRENT LEVEL OF PERFORMANCE	
Labor hours to complete	2,000
PROPOSED LEVEL OF PERFORMANCE	
Labor hours to complete	1,200
BENEFIT	
Capital labor savings hours	800
Capital labor savings dollars	$28,846
CORPORATE METRICS IMPACTED	
Capital spending	

Table 12.4c Business case processes: *Asset management*

AREA OF SAVINGS	
Use of the GIS for asset management	
DESCRIPTION OF PROCESS IMPROVEMENT	
Eliminate the use of maintenance tables	
CURRENT LEVEL OF PERFORMANCE	
Current maintenance costs	$132,125,000
Capital costs related to delivery system	$81,328,125
PROPOSED LEVEL OF PERFORMANCE	
Improvement in maintenance labor and material costs	0.50%
Improvement in capital spending	1%
BENEFIT	
Expense labor costs savings (overtime)	$50,625
Expense materials savings	$150,000
Expense savings in fleet costs	$45,000
Expense reduction in contractor costs	$40,000
Capital material savings	$813,281
CORPORATE METRICS IMPACTED	
Earnings per share, operations and maintenance spending, capital spending, average percent overtime per employee	

Table 12.4d   Business case processes: *Engineering*

AREA OF SAVINGS	
Use of the GIS for engineering	
DESCRIPTION OF PROCESS IMPROVEMENT	
Uses legacy AM/FM system to plot designs, then create hard copy maps for crews and designers	
CURRENT LEVEL OF PERFORMANCE	
Number of engineering work orders per year	1,500
Average time to complete per work order in hours	40
Total hours for engineering work orders	60,000
PROPOSED LEVEL OF PERFORMANCE	
Labor hours per work order using automated placement tools and design optimization	20
Improvement in capital spending	0.5%
BENEFIT	
Labor hours savings	30,000
Expense labor dollar savings (delivery system)	$1,081,731
Capital labor savings (delivery system)	$406,641
CORPORATE METRICS IMPACTED	
Earnings per share, operations and maintenance spending, capital spending, average percent overtime per employee	

Table 12.4e   Business case processes: *Rights, permits, and easements*

AREA OF SAVINGS	
Use of the GIS for rights, permits and easement processing	
DESCRIPTION OF PROCESS IMPROVEMENT	
Automate process to draft custom plans for permits	
CURRENT LEVEL OF PERFORMANCE	
Number of hours in the rights and survey group preparing plans from scratch in hours per year (no overtime)	15,000
Number of people in the group	12
PROPOSED LEVEL OF PERFORMANCE	
Plans prepared using automated templates in hours	8,000
BENEFIT	
Hours saved	7,000
Capital labor dollars savings	$252,404
CORPORATE METRICS IMPACTED	
Capital spending, average percent overtime per employee	

Table 12.4f   Business case processes: *Distribution design/routine work*

AREA OF SAVINGS	
Use of the GIS for distribution design/routine work orders including new customer connections for gas and electric services	
DESCRIPTION OF PROCESS IMPROVEMENT	
Eliminate manual sketches on plots from the AM/FM system communicated to the field by fax	
CURRENT LEVEL OF PERFORMANCE	
Work orders produced per year	12,000
Hours per work order including designer and admin support (includes overtime)	4
Hours per work order posting as-built data from the field and updating AM/FM system	1.5
Total labor hours	66,000
PROPOSED LEVEL OF PERFORMANCE	
Hours per work order total (design and updating the GIS)	1.5
BENEFIT	
Labor hours savings	48,000
Capital labor dollar savings (overtime)	$2,596,154
CORPORATE METRICS IMPACTED	
Capital spending, average percent overtime per employee	

Table 12.4g   Business case processes: *Construction*

AREA OF SAVINGS	
Use of the GIS for construction	

DESCRIPTION OF PROCESS IMPROVEMENT	
Correct the regular missteps in construction that result in additional labor	

CURRENT LEVEL OF PERFORMANCE	
Field workers involved in delivery system construction	400
Average days per year worked	250
Minimum hours of wasted effort per day per worker due to inaccurate records and poor designs due to lack of good records	1
Total wasted hours per year	100,000

PROPOSED LEVEL OF PERFORMANCE	
Reduction in wasted time due to inaccurate records and designs based on the records	15%

BENEFIT	
Hours of wasted time saved	15,000
Capital labor savings (overtime)	$811,298

CORPORATE METRICS IMPACTED	
Capital spending, average percent overtime per employee	

Table 12.4h   Business case processes: *Electric transmission right-of-way data management*

AREA OF SAVINGS	
Use of the GIS to manage the electric transmission right-of-way data	
DESCRIPTION OF PROCESS IMPROVEMENT	
An integrated GIS to keep track of the rights of way parcel ownership and access roads	
CURRENT LEVEL OF PERFORMANCE	
Manual transmission strip plans maintained by the real estate department with people processing all the requests from legal to research easements, ownership and rights	
Number of people manually doing research and reporting	2
Electrical transmission maintenance crews	20
Workers per crew	2
Average hours spent searching for access roads per week	3
Weeks working per year	50
Total transmission maintenance crew hours looking for access roads	6,000
PROPOSED LEVEL OF PERFORMANCE	
Elimination of the two positions to research claims and licenses. One part-time employee to handle all requests. Full-time equivalent savings	1.5
Reduction in wasted time for the transmission crews	15%
BENEFIT	
Expense labor savings in the real estate department	$112,500
Hours saved	900
Expense labor dollar savings (overtime)	$48,678
CORPORATE METRICS IMPACTED	
Operations and maintenance spending, earnings per share, average percent overtime per employee	

Table 12.4i **Business case processes:** *Vegetation management*

AREA OF SAVINGS	
Use of GIS to improve vegetation management	

DESCRIPTION OF PROCESS IMPROVEMENT	
GIS used to analyze the optimal cycle times for right of way and electric distribution tree trimming	

CURRENT LEVEL OF PERFORMANCE	
Transmission right of way vegetation management performed on a scheduled basis with no analysis of need. Distribution system tree trimming scheduled on a four-year cycle by circuit	

PROPOSED LEVEL OF PERFORMANCE	
Intelligent vegetation management using GIS with historic rail fall data and intelligent satellite image processing to organize fast growing trees. Savings on vegetation management program	5%
Improvement in distribution reliability due to optimized tree maintenance	5%

BENEFIT	
System Average Interruption Duration Index improvement per year in minutes	6
Expense savings in vegetation management program per year	$1,000,000

CORPORATE METRICS IMPACTED	
Operations and maintenance spending, earnings per share, reliability	

Table 12.4j Business case processes: *Environmental management*

AREA OF SAVINGS	
Use of GIS for better environmental management	

DESCRIPTION OF PROCESS IMPROVEMENT	
GIS and Web services used to accurately delineate wetlands and sensitive areas	

CURRENT LEVEL OF PERFORMANCE	
Average number of hazardous liquid spills into environmentally sensitive areas where AnyTown Energy did not have good records of sensitive areas	10

PROPOSED LEVEL OF PERFORMANCE	
Reduction in spills per year	50%

BENEFIT	
Number of spills	5

CORPORATE METRICS IMPACTED	
Negative environmental reports in the media	

Table 12.4k Business case processes: *Inspection and maintenance management*

AREA OF SAVINGS	
Use of the GIS to manage inspection and maintenance	

DESCRIPTION OF PROCESS IMPROVEMENT	
GIS used with field devices to better maintain the electric and gas systems with accurate, up-to-date information	

CURRENT LEVEL OF PERFORMANCE	
Crews work on maintenance and inspection. Maintenance is performed using an automated work/maintenance management system but it is not integrated with spatial information. As-built information is consistently out of date so maintenance crews spend additional time verifying location and proper equipment	200
Number of workers per crew	2
Hours worked per year per worker	1,500
Total maintenance straight time labor hours	600,000

PROPOSED LEVEL OF PERFORMANCE	
Improvement in crew maintenance activity	3%
Reduction in maintenance material used	2%

BENEFIT	
Labor hours saved	18,000
Expense crew labor savings	$649,038
Expense material cost savings	$600,000

CORPORATE METRICS IMPACTED	
Operations and maintenance spending, earnings per share, average percent overtime per employee	

Table 12.4l   Business case processes: *Call before you dig*

AREA OF SAVINGS	
Use of the GIS to improve call before you dig processes	

DESCRIPTION OF PROCESS IMPROVEMENT	
GIS manages the call before you dig processes	

CURRENT LEVEL OF PERFORMANCE	
People assigned to call before you dig group	10
AnyTown Energy receives faxes from the call before you dig agency. People have to look up the area on the AM/FM system, and then have to check the backlog of un-posted work orders to make sure there hasn't been a recent underground installation. Hand drawn sketches are given to mark out contractors.	

PROPOSED LEVEL OF PERFORMANCE	
Process automatically integrates the information from the call before you dig agency into the GIS to produce the one call work orders directly to the contractor.	
People to manage the process.	4

BENEFIT	
Full time equivalent savings	6
Expense labor dollar savings	$450,000

CORPORATE METRICS IMPACTED	
Operations and maintenance spending, earnings per share, average percent overtime per employee	

Table 12.4m   Business case processes: *Outage management*

AREA OF SAVINGS	
Integration of the GIS for outage management	

DESCRIPTION OF PROCESS IMPROVEMENT	
Current GIS data forms the outage management system data	

CURRENT LEVEL OF PERFORMANCE	
No integration of AM/FM system with the outage management system	
People entering data into the outage management system	2
Outages frequently get extended due to lack of good information and large backlogs of un-posted information.	
Switching errors due to incorrect or out-of-date information	4
Complaints filed with the public utilities commission related to poor outage response	200

PROPOSED LEVEL OF PERFORMANCE	
No manual processing of system changes in the outage management system	
Reduction in outage related complaints to the public utilities commission	25%
Reduction in System Average Interruption Duration Index (SAIDI)	10%
Improvement in customer satisfaction ratings	10%
Switching errors	3

BENEFIT	
Labor savings full-time equivalent.	2
Expense labor dollars savings	$150,000
System Average Interruption Duration Index reduction in minutes	12
Reduction in complaints to the public utilities commission	50
Improvement in customer satisfaction rating	0.25
Reduction in switching errors	1

CORPORATE METRICS IMPACTED	
Operations and maintenance spending, earnings per share, reliability, outage complaints to the public utilities commission, customer satisfaction, switching errors	

Table 12.4n   Business case processes: *Gas leak management*

AREA OF SAVINGS	
Integration of the GIS gas leak management	

DESCRIPTION OF PROCESS IMPROVEMENT	
Gas leaks included in the GIS	

CURRENT LEVEL OF PERFORMANCE	
Separately maintained non spatial gas leak management system. Not integrated with AM/FM system, managed and maintained by two people.	
Gas explosions per year resulting in property damage	4
Average damage per explosion	$100,000
Technicians to inspect for leaks, file manual reports, and regularly earn overtime	30

PROPOSED LEVEL OF PERFORMANCE	
Elimination of the leak management system. Complete automation using the GIS with spatially enabled mobile field data capturing system	
Gas explosions per year resulting in property damage	2
Improvement in gas technician productivity	2%

BENEFIT	
Labor savings full-time equivalent	2
Expense labor savings dollars	$150,000
IT savings for server maintenance and backup systems	$10,000
Expense savings in property damage	$200,000
Labor savings of gas technicians	$67,500
Reduction in gas explosions	2

CORPORATE METRICS IMPACTED	
Operations and maintenance spending, earnings per share, reliability, outage complaints to the public utilities commission, customer satisfaction	

Table 12.4o Business case processes: *New customer connections*

AREA OF SAVINGS	
Integration of the GIS to improve new customer connections	

DESCRIPTION OF PROCESS IMPROVEMENT	
Integrate GIS into the call center and implement a Web service to bring in data from the local permitting agencies	

CURRENT LEVEL OF PERFORMANCE	
Average number of days to obtain electric service from time call made	20
Average number of days to obtain gas service from time call	60

PROPOSED LEVEL OF PERFORMANCE	
Improvement in electric connection time	25%
Improvement in gas connection time	25%
Improvement in customer satisfaction	3%

BENEFIT	
Reduction in new customer connect times electric in days	5
Reduction in new customer connect times gas in days	15
Increase in customer satisfaction ratings	0.075

CORPORATE METRICS IMPACTED	
Average time for customer connection, customer satisfaction	

Table 12.4p   Business case processes: *Pipeline integrity*

AREA OF SAVINGS

Application of GIS for pipeline integrity management

DESCRIPTION OF PROCESS IMPROVEMENT

Abandon CAD for pipeline alignment sheets and for filing integrity management plans with the department of transportation

CURRENT LEVEL OF PERFORMANCE

Expense labor hours to update CAD based alignment sheets	4800
Average time to file integrity management plans in months	12

PROPOSED LEVEL OF PERFORMANCE

Reduction in time to complete update	50%
Reduction in time to file to the department of transportation	50%

BENEFIT

Expense labor hours savings	$86,538
Reduction department of transportation filing time in months	6

CORPORATE METRICS IMPACTED

Average time for customer connection, customer satisfaction

Table 12.4q   Business case processes: *Logistics and fleet*

AREA OF SAVINGS	
Use of GIS to improvement logistics and fleet management	

DESCRIPTION OF PROCESS IMPROVEMENT	
Intelligently route crews	

CURRENT LEVEL OF PERFORMANCE	
No use of GIS for logistics	
Vehicles	2,000
Average miles driven per year	20,000
Average cost per year to maintain and operate each vehicle including leases and fuel	$15,000
Average speed per vehicle in miles per hour	25
Total miles driven	40,000,000
Average number of employees in vehicle	2
Total labor hours during travel	2,400,000
Total number of responsible (at fault) motor vehicle accidents per year	50

PROPOSED LEVEL OF PERFORMANCE	
Using intelligent routing, travel mileage reduction	5%
Reduction in responsible motor vehicle accidents	5%

BENEFIT	
Expense savings in fleet costs	$1,125,000
Capital savings in fleet costs	$375,000
Reduction in responsible motor vehicle accidents	2.5
Expense labor savings (overtime)	$4,867,788
Capital labor savings (overtime)	$1,622,596

CORPORATE METRICS IMPACTED
Operations and maintenance spending, capital spending, earnings per share, average overtime hours, responsible motor vehicle accidents

Table 12.4r   Business case processes: *Plant accounting*

AREA OF SAVINGS
GIS integrated with plant accounting

DESCRIPTION OF PROCESS IMPROVEMENT
Integrate GIS into the financial systems to automate recording of new and removed plant from the system

CURRENT LEVEL OF PERFORMANCE

Manual process of reviewing the work management printouts with the updated prints from the AM/FM system

Average time to file integrity management plans in months	5
Contactor cost per hour	$60
Average hours per year contactor worked	1,500

PROPOSED LEVEL OF PERFORMANCE
Automate the movement of data from the GIS into the plant accounting financial system. Eliminate the need for contactors

BENEFIT

Expense contractor savings	$450,000

CORPORATE METRICS IMPACTED
Earnings per share, operations and maintenance

Table 12.4s   **Business case processes:** *Collections system*

AREA OF SAVINGS	
GIS integrated with collections system	
DESCRIPTION OF PROCESS IMPROVEMENT	
Use GIS to optimize collections associated with debt prior to selling receivable to collection agency	
CURRENT LEVEL OF PERFORMANCE	
Annual bad debt	$10,000,000
PROPOSED LEVEL OF PERFORMANCE	
Improve collection performance	0.5%
BENEFIT	
Expense savings in bad debt	$50,000
CORPORATE METRICS IMPACTED	
Earnings per share, operations and maintenance	

Table 12.5 summarizes the annual benefits of an enterprise GIS based on the AnyTown Energy profile. These savings compare very favorably with the costs of the GIS. In fact, the savings alone far exceed the actual total costs of the GIS in the first year. Since this is a case with fictional workflows, costs, and savings, the balance sheet for a comparably sized utility are likely to be quite different. To complete the business case, the costs of the GIS can be subtracted from the savings to show the complete impact on the metrics for the company. Since all of the costs of the GIS are subtracted from the expense and capital plan in one year, the reduction in gaps in the following year would be much higher. In practice, the GIS would be implemented over more than a single calendar year and the benefits would likely not be immediate. However, for the sake of simplicity, all costs and benefits are booked into a single year financial view. No attempt has been made to perform a rigorous financial analysis.

The net savings, taking into account the difference between expense and capital, are as follows:

- Expense savings minus cost of GIS implementation: $7,924,399
- Capital savings minus cost of GIS implementation: $4,096,977

Enterprise GIS is about transforming the utility. If that is so, then it should have a significant impact on the things that are most important to a utility. Table 12.6 shows the corporate metrics along with an extra column that shows the improvements in performance of the company after it implemented enterprise GIS.

Table 12.5 Summary of benefits

Category	Value
System Average Interruption Duration Index (SAIDI) reduction in minutes	18.00
Reduction in the number of spills	5
Improvement in customer satisfaction rating	0.325
Reduction in switching errors	1
Reduction in responsible motor vehicle accidents	2.5
Reduction in gas explosions	2
Reduction in new customer connect times electric in days	5
Reduction in new customer connect times gas in days	15
Reduction in department of transportation filing time in months	6
Reduction in complaints to the public utilities commission	50
Expense labor savings	$ 7,714,399
Capital labor savings	5,721,977
Capital material savings	943,281
Expense material savings	750,000
Expense fleet savings	1,170,000
Capital fleet savings	375,000
Expense savings in contractor costs	490,000
Expense savings on vegetation management	1,000,000
Expense savings on bad debt	50,000
Reduction in overtime	9,997,139
Total expense savings	**$ 11,174,399**
Total capital savings	**$ 6,096,977**

Table 12.6   Corporate metrics with GIS

Goal	Actual	Target	Gap	After GIS
SHAREHOLDER				
Earnings per share	$1.18	$1.30	$0.12	$1.23
Average percent overtime per employee	15%	10%	5%	10.56%
Operations and maintenance spending	$330,312,500	$300,000,000	$30,312,500	$322,388,101
Total annual capital spending	$108,437,500	$100,000,000	$8,437,500	$104,340,523
CUSTOMER				
Average days to complete new electric customer connection	20	10	10	15
Average days to complete new gas customer connection	60	30	30	45
Reliability—System Average Interruption Duration Index (SAIDI)	120	90	30	102
Response time to gas leaks in minutes	20	15	5	20
Customer satisfaction (scale of 1 to 5)	2.5	4	−2	2.825
COMMUNITY				
Hazardous liquid spills into environmentally sensitive areas	10	5	5	5
Complaints to the local public utility commission	200	125	75	150
Time to prepare integrity management filings to the DOT in months	12	6	6	6
EMPLOYEE				
Reportable injuries and motor vehicle accidents	50	40	10	47.5
Switching errors	4	0	4	3
Gas explosions	5	0	5	3

The business case for GIS

GIS is not only about making maps. It's about using spatial information to empower the utility to improve its overall performance. Yes, GIS produces maps, but those maps are often in the form of visualizing better ways to operate, improve crew utilization, and avoid costly mistakes. If GIS were just about automating map production or improving a single department—like AnyTown Energy's original justification for its AM/FM system—then the impact on the company would be fairly small. Since GIS is a strategic platform, it's not surprising that it has strategic impact on the corporation, as shown by the business case. Once the utility builds the GIS platform, it will discover additional benefits. In fact, by using the powerful analytical tools of GIS, utilities may discover new things about their systems and operations never before imagined.

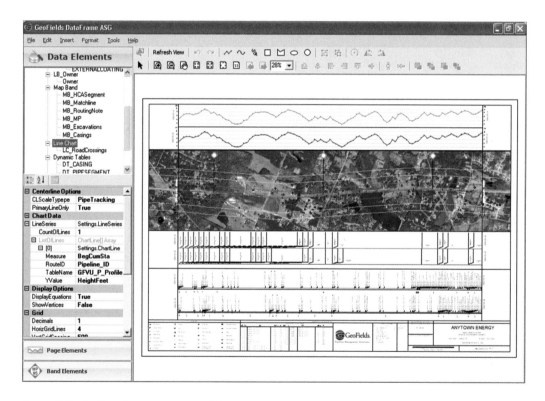

Figure 12.7   AnyTown Energy can now use GIS to create a gas transmission pipeline alignment sheet on the fly from GIS.

Courtesy of GeoFields

References

Adams, M. 2005. Web-based GIS: The easier solution. Transactions of GITA.

Alfonso, M. A. 2003. Deploying a full GIS in a utility company in eighteen months. Paper presented at the ESRI International User Conference, July 7–11 in San Diego, Calif.

_____. 2004. GIS for underground network. Paper presented at the ESRI International User Conference, August 9–13 in San Diego, Calif.

Ballieu, B., and E. Thijs. 2003. The complexity of the network. Paper presented at the ESRI International User Conference, July 7–11 in San Diego, Calif.

Beck, K., and R. Mathieu. 2004. Can power companies use space patrols to monitor transmission corridors? Paper presented at the ESRI International User Conference, August 9–13 in San Diego, Calif.

Borchert, R. 2003. Geometric network: What is it and how to make it? Paper presented at the ESRI International User Conference, July 7–11 in San Diego, Calif.

_____. 2006. QA/QC: Assuring quality and control with a checklist. Paper presented at the ESRI International User Conference, August 7–11 in San Diego, Calif.

Bradbury, D. 2005. Data quality triage. Transactions of GITA.

Brewington, J., and S. Higgins. 2003. Business process and geodatabase version management at the utility. Paper presented at the ESRI International User Conference, July 7–11 in San Diego, Calif.

Brummels, G., T. Acker, and S. Williams. 2006. Navajo wind energy development exclusions: An analysis of land suitable for wind energy development on the Navajo nation. Paper presented at the ESRI International User Conference, August 7–11 in San Diego, Calif.

Brush, R. 2004. Applying GIS to the new gas HCA rule. Transactions of GITA.

Cantwell, B., J. Kuiper, and M. Nesta. 2006. The application of spatial analysis in selecting energy transmission corridors. Paper presented at the ESRI International User Conference, August 7–11 in San Diego, Calif.

Carlson, P. 2005. The history of the Lake Country Power Initiative. Paper presented at the ESRI International User Conference, July 25–29 in San Diego, Calif.

Casella, M., and S. Kerr. 2006. Enterprise asset management (EAM) driven GIS: An alternative approach. Paper presented at the ESRI International User Conference, August 7–11 in San Diego, Calif.

Cederholm, M. 2005. Synchronizing small world data with ArcGIS. Paper presented at the ESRI International User Conference, July 25–29 in San Diego, Calif.

Chester, J. 2005. Power plant suitability analysis made easier with ModelBuilder. Paper presented at the ESRI International User Conference, July 25–29 in San Diego, Calif.

Childs, D., and M. Mohseni. 2005. Building the business case for an enterprise GIS. Paper presented at the ESRI International User Conference, July 25–29 in San Diego, Calif.

Cover, C. 2006. Using GIS to help manage a national energy program. Paper presented at the ESRI International User Conference, August 7–11 in San Diego, Calif.

Cox-Drake, R. 2004. The value of time. Transactions of GITA.

_____. 2005. Protecting critical infrastructure: A key role for GIS. Transactions of GITA.

Dangermond, J. 2004. The role of geospatial information: Its future for utilities. Transactions of GITA.

_____. 2005. GIS is just getting started. Transactions of GITA.

_____. 2006. GIS enterprise architecture: Unifying the utility. Transactions of GITA.

_____. 2007. Enterprise GIS: Exploring the possibilities of mission critical operations. Transactions of GITA.

Duswalt, J. 2003. PSEG: Spatial data QA: Data and processes. Transactions of GITA.

Fitzgerald, I. 2003. How accounting practices have driven GIS maintenance at Truckee Donner. Paper presented at the ESRI International User Conference, July 7–11 in San Diego, Calif.

Foresman, T. 1998. History of Geographic Information Systems: Perspectives from the Pioneers. Upper Saddle River, N.J.: Prentice Hall PTR.

Fortich, C., and J. Armstrong. 2006. Lessons learned in building an overhead primary and secondary network. Paper presented at the ESRI International User Conference, August 7–11 in San Diego, Calif.

Frantz, B., and C. Findley. 2005. Quantifying municipal electric infrastructure for GASB34 compliance. Paper presented at the ESRI International User Conference, July 25–29 in San Diego, Calif.

Frymyer, R. 2002. Leveraging capital projects for GIS success. Transactions of GITA.

Glasgow, J. 2004. Siting linear facilities with geographic information systems. Paper presented at the ESRI International User Conference, August 9–13 in San Diego, Calif.

Gomide, A., and G. Kissula. 2006. Using geocoding to improve data quality. Paper presented at the ESRI International User Conference, August 7–11 in San Diego, Calif.

Grisé, S. 2004. Web services: A replacement for desktop GIS? Transactions of GITA.

Hahne, R. 2004. Integration of GIS and EAM. Transactions of GITA.

Hall, W. 2005. Enterprise benefits through automated routing and scheduling. Transactions of GITA.

Helmer, T. 2004. Using GIS technology to maximize operations data marts. Transactions of GITA.

Hershman, J. 2004. Using Web services to integrate GIS into the enterprise. Transactions of GITA.

Hierholzer, J., and K. Irwin. 2003. Challenging CAD conversion issues at Gulf Power. Paper presented at the ESRI International User Conference, July 7–11 in San Diego, Calif.

Hill, C. 2004. Lessons learned in building a foundation for technology-enabled business transformation of utility operations. Transactions of GITA.

Hoel, E. 1999. Building dynamic network models with GIS software components. Transactions of GITA.

Horne, C. 2005. Understanding mystery conflicts. Paper presented at the ESRI International User Conference, July 25–29 in San Diego, Calif.

Hughes, T., and B. Moreira. 2006. GIS applications for wind farm development, siting, and permitting. Paper presented at the ESRI International User Conference, August 7–11 in San Diego, Calif.

Ingram, D., and C. Shankland. 2006. Utilizing videography and GIS for right-of-way issue identification. Paper presented at the ESRI International User Conference, August 7–11 in San Diego, Calif.

Johnson, J. 2001. Are we there yet? Experiences and lessons in a GIS conversion project. Transactions of GITA.

Kersting A. P., J. Kersting, C. F. Filho, and M. Müller. 2005. Airborne lidar and GIS tools in transmission line re-rating projects. Paper presented at the ESRI International User Conference, July 25–29 in San Diego, Calif.

Kircher, T., G. Garcia, and A. Little. 2003. Streamlining gas transmission management at PNM. Paper presented at the ESRI International User Conference, July 7–11 in San Diego, Calif.

Kolosvary, R., and D. Desmarais. 2003. GIS for joint-use field data collection. Paper presented at the ESRI International User Conference, July 7–11 in San Diego, Calif.

Ladha, N., S. Jiwani, and S. Kumra. 2005. Enterprise GIS at one of North America's largest electricity networks. Paper presented at the ESRI International User Conference, July 25–29 in San Diego, Calif.

Lariviere, F., T. Thistoll, and W. Warren. 2005. Rapid data capture and asset inspections: Saving money. Paper presented at the ESRI International User Conference, July 25–29 in San Diego, Calif.

Lembo, A., L. Nozick, and T. O'Rourke. 2003. Optimizing gas main expansion with spatial analysis and operations research. Paper presented at the ESRI International User Conference, July 7–11 in San Diego, Calif.

MacNaughton, J., J. Schick, N. Kernohan, and R. Menon. 2004. Electrical designing in the field using ArcGIS and ArcFM. Paper presented at the ESRI International User Conference, August 9–13 in San Diego, Calif.

MacPhee, A. 2006. Innovative tools for data reconciliation/production use. Paper presented at the ESRI International User Conference, August 7–11 in San Diego, Calif.

Maguire, D. 1999. Object-component GIS: The new standards. Transactions of GITA.

_____. 2001. Building domain data models for AM/FM/GIS. Transactions of GITA.

_____. 2002. Re-thinking topology in AM/FM/GIS. Transactions of GITA.

_____. 2005. Enterprise geographic information servers: A new information system architecture. Transactions of GITA.

Martin, B. 2005. Leveraging work and maintenance management systems as an integral component of your asset management strategy. Transactions of GITA.

May, C., and J. Henry. 2006. Integrating GIS into a pole replacement workflow system. Paper presented at the ESRI International User Conference, August 7–11 in San Diego, Calif.

Meehan, W. 1989. Moving from utility CAD to AM/FM. Transactions of AM/FM International (April).

_____. 1991. AM/FM electric model using a geographic information system. Transactions of AM/FM International (April).

_____. 1992. Boston Edison's AM/FM/GIS: The key to providing better service. GeoInfo Systems (April).

_____. 1992. Distribution dispatching using AM/FM/GIS. Transactions of AM/FM International (April).

_____. 1993. Re-engineering work processes using AM/FM/GIS. Transactions of AM/FM International (April).

_____. 1994. AM/FM/GIS: Enabling redesign of the electric utility operations. Transactions of AM/FM International (March).

_____. 1995. Anatomy of a large electric AM/FM/GIS project—halfway. Transactions of AM/FM International (March).

_____. 1996. Training critical in AM/FM/GIS. Transactions of AM/FM International (March).

_____. 1997. After the thrill is gone: Institutionalizing GIS, Transactions of AM/FM International (March).

_____. 1998. GIS plays a role in industry restructuring. Transmission and Distribution World (February).

_____. 1999. Stop your GIS project now. Transactions of GITA.

_____. 2003. Shredding the Map. DistribuTech Conference Proceedings. Dusseldorf, Germany: Pennwell Publishing.

_____. 2005. Enterprise GIS: If you build it, it will fund. Geoworld (March).

_____. 2006. Transforming utilities. Geo Connections International (July).

Meehan, W., and D. Frye. 2004. GIS: A must for assessing pipeline integrity. Transactions of GITA.

Meehan, W., and C. Salas. 2004. Modeling high-pressure distribution for integrity management. Transactions of GITA Oil and Gas Conference.

Meyer, W. 2001. Gas compliance/maintenance process improvement utilizing GIS. Transactions of GITA.

Meyers, J. 2002. Ten things I hate about you: The worst mistakes in GIS project history (and how to avoid them). Transactions of GITA.

_____. 1999. Rule-based technology for GIS applications. Transactions of GITA.

_____. 2003. Building Your ArcFM, 2nd Edition. Fort Collins, Colo.: Miner & Miner Publications.

_____. 2004. Wars and rumors of wars: Change management and enterprise GIS implementation. Transactions of GITA.

Miller, A. 2005. Merging two GIS platforms for utility data into one. Paper presented at the ESRI International User Conference, July 25–29 in San Diego, Calif.

Montgomery, R. 2004. Innovative economic development. Transactions of GITA.

Morgan, G. 2003. Facilities inspection and maintenance. Paper presented at the ESRI International User Conference, July 7–11 in San Diego, Calif.

Müller-Bertram, O., and P. Grüninger. 2006. Migrating Germany's third largest energy company. Paper presented at the ESRI International User Conference, August 7–11 in San Diego, Calif.

Nix, G., and T. Craig. 2007. GIS and your AMR system. Paper presented at TechAdvantage, March 15–18 in Las Vegas, Nev.

Noonan, J. 2005. Spatial load forecasting: Bringing GIS to T&D Asset Management. Paper presented at the ESRI International User Conference, July 25–29 in San Diego, Calif.

Park, N. 2003. Terrestrial spill modeling: Increasing confidence in the estimation of high consequence area (HCA) impact. Transactions of GITA.

Pertot, B., and B. Abou-El-Hassan. 2004. A fundamental utility restoration and evolution using GIS. Paper presented at the ESRI International User Conference, August 9–13 in San Diego, Calif.

Peters, D. 2005. Planning for productive enterprise GIS operations. Transactions of GITA.

———. 2004. System architecture alternatives for enterprise AM/FM operations. Transactions of GITA.

Porter, B. 2001. The metamorphosis of GIS: Is AM/FM dead? Transactions of GITA.

———. 1999. Interfacing AM/FM/GIS with enterprise and operations systems. Transactions of GITA.

Porter, R. 2004. Considering the life in project life cycle: The human perspective. Transactions of GITA.

Portillo, D. 2006. An ArcGIS schematics application for an electric utility. Paper presented at the ESRI International User Conference, August 7–11 in San Diego, Calif.

Presti, J. 2003. Work management integration with ERP and GIS. Transactions of GITA.

Schmidt, A. 2005. Integration of GIS with asset management: Creating a road map for success. Paper presented at the ESRI International User Conference, July 25–29 in San Diego, Calif.

Seiler, K. 2004. Integration of spatial technology for the purposes of visualization, analysis, and planning. Transactions of GITA.

Shaw, W. 2003. Migrating legacy GIS: An evolutionary approach. Transactions of GITA.

Stasik, M. 2005. The last mile of field work: Integrating spatial data back into the office. Transactions of GITA.

Stover, D., and B. Beaver. 2005. ArcView and SynerGEE work together in a gas COS application. Paper presented at the ESRI International User Conference, July 25–29 in San Diego, Calif.

Taber, T., and S. Koehler. 2003. Multispeak integration strategies. Paper presented at the ESRI International User Conference, July 7–11 in San Diego, Calif.

Thomas, C., and M. Ospina. 2004. Measuring Up: The Business Case for GIS. Redlands, Calif.: ESRI Press.

Thorne, M. 2005. Quantitative pipeline risk assessment. Transactions of GITA.

Tomlinson, R. 2003. Thinking About GIS. Geographic Information System Planning for Managers. Redlands, Calif.: ESRI Press.

Tram, H. 2004. Integrated resource planning for multi-utility services. Transactions of GITA.

Reece, C. 2003. Integrating real-time weather into outage management. Paper presented at the ESRI International User Conference, July 7–11 in San Diego, Calif.

Robertson, T., and J. Luera. 2004. GIS data conversion, training, and layer development. Paper presented at the ESRI International User Conference, August 9–13 in San Diego, Calif.

Rogers, C. 2002. The tricks and traps of managing an enterprise GIS. Transactions of GITA.

Wallace, B., and E. Fulcher. 2004. Bridging the gap between GIS and ERP at Alagasco. Paper presented at the ESRI International User Conference, August 9–13 in San Diego, Calif.

Wilke, L. 2004. Taking Tablet PCs and the enterprise geodatabase to the field. Paper presented at the ESRI International User Conference, August 9–13 in San Diego, Calif.

Zeiler, M. 1999. Patterns for building utility data models. Transactions of GITA.

Glossary

alignment sheets   Manually prepared drawings that display segments of pipe over particular sections.

AM/FM *(automated mapping/facility management)*   GIS or CAD-based systems used by utilities and public-works organizations for storing, manipulating, and mapping facility information such as the location of geographically dispersed assets.

AMI *(advanced metering infrastructure)*   Closely related to AMR and refers to systems that measure, collect, and analyze energy usage. AMI is often one component in what is referred to as the intelligent or smart grid.

AMR *(automatic meter reading)*   The technology of automatically collecting data from utility metering devices and transferring that data to a central database for billing and/or analyzing.

asset management   The process of making informed decisions about repairing or replacing equipment, assessing the risks concerning when to repair or replace, and prioritizing all work within the system for budgeting and forecasting.

CAD *(computer-aided design)*   A computer-based system for the design, drafting, and display of graphical information. Also known as computer-aided drafting, such systems are most commonly used to support engineering, planning, and illustrating activities.

CAIDI *(Customer Average Interruption Duration Index)*   Measures how long it takes a utility to restore service after an interruption. The average is derived by adding the durations of each outage in a year and dividing that by the total number of customer service interruptions.

CIS *(customer information system)*   The CIS in a utility manages the customer interaction with the utility and is closely associated with the billing and meter information.

CP *(cathodic protection)*   A pipe corrosion protection system that establishes a low voltage electrical negative potential on the metal pipes that repels electrons from corrosive materials present in the soil. The CP system consists of positively charged anodes, an electric source, and wire buried with the pipe.

CRM *(customer relationship management)*   CRM is a system that manages customer interaction. In a utility, CRM is often handled by the billing or customer information system.

database management system   A set of software applications used to create and maintain databases according to a schema. Database management systems provide tools for adding, storing, changing, deleting, and retrieving data.

data model   A set of database design specifications for objects in a GIS application. A data model describes the thematic layers used in the application, their spatial representation, their integrity rules and relationships, their cartographic portrayal, and their metadata requirements.

distribution system   The stage in electric power delivery from the substation to the consumer that involves medium-voltage (less than 50 kV) power lines, substations, pole-mounted transformers, low-voltage (less than 1000 V) distribution wiring, and meters.

EAI *(enterprise application integration)*   A business computing term for the plans, methods, and tools aimed at modernizing, consolidating, and coordinating the computer applications in an enterprise.

EMF *(electric and magnetic field)*   Forces that surround electrical devices. Transmission and distribution lines, electrical wiring, and electrical equipment produce EMF. The intensity of the fields decrease as the distance from the devices decrease.

enterprise GIS   A geographic information system that is integrated through an entire organization so that a large number of users can manage, share, and use spatial data and related information to address a variety of needs, including data creation, modification, visualization, analysis, and dissemination.

ERP *(enterprise resource planning)*   The broad set of activities supported by multimodule application software that helps a company manage product planning, parts purchasing, maintaining inventories, interacting with suppliers, providing customer service, tracking orders, and other key functions. ERP can also include application modules for the finance and human resources aspects of a business.

geodataset   Any organized collection of data in a geodatabase with a common theme. For a utility, a geodataset includes all the land, facility, and imagery data that pertains to the utility's operating area.

GPS *(Global Positioning System)*   A system of geosynchronous, radio-emitting and receiving satellites used for determining positions on the earth. The orbiting satellites transmit signals that allow a GPS receiver anywhere on earth to calculate its own location through triangulation. Used in navigation, mapping, surveying, and other applications requiring precise positioning.

HCA *(high consequence area)*   Pipeline safety regulations identify these sensitive areas where a natural gas or hazardous liquid release could have the most significant consequences. Once identified, operators are required to devote additional attention, efforts, and analysis in HCAs to ensure the integrity of pipelines.

high-pressure transmission lines   Pipelines that transport natural gas to the distribution system via a mostly underground network.

intelligent grid   A concept where the electric utility system reaches into the customer base, is self-healing, automated, and can predict weaknesses before problems arise. Also referred to as the smart grid.

IVR *(interactive voice response)*   A computerized system that allows a person, typically a telephone caller, to select an option from a voice menu and otherwise interface with a computer system

load forecasting   Projecting future energy needs for a particular service area.

low-pressure mains   Pipelines that distribute natural gas from the regulator station to the customer.

OMS *(outage management system)*   An OMS efficiently identifies and resolves utility outages and generates and reports valuable historical information. It also helps the utility inform the customer of the outage situation and restoration status rather than the customer informing the utility.

photovoltaic cells   Converts the sun's energy into direct current electricity. Systems that use photovoltaic cells are the most common source of solar power.

SAIDI *(System Average Interruption Duration Index)*   Commonly used as a reliability indicator by electric power utilities. SAIDI is the average outage duration for each customer served, and is calculated by dividing the sum of all customer interruption durations by the total number of customers served. SAIDI is measured in units of time, often minutes or hours.

SCADA *(supervisory control and data acquisition)*   The term refers to a large-scale, distributed measurement and control system. SCADA systems are used to monitor or control electric power distribution and generation, gas and oil pipelines, and other distributed processes.

smart grid   *See* intelligent grid.

substation The subsidiary facility of an electricity generation, transmission, and distribution system where voltage is transformed from high to low or the reverse using transformers.

supply chain logistics The effective movement of material and people for the purpose of performing a utility's work.

transmission system Sometimes called the grid, transmission systems deliver electricity from the power plant to the bulk distribution supply substation over high voltage (110 kV or above) lines.

UML *(unified modeling language)* A modeling language that uses a series of diagrams to model objects in a system.

URD *(underground residential distribution)* An underground utility system that consists of above-ground cabinets that house electrical equipment, such as transformers and switches, connected by buried conduit.

Index

Related titles from ESRI Press

A to Z GIS
ISBN 978-1-58948-140-4

Confronting Catastrophe: A GIS Handbook
ISBN 978-1-58948-040-7

Designing Geodatabases
ISBN 978-1-58948-021-6

GIS Spatial Analysis and Modeling
ISBN 978-1-58948-130-5

The ESRI Guide to GIS Analysis volume 1
ISBN 978-1-879102-06-4

The ESRI Guide to GIS Analysis volume 2
ISBN 978-1-58948-116-9

Integrating GIS and the Global Positioning System
ISBN 978-1-879102-81-1

Measuring Up: The Business Case for GIS
ISBN 978-1-58948-088-9

Modeling Our World
ISBN 978-1-879102-62-0

Remote Sensing
ISBN 978-1-58948-081-0

ESRI Press publishes books about the science, application, and technology of GIS. Ask for these titles at your local bookstore or order by calling 1-800-447-9778. You can also read book descriptions, read reviews, and shop online at www.esri.com/esripress. Outside the United States, contact your local ESRI distributor.